LA DEMOCRATIE

The first part of Channel Zero is set in NYC right now. Broadcast and print media have been taken over by the government, giving them control over content. This came in the form of the Clean Act, a bill that was forced through Congress and signed into law under pressure from special interest groups, most notably the Christian Right and Pro-Censorship Parents groups. Most of the populace went along with the change, either in support of it, or too lazy to do anything about it. This demonstates the dangers of apathy.

The protagonist is Jennie 2.5, an ex-performance artist made obsolete by the Clean Act, who cannot understand or accept the fact that her friends and peers just sit by while the government censors their lives. With a little help from a tiny struggling anti-government underground resistance, she comes up with a plan to broadcast a pirate television show, public-access style, in hopes of reaching people brainwashed by the propaganda that's around them, and convince them they need to take action, regain control of their lives. Her motives cannot be so pure, however, and a certain amount of ego and a desire to be famous comes very close to overpowering her "moral desire to do what's right."

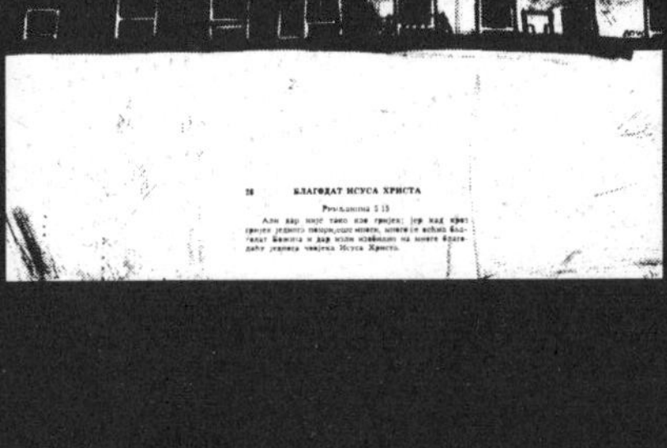
БЛАГОДАТ ИСУСА ХРИСТА

Also by Brian Wood:

Public Domain: A Channel Zero Designbook

Channel Zero: Jennie One
(with Becky Cloonan)

Demo (the monthly series)
Demo: The Twelve Original Scripts
Demo: The Collection
(with Becky Cloonan)

Couscous Express *(with Brett Weldele)*

The Couriers 01
The Couriers 02: Dirtbike Manifesto
The Couriers 03: The Ballad Of Johnny Funwrecker
(with Rob G)

Available from AiT/Planet Lar

CHANNEL ZERO
Written and illustrated by Brian Wood

Published by AiT/Planet Lar, 2034 47th Avenue, San Francisco, CA 94116

First edition: September 2000
Second edition: June 2001
Third edition: January 2003
Fourth edition: February 2006
Fifth edition: May 2007
10 9 8 7 6 5

Publication design by Brian Wood

ISBN: 0-9676847-4-9

Printed and bound in Canada by Lebonfon Printing.

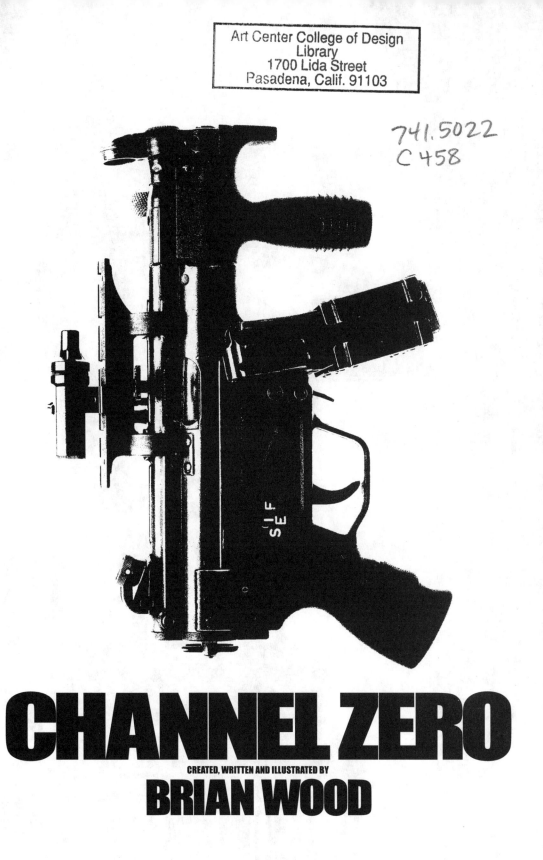

CHANNEL ZERO

CREATED, WRITTEN AND ILLUSTRATED BY
BRIAN WOOD

SAN FRANCISCO

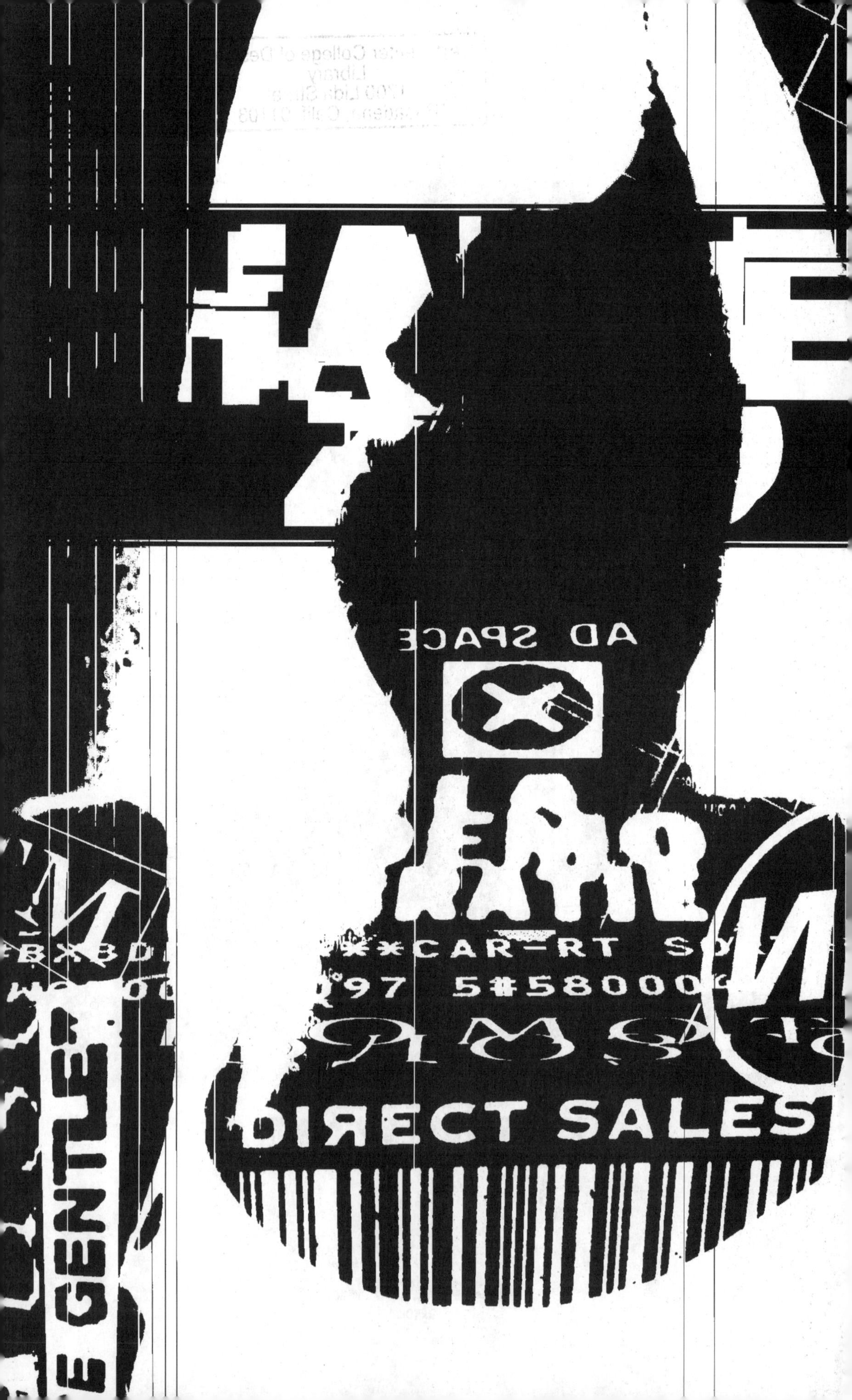
AD SPACE
**CAR-RT
97 5#58000
DIRECT SALES
GENTLE

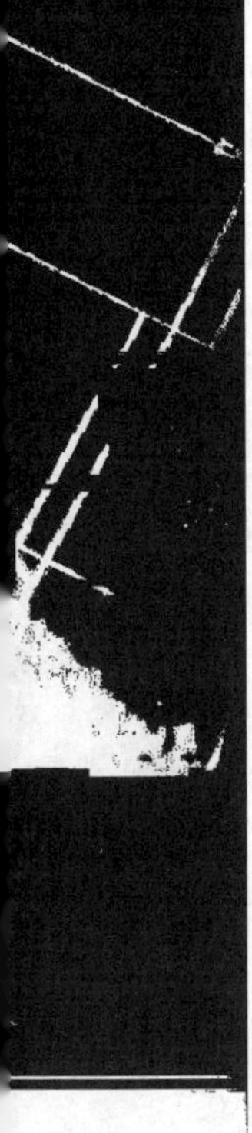

CHANNEL ZERO

INTRODUCTION BY WARREN ELLIS

Pop culture rolled over and died some time ago. Some people actually think Marilyn Manson is scary, that Kurt Cobain had something to do with rebellion, that Bret Easton Ellis is a dangerous writer, that it's a good thing that you can buy McDonald's in Prague, that movies are somehow relevant to our lives.

Television is our stage and our anaesthetic. Real life happens on television in preference to our homes and streets. People resolve their relationships on freakshow chatshows instead of in living rooms or beds or even goddamn bars.

And it spreads. Rupert Murdoch beams his shit into Asia, English children are taught that Z is pronounced Zee by goddamn Barney, and all of a sudden, world cultures become the Monoculture, the same conversation, the same clothes, the same show. All tuned to Channel Zero.

And, all over the world, one by one, we quit fighting it. We sit and we put the book we're reading down and laugh at the arseholes on Jerry Springer, snigger at Matthew Perry, get our news managed for us by CNN, and suddenly we're like all the rest. We're in cultural lockstep, taking holidays in other people's misery, asking for our stinking badges, dead heads nodding over phosphordot fixes.

Someone's remembered what comics are for.

In goddamn America, of all places.

Meet Brian Wood.

Over here in comics, things are different, you see. Sometimes we're an outlaw medium. Sometimes we're just the preferred tiny place for neurotics and losers to gibber in. Either way, we're an outside art, a fringe medium watched by no-one but the more voracious cultural commentators and the aficionados. We don't have huge corporations trembling at our every movement, because we make no money compared to the other visual narrative media. That vast commercial pressure isn't brought to bear on comics. Which means, often, that we can say what we want without rich men's scissors attacking our work until it's safe for little Tommy in Dogshit, Nebraska. I hate little Tommy in Dogshit, Nebraska. I want to kill little Tommy in Dogshit, Nebraska. And so does Brian Wood.

Brian Wood remembers how to be angry. He remembers how to wake up in the morning and look out at this plastic MTV-soundtracked world we've agreed to exist in and get pissed off with it. And he goes to his desk and makes buzzing, scratchy, shuddering people, the innards of the people-shaped things he sees lockstepping down the street outside, and he puts them in a crazed, broken America that really is just the America we know seen through a cleaner window, and he makes those people move the way they should. He makes them talk about revolution. He makes them spark and snarl and scheme and scream the way pop culture icons are supposed to. They rant and rail against the dying of the light the way people should.

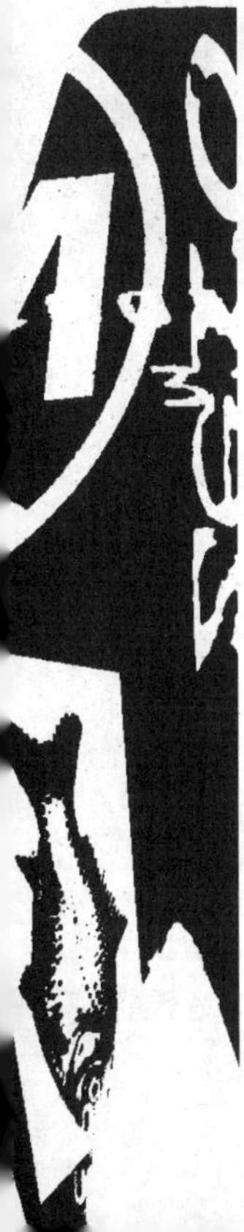

The longer CHANNEL ZERO runs, the purer it becomes. It grows dominated by symbols, huge dark images of a beaten world filled with a beaten generation, the place that, like Ginsberg howled, saw its best minds destroyed. Black things grow out of the pages, looming over and burying Jennie 2.5 and Channel Zero's other hopeful monsters. The semiotics of a heartdead world hit like gunfire -- but, in the interstices, you begin to hear music. Anger and passion rise up again.

For all its black and white somber mien, CHANNEL ZERO is, to me, one of the most uplifting comics of the Nineties. CHANNEL ZERO is about winning. It's about learning how to give a shit again, about finding ways to make things better. It's about anger as a positive force of creation. It's about your right to not have to live in the world they've built for you.

It's about turning off the television.

Warren Ellis is the creator of Transmetropolitan, Planetary, Desolation Jones, Fell, and Global Frequency. He can be found at www.warrenellis.com

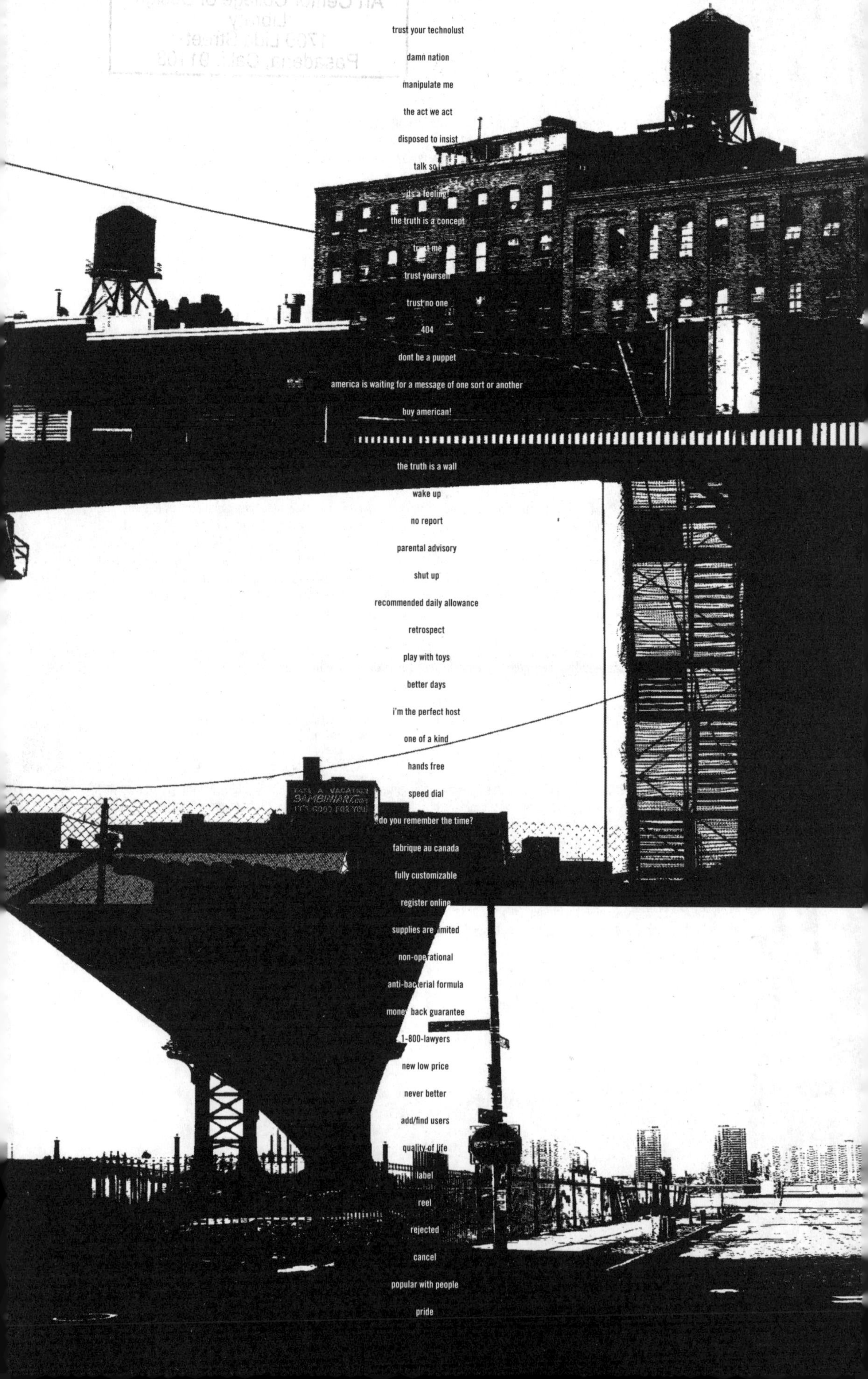
trust your technolust
damn nation
manipulate me
the act we act
disposed to insist
talk so
its a feeling!
the truth is a concept
trust me
trust yourself
trust no one
404
dont be a puppet
america is waiting for a message of one sort or another
buy american!
the truth is a wall
wake up
no report
parental advisory
shut up
recommended daily allowance
retrospect
play with toys
better days
i'm the perfect host
one of a kind
hands free
speed dial
do you remember the time?
fabrique au canada
fully customizable
register online
supplies are limited
non-operational
anti-bacterial formula
money back guarantee
1-800-lawyers
new low price
never better
add/find users
quality of life
label
reel
rejected
cancel
popular with people
pride

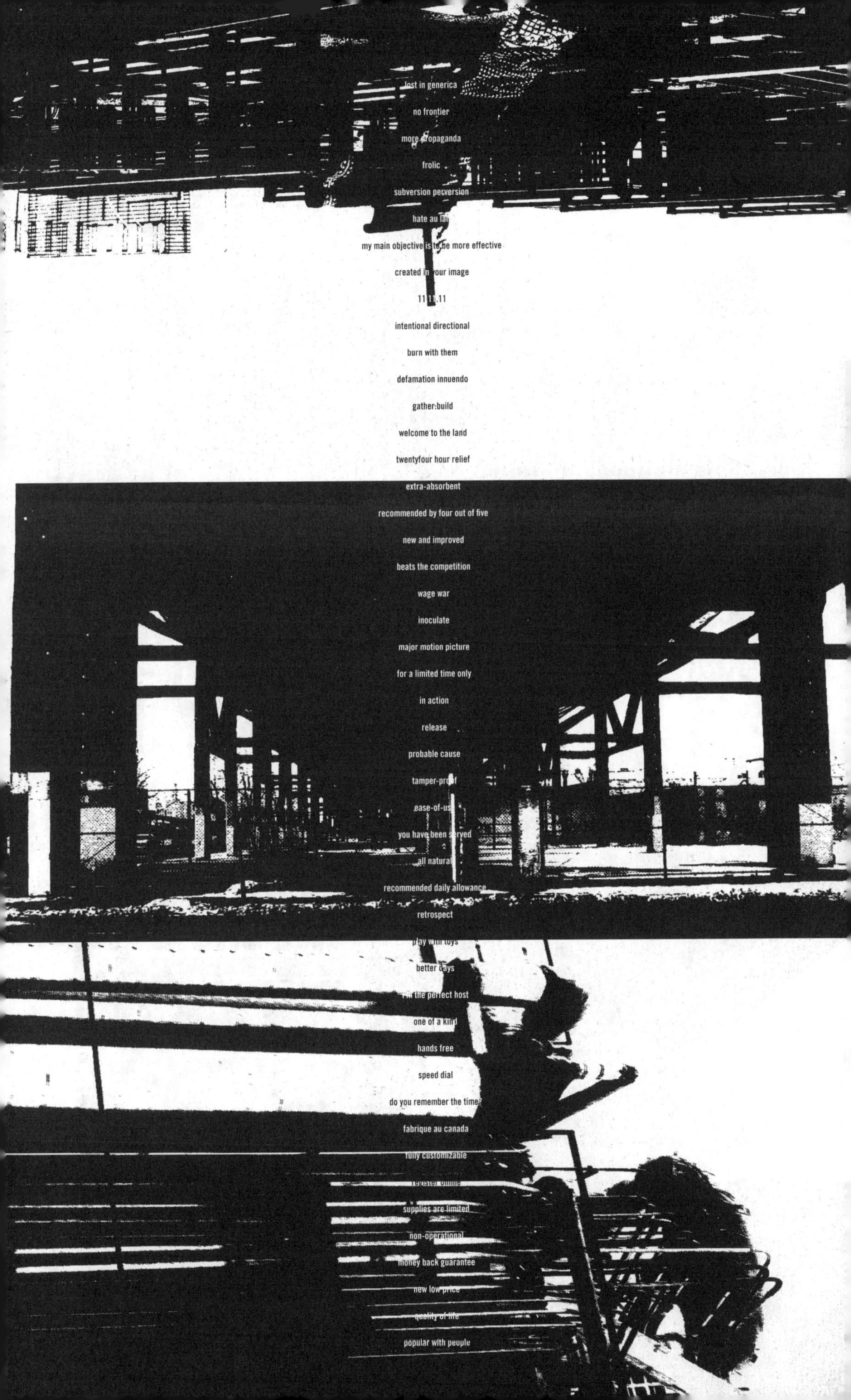
lost in generica
no frontier
more propaganda
frolic
subversion perversion
hate au lai
my main objective is to be more effective
created in your image
11.11.11
intentional directional
burn with them
defamation innuendo
gather:build
welcome to the land
twentyfour hour relief
extra-absorbent
recommended by four out of five
new and improved
beats the competition
wage war
inoculate
major motion picture
for a limited time only
in action
release
probable cause
tamper-proof
ease-of-use
you have been served
all natural
recommended daily allowance
retrospect
play with toys
better days
i'm the perfect host
one of a kind
hands free
speed dial
do you remember the time
fabrique au canada
fully customizable
register online
supplies are limited
non-operational
money back guarantee
new low price
quality of life
popular with people

PHOTOCOPY THIS PAGE!

These are copyright-free images you can use for stickers, flyers, t-shirts, and petty vandalism. They may not be used for profit, or altered in any way. Scratchbomb the system! Help spread the message.

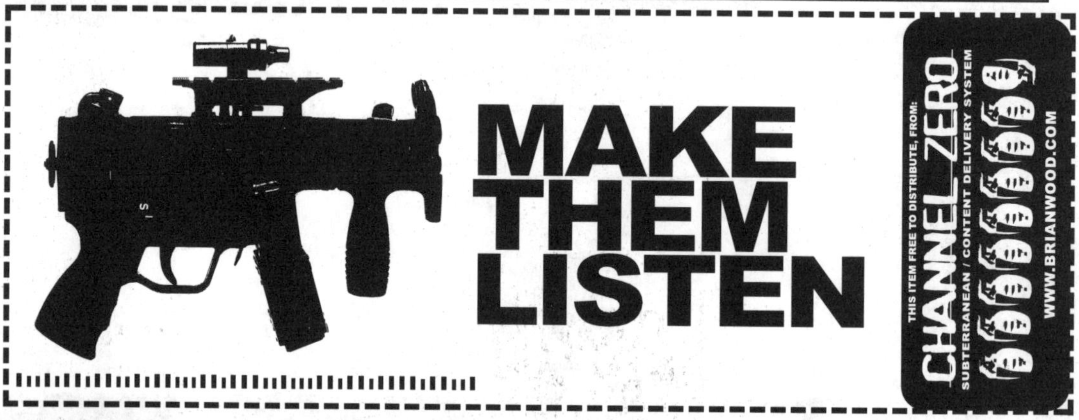
MAKE
THEM
LISTEN
THIS ITEM FREE TO DISTRIBUTE, FROM:
CHANNEL ZERO
SUBTERRANEAN / CONTENT DELIVERY SYSTEM
WWW.BRIANWOOD.COM

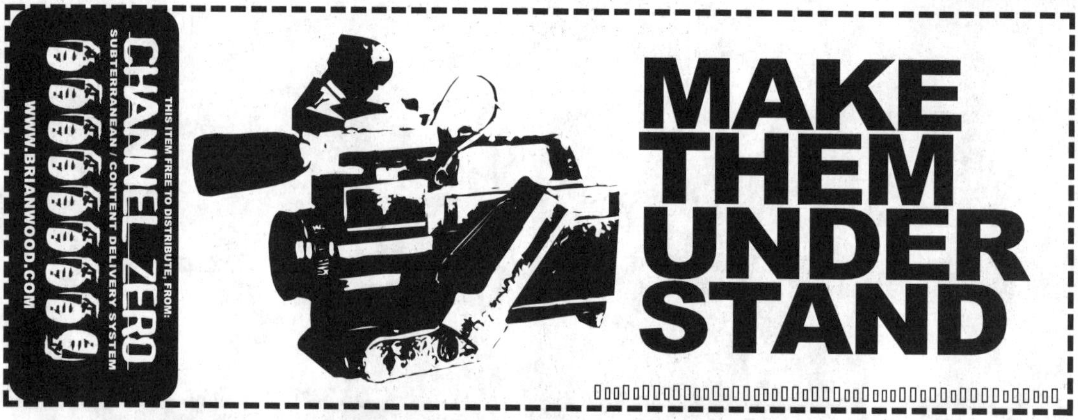
MAKE
THEM
UNDER
STAND
THIS ITEM FREE TO DISTRIBUTE, FROM:
CHANNEL ZERO
SUBTERRANEAN / CONTENT DELIVERY SYSTEM
WWW.BRIANWOOD.COM

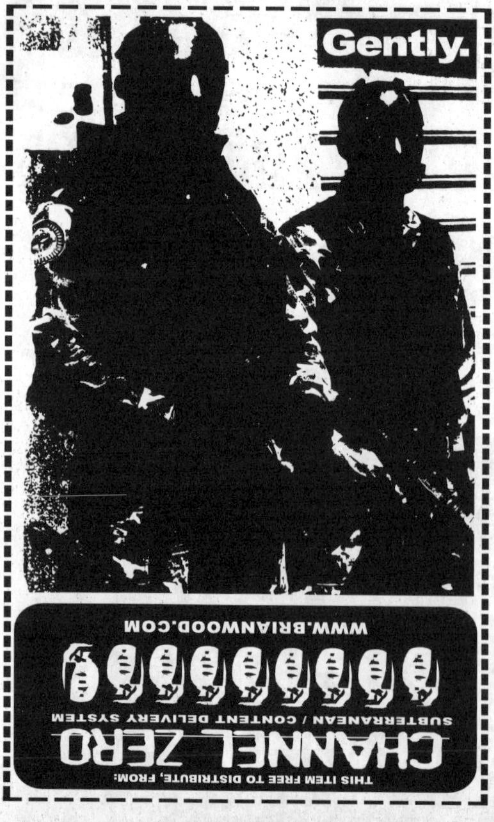
Gently.
THIS ITEM FREE TO DISTRIBUTE, FROM:
CHANNEL ZERO
SUBTERRANEAN / CONTENT DELIVERY SYSTEM
WWW.BRIANWOOD.COM

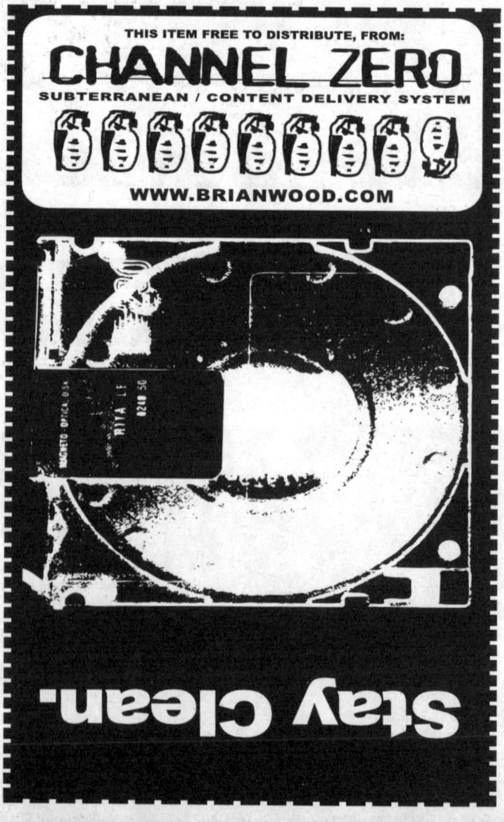
THIS ITEM FREE TO DISTRIBUTE, FROM:
CHANNEL ZERO
SUBTERRANEAN / CONTENT DELIVERY SYSTEM
WWW.BRIANWOOD.COM
Stay clean.

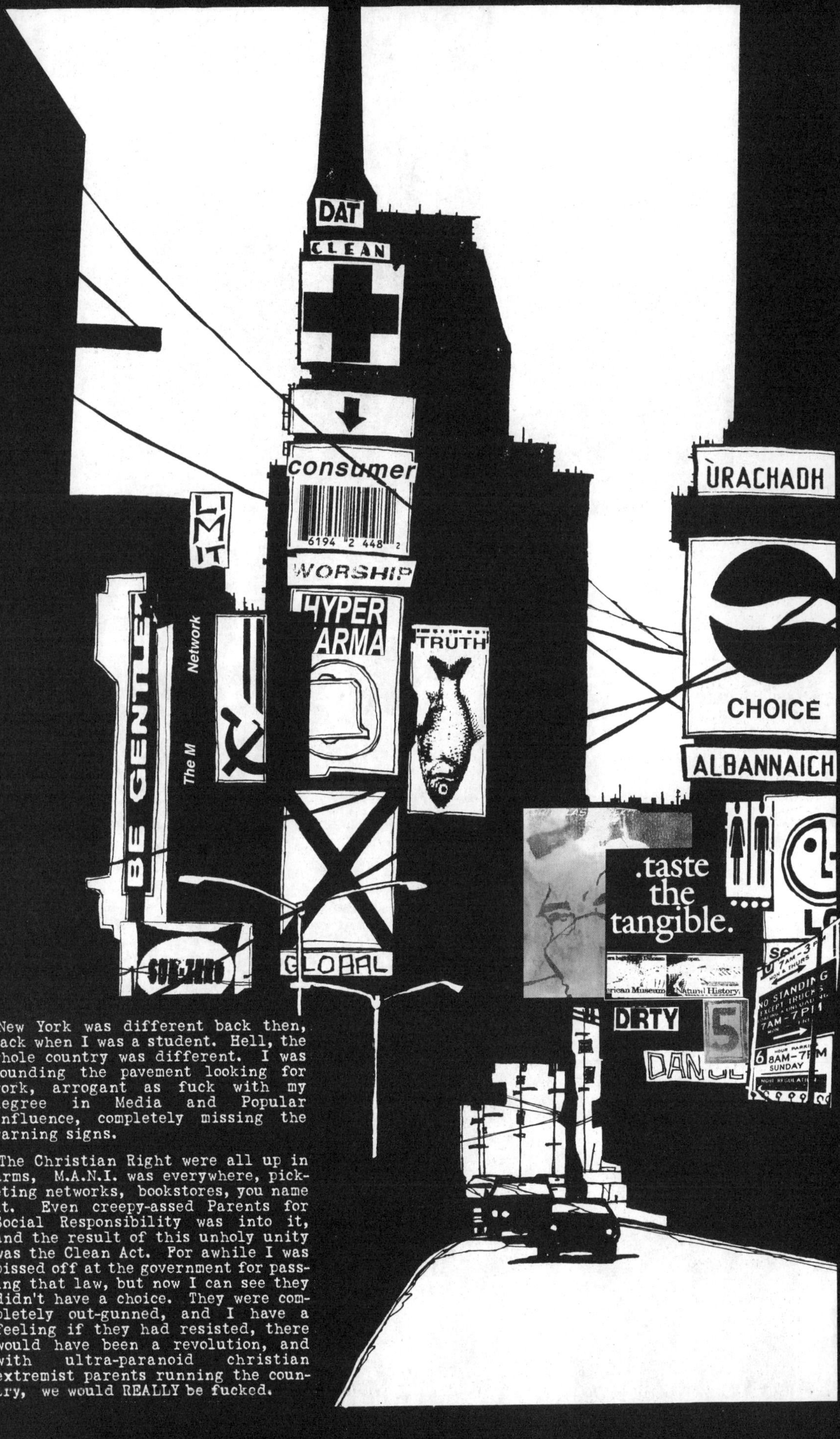
DAT
CLEAN
consumer
6194 2 448 2
WORSHIP
HYPER ARMA
TRUTH
LIMIT
BE GENTLE
The M Network
GLOBAL
ÙRACHADH
CHOICE
ALBANNAICH
.taste the tangible.
DRTY
5

"New York was different back then, back when I was a student. Hell, the whole country was different. I was pounding the pavement looking for work, arrogant as fuck with my degree in Media and Popular Influence, completely missing the warning signs.

"The Christian Right were all up in arms, M.A.N.I. was everywhere, picketing networks, bookstores, you name it. Even creepy-assed Parents for Social Responsibility was into it, and the result of this unholy unity was the Clean Act. For awhile I was pissed off at the government for passing that law, but now I can see they didn't have a choice. They were completely out-gunned, and I have a feeling if they had resisted, there would have been a revolution, and with ultra-paranoid christian extremist parents running the country, we would REALLY be fucked.

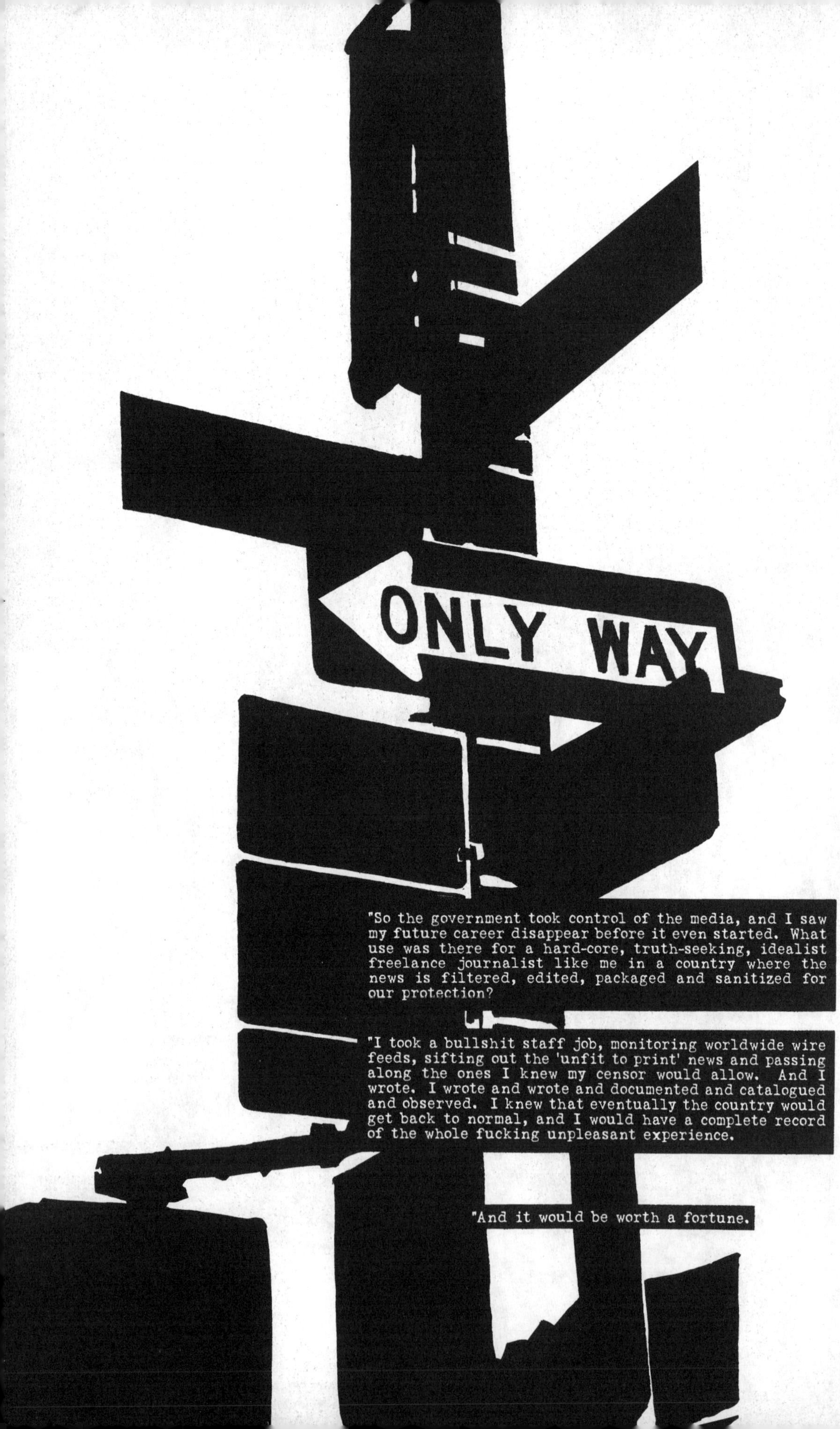
ONLY WAY
"So the government took control of the media, and I saw my future career disappear before it even started. What use was there for a hard-core, truth-seeking, idealist freelance journalist like me in a country where the news is filtered, edited, packaged and sanitized for our protection?
"I took a bullshit staff job, monitoring worldwide wire feeds, sifting out the 'unfit to print' news and passing along the ones I knew my censor would allow. And I wrote. I wrote and wrote and documented and catalogued and observed. I knew that eventually the country would get back to normal, and I would have a complete record of the whole fucking unpleasant experience.
"And it would be worth a fortune.

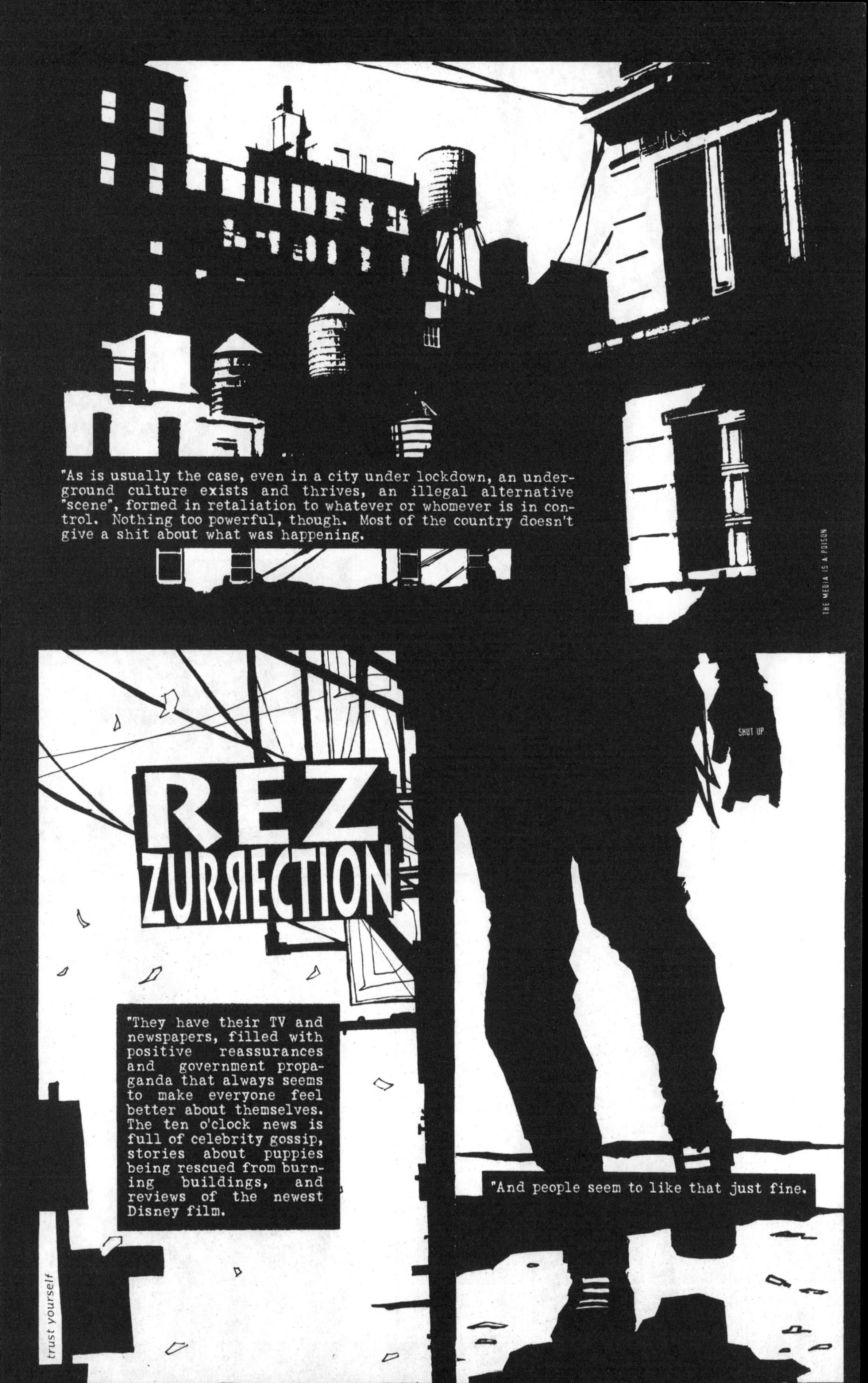

"As is usually the case, even in a city under lockdown, an underground culture exists and thrives, an illegal alternative "scene", formed in retaliation to whatever or whomever is in control. Nothing too powerful, though. Most of the country doesn't give a shit about what was happening.
THE MEDIA IS A POISON
SHUT UP
REZ ZURRECTION
"They have their TV and newspapers, filled with positive reassurances and government propaganda that always seems to make everyone feel better about themselves. The ten o'clock news is full of celebrity gossip, stories about puppies being rescued from burning buildings, and reviews of the newest Disney film.
"And people seem to like that just fine.
trust yourself

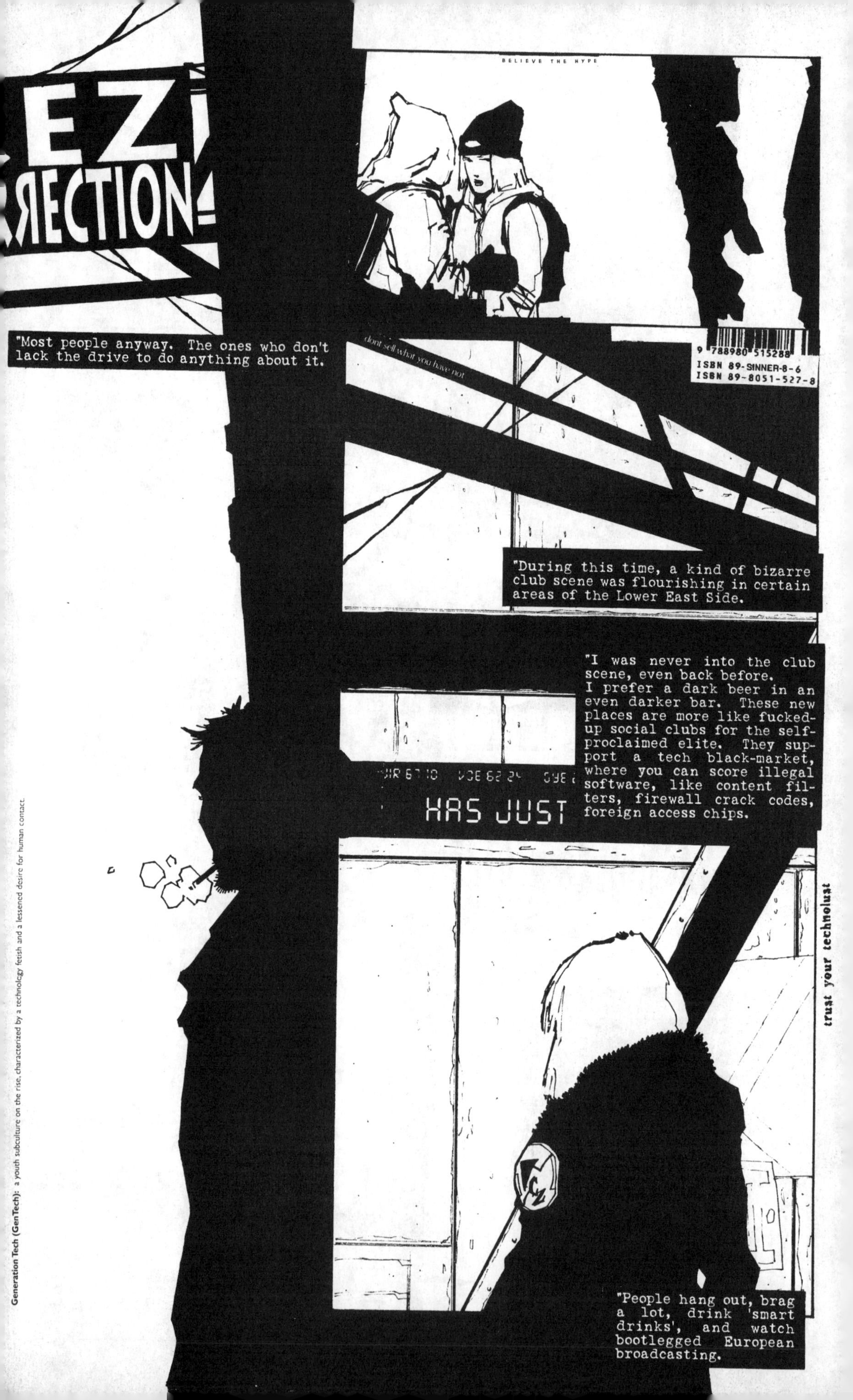

EZ
RECTION
BELIEVE THE HYPE
"Most people anyway. The ones who don't lack the drive to do anything about it.
dont sell what you have not
ISBN 89-SINNER-8-6
ISBN 89-8051-527-8
"During this time, a kind of bizarre club scene was flourishing in certain areas of the Lower East Side.
"I was never into the club scene, even back before.
I prefer a dark beer in an even darker bar. These new places are more like fucked-up social clubs for the self-proclaimed elite. They support a tech black-market, where you can score illegal software, like content filters, firewall crack codes, foreign access chips.
HAS JUST
"People hang out, brag a lot, drink 'smart drinks', and watch bootlegged European broadcasting.
trust your technolust

Generation Tech (GenTech): a youth subculture on the rise, characterized by a technolcgy fetish and a lessened desire for human contact.

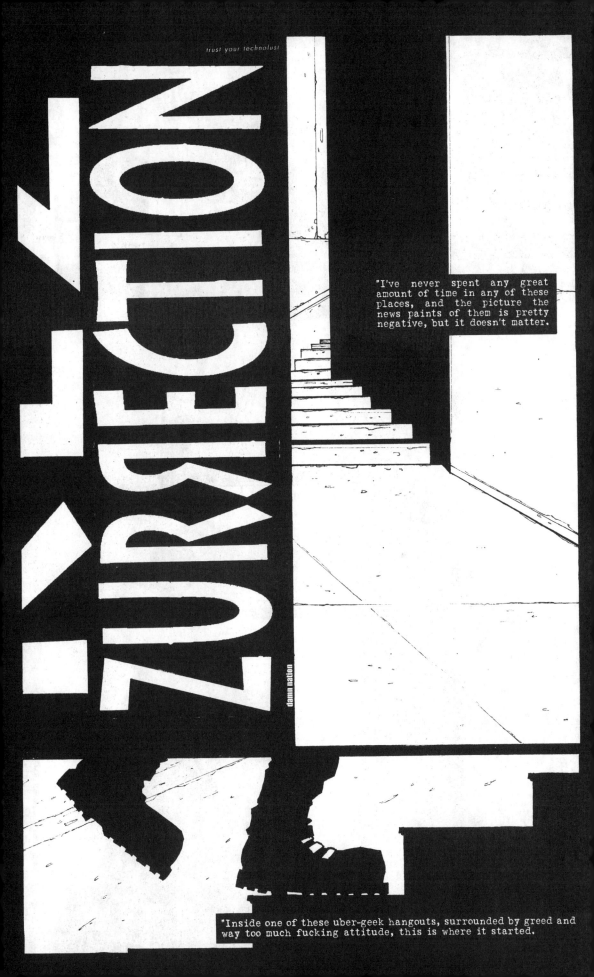

trust your technolust

INSURRECTION

damn nation

"I've never spent any great amount of time in any of these places, and the picture the news paints of them is pretty negative, but it doesn't matter.

"Inside one of these uber-geek hangouts, surrounded by greed and way too much fucking attitude, this is where it started.

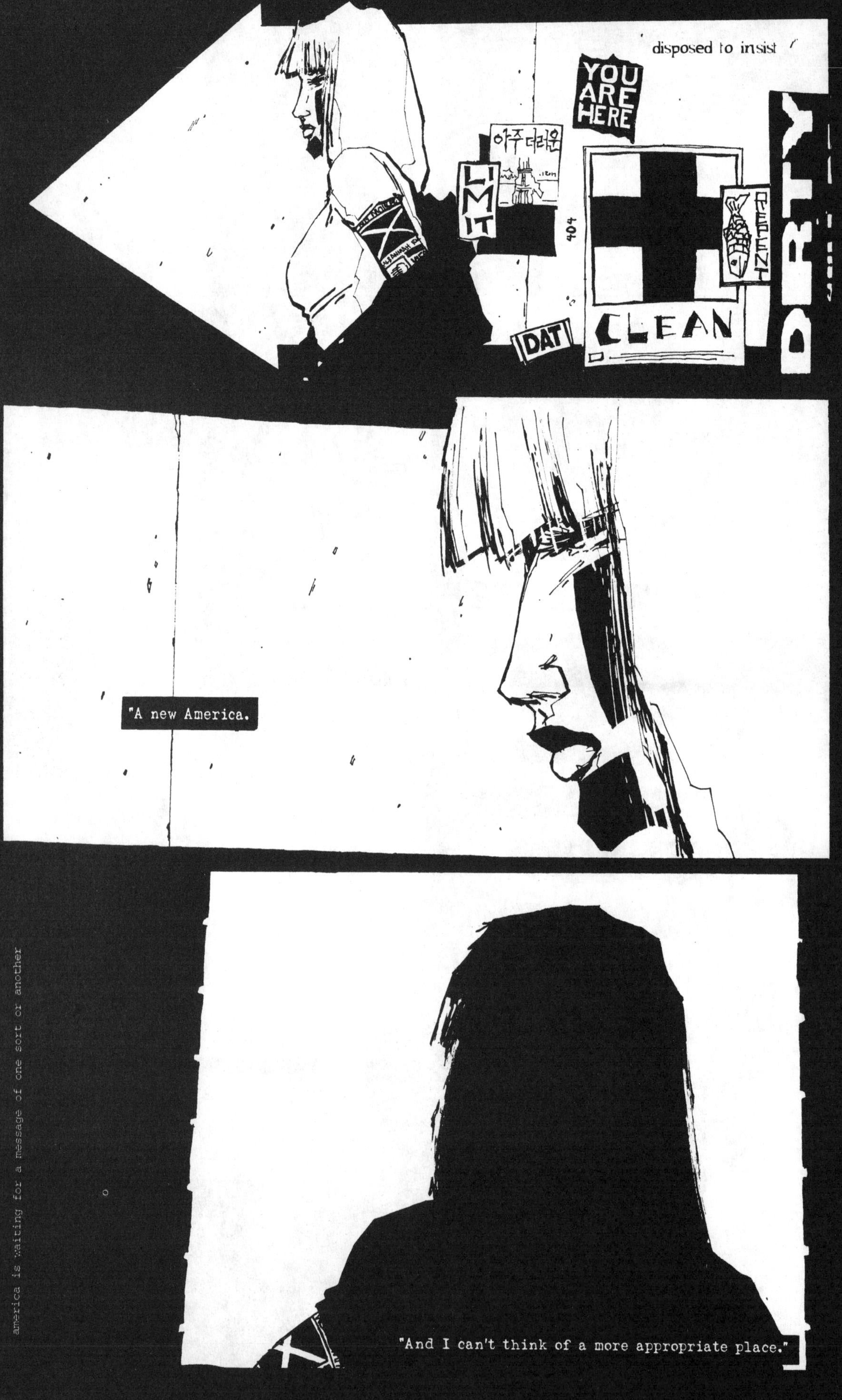
disposed to insist
YOU ARE HERE
아주더러운
LIMIT
404
REPENT
CLEAN
DAT
DRTY
"A new America.
"And I can't think of a more appropriate place."

america is waiting for a message of one sort or another

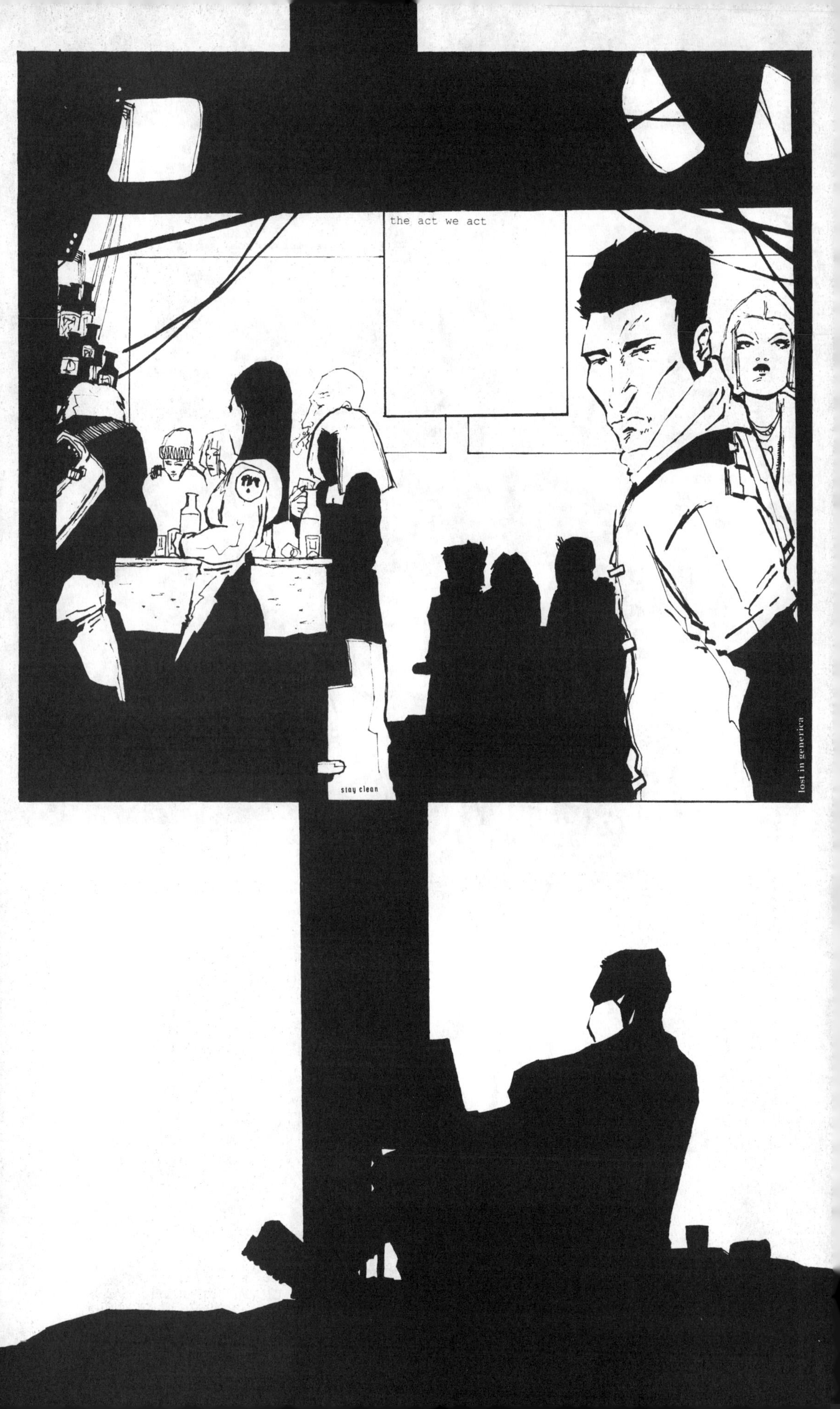
the act we act
stay clean
lost in generica

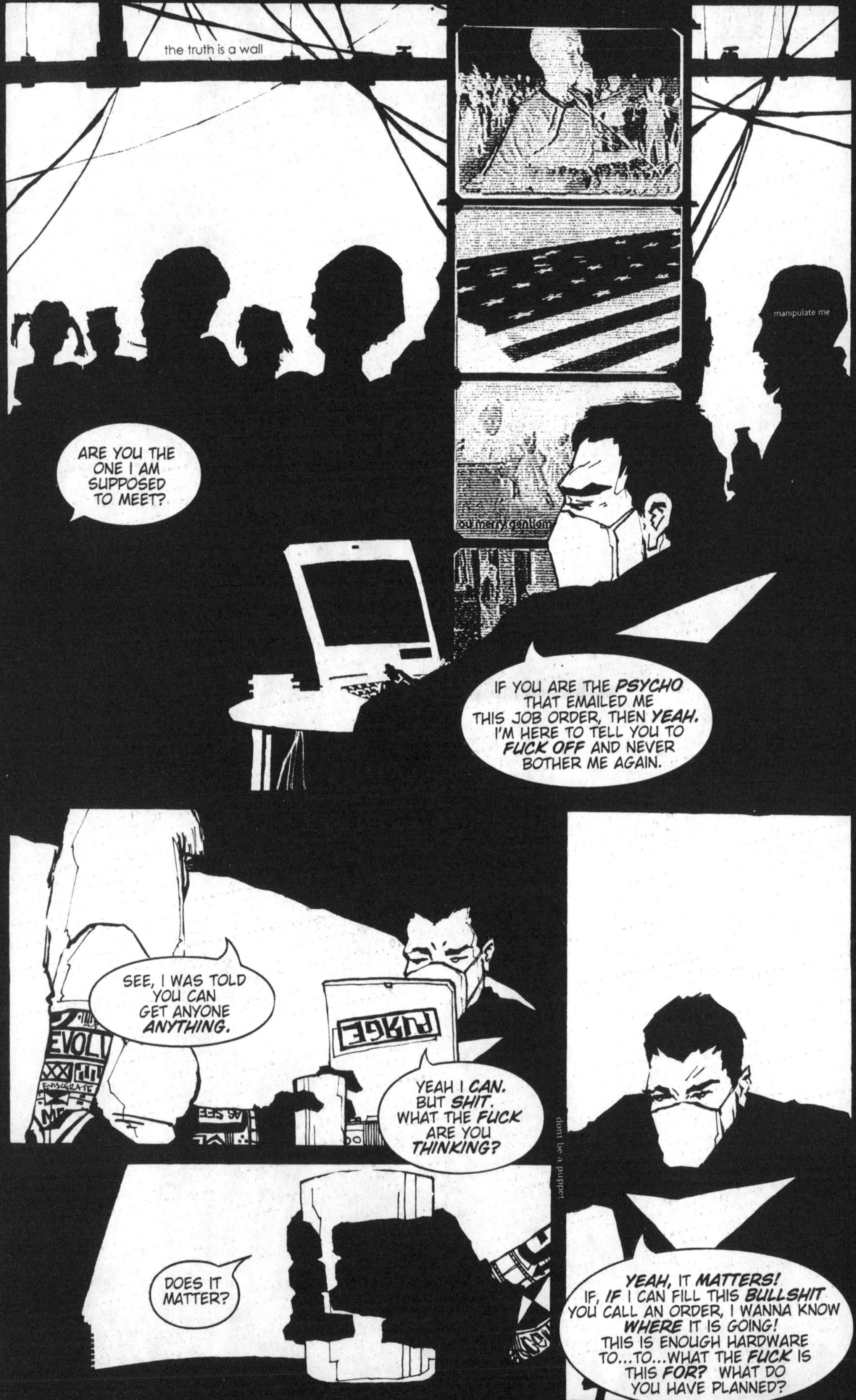
the truth is a wall
manipulate me
ARE YOU THE ONE I AM SUPPOSED TO MEET?
IF YOU ARE THE PSYCHO THAT EMAILED ME THIS JOB ORDER, THEN YEAH. I'M HERE TO TELL YOU TO FUCK OFF AND NEVER BOTHER ME AGAIN.
SEE, I WAS TOLD YOU CAN GET ANYONE ANYTHING.
YEAH I CAN. BUT SHIT. WHAT THE FUCK ARE YOU THINKING?
DOES IT MATTER?
dont be a puppet
YEAH, IT MATTERS! IF, IF I CAN FILL THIS BULLSHIT YOU CALL AN ORDER, I WANNA KNOW WHERE IT IS GOING! THIS IS ENOUGH HARDWARE TO...TO...WHAT THE FUCK IS THIS FOR? WHAT DO YOU HAVE PLANNED?

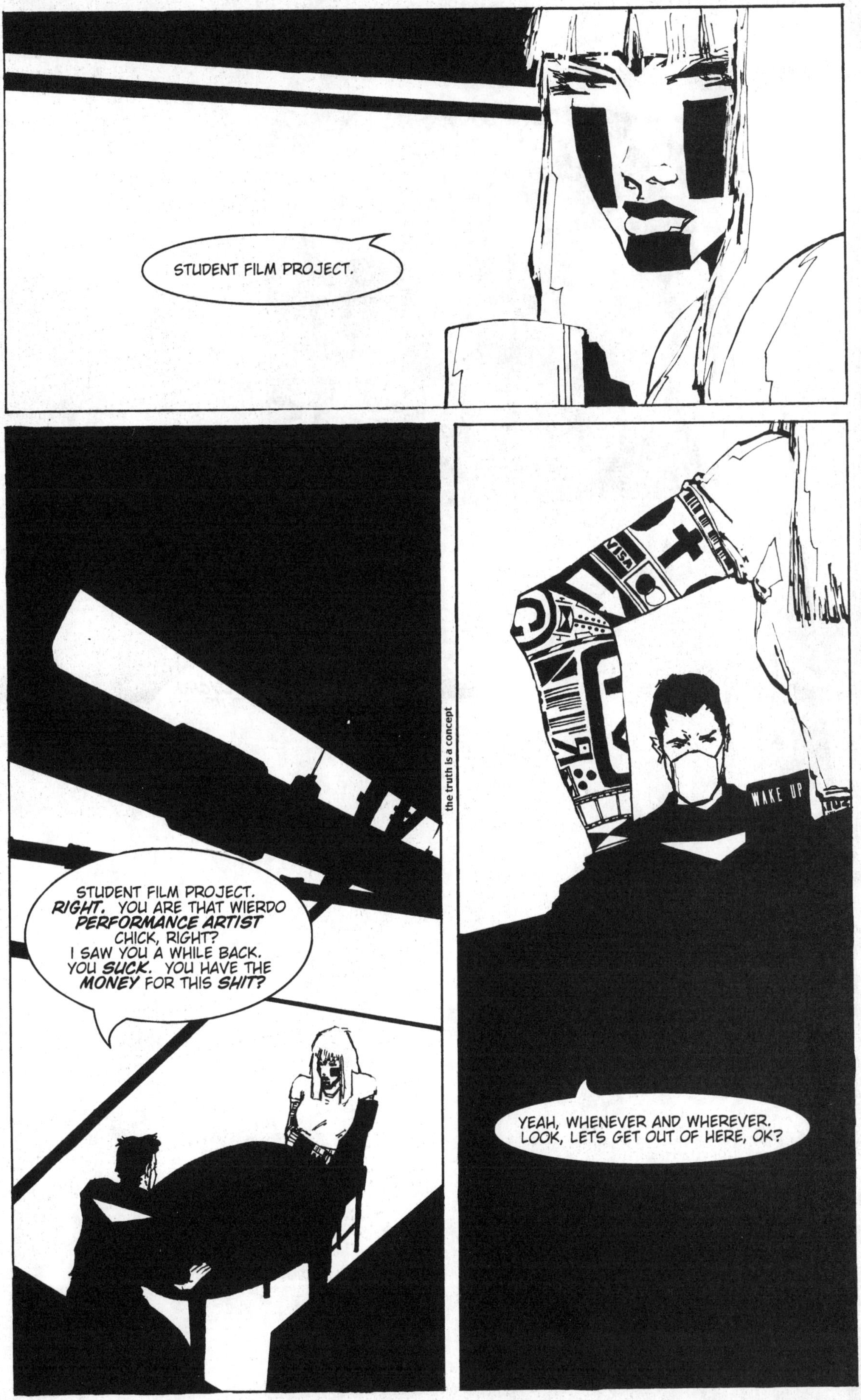
STUDENT FILM PROJECT.
STUDENT FILM PROJECT. RIGHT. YOU ARE THAT WIERDO PERFORMANCE ARTIST CHICK, RIGHT? I SAW YOU A WHILE BACK. YOU SUCK. YOU HAVE THE MONEY FOR THIS SHIT?
the truth is a concept
VISA
WAKE UP
YEAH, WHENEVER AND WHEREVER. LOOK, LETS GET OUT OF HERE, OK?

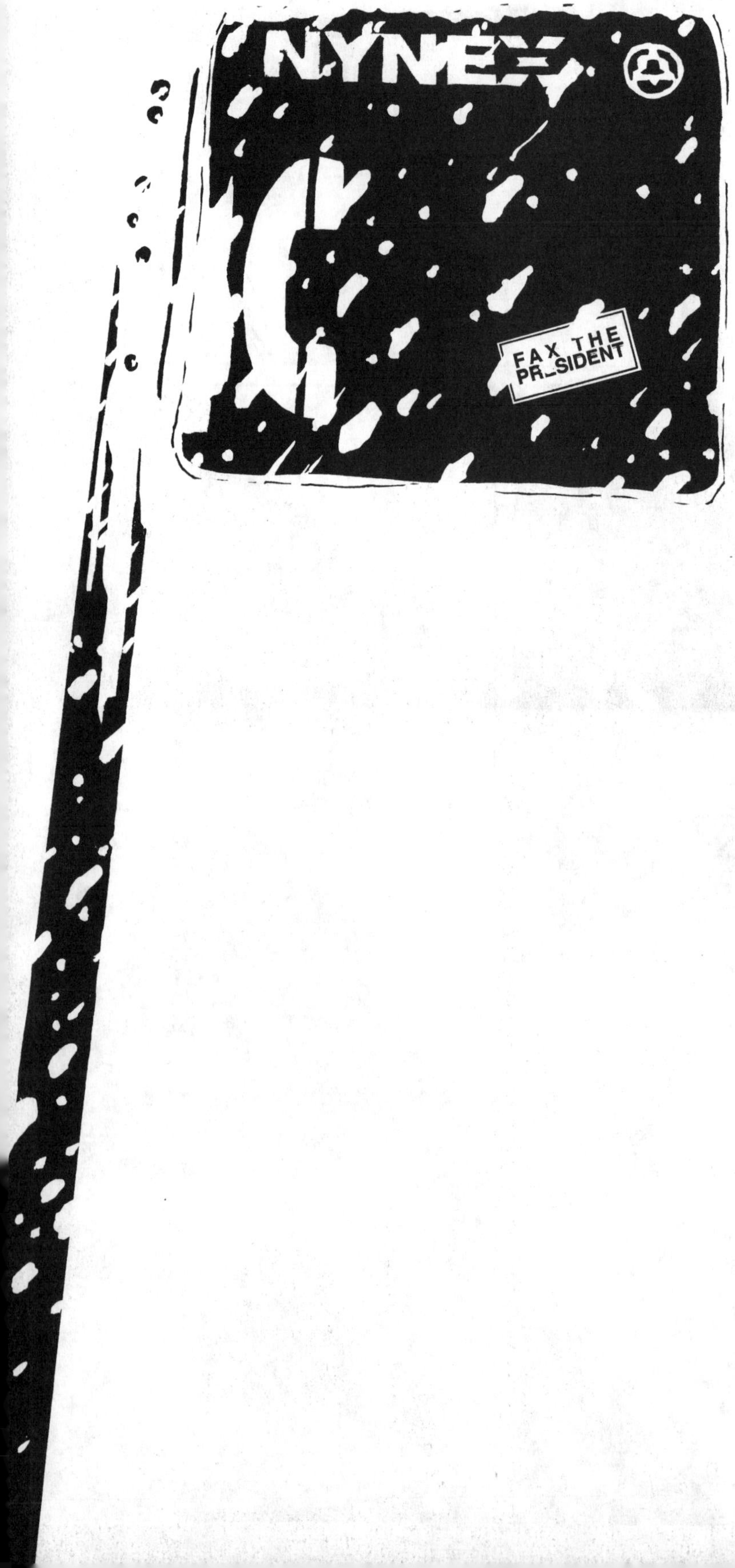
NYNEX
FAX THE
PRESIDENT

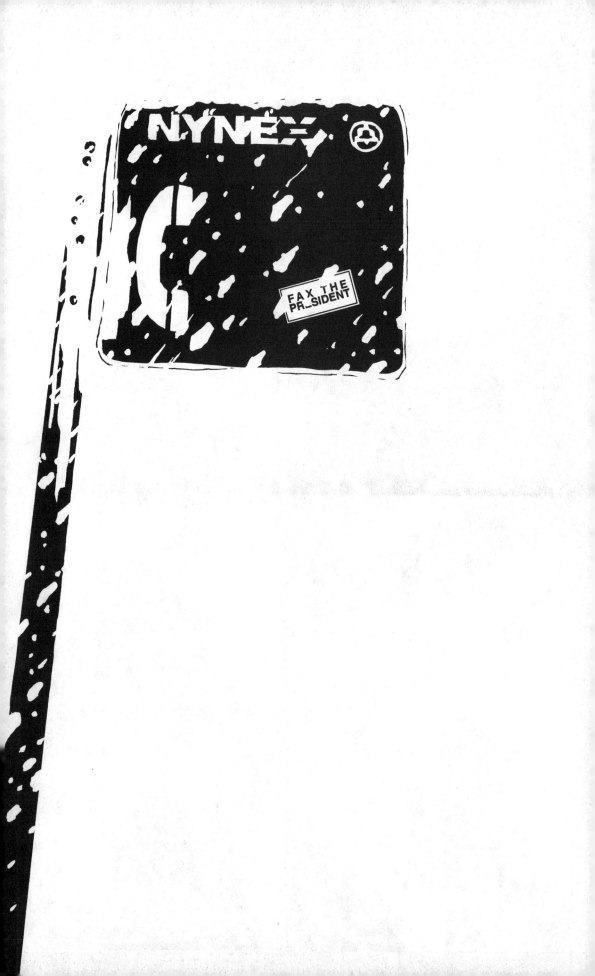

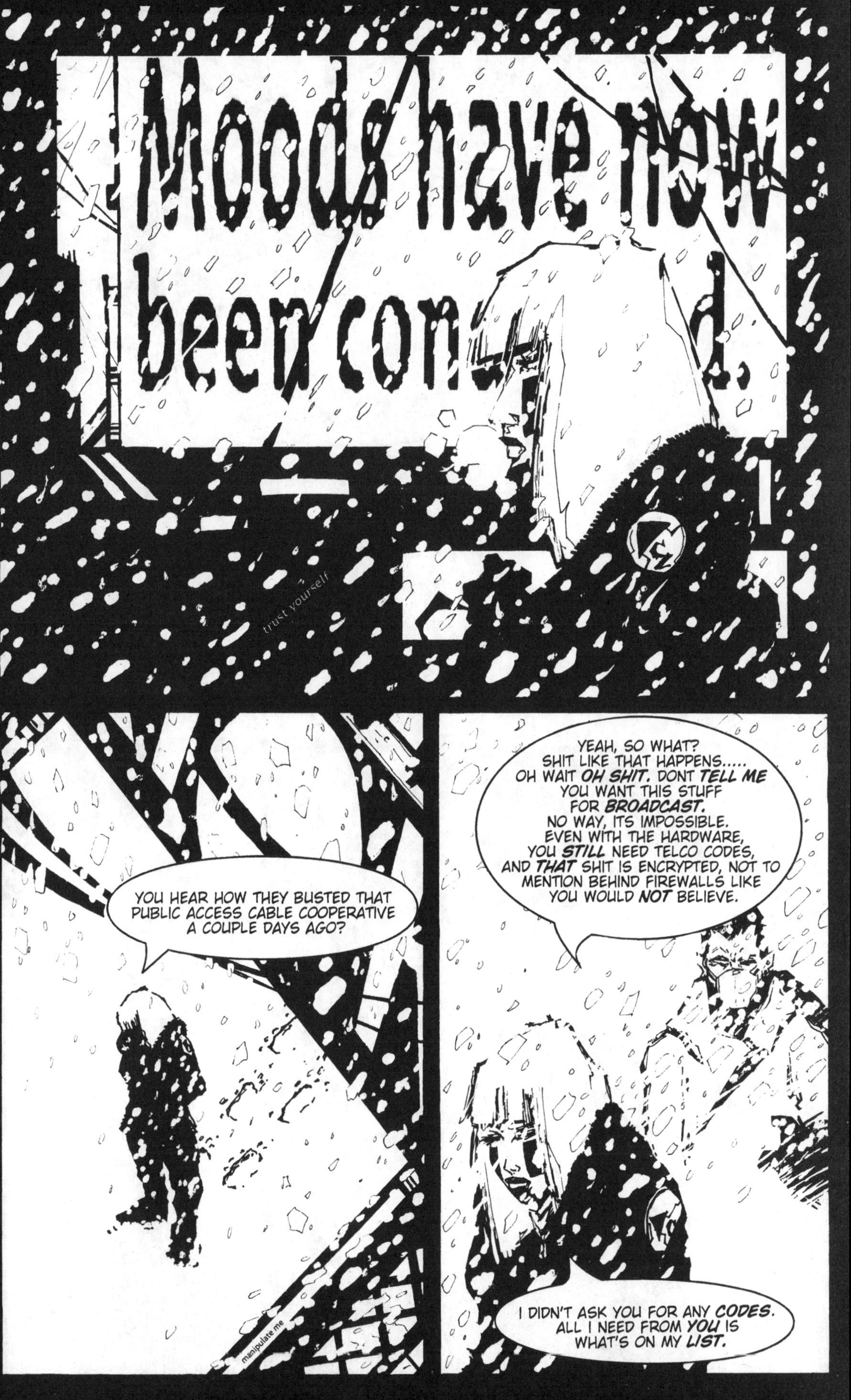
Moods have now
been con d.
trust yourself
YOU HEAR HOW THEY BUSTED THAT PUBLIC ACCESS CABLE COOPERATIVE A COUPLE DAYS AGO?
manipulate me
YEAH, SO WHAT? SHIT LIKE THAT HAPPENS..... OH WAIT *OH SHIT.* DONT *TELL ME* YOU WANT THIS STUFF FOR *BROADCAST.* NO WAY, ITS IMPOSSIBLE. EVEN WITH THE HARDWARE, YOU *STILL* NEED TELCO CODES, AND *THAT* SHIT IS ENCRYPTED, NOT TO MENTION BEHIND FIREWALLS LIKE YOU WOULD *NOT* BELIEVE.
I DIDN'T ASK YOU FOR ANY *CODES.* ALL I NEED FROM *YOU* IS WHAT'S ON MY *LIST.*

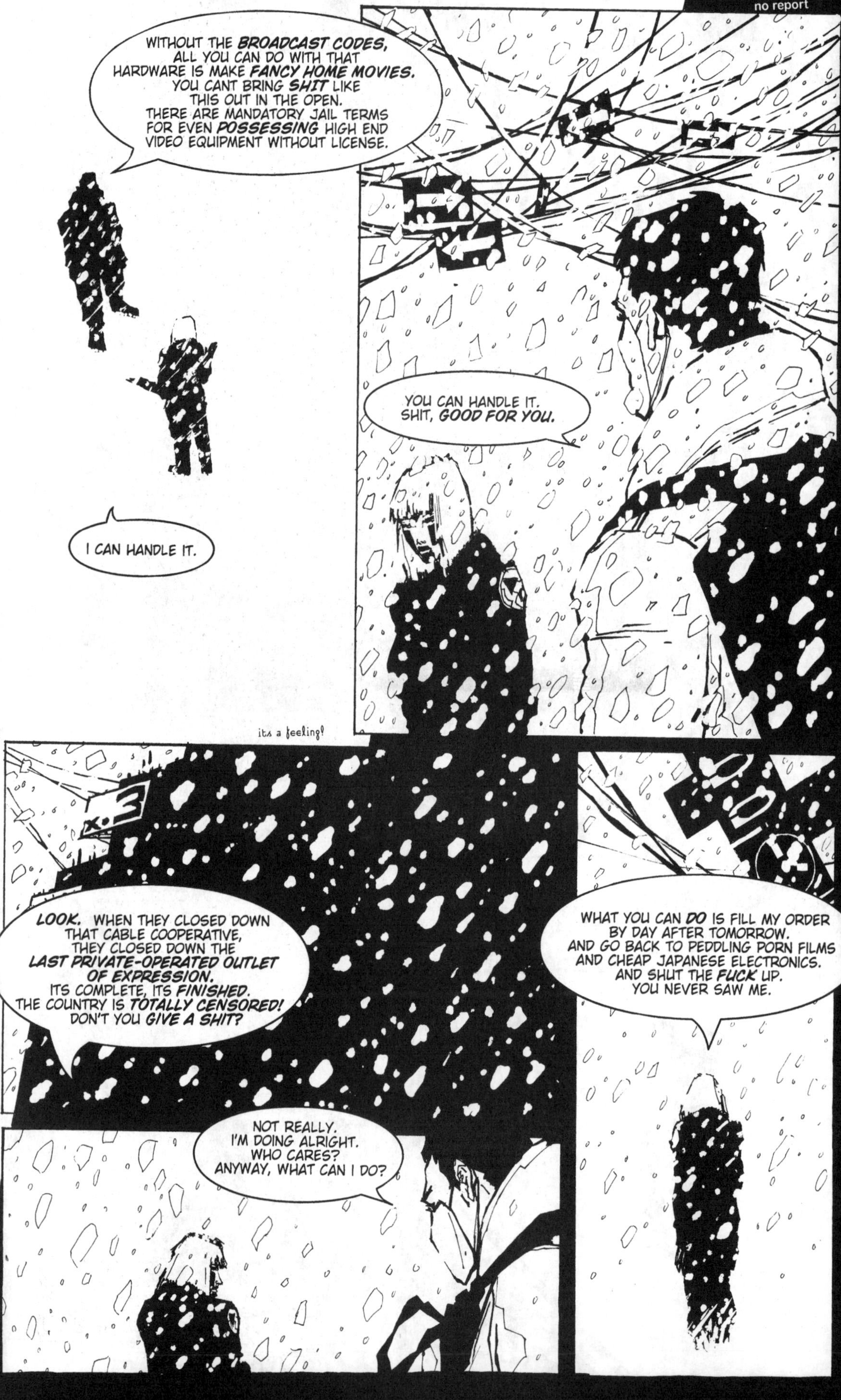
WITHOUT THE BROADCAST CODES, ALL YOU CAN DO WITH THAT HARDWARE IS MAKE FANCY HOME MOVIES. YOU CANT BRING SHIT LIKE THIS OUT IN THE OPEN. THERE ARE MANDATORY JAIL TERMS FOR EVEN POSSESSING HIGH END VIDEO EQUIPMENT WITHOUT LICENSE.
I CAN HANDLE IT.
YOU CAN HANDLE IT. SHIT, GOOD FOR YOU.
its a feeling!
LOOK. WHEN THEY CLOSED DOWN THAT CABLE COOPERATIVE, THEY CLOSED DOWN THE LAST PRIVATE-OPERATED OUTLET OF EXPRESSION. ITS COMPLETE, ITS FINISHED. THE COUNTRY IS TOTALLY CENSORED! DON'T YOU GIVE A SHIT?
NOT REALLY. I'M DOING ALRIGHT. WHO CARES? ANYWAY, WHAT CAN I DO?
WHAT YOU CAN DO IS FILL MY ORDER BY DAY AFTER TOMORROW. AND GO BACK TO PEDDLING PORN FILMS AND CHEAP JAPANESE ELECTRONICS. AND SHUT THE FUCK UP. YOU NEVER SAW ME.

SUBVERTISEMENT

POINT AND SHOOT

w h e n   y o u   s p e a k ,   t h e   s o u n d   o f   y o u r   v o i c e   c a n c e l s   o u t   a l l   o t h e r s

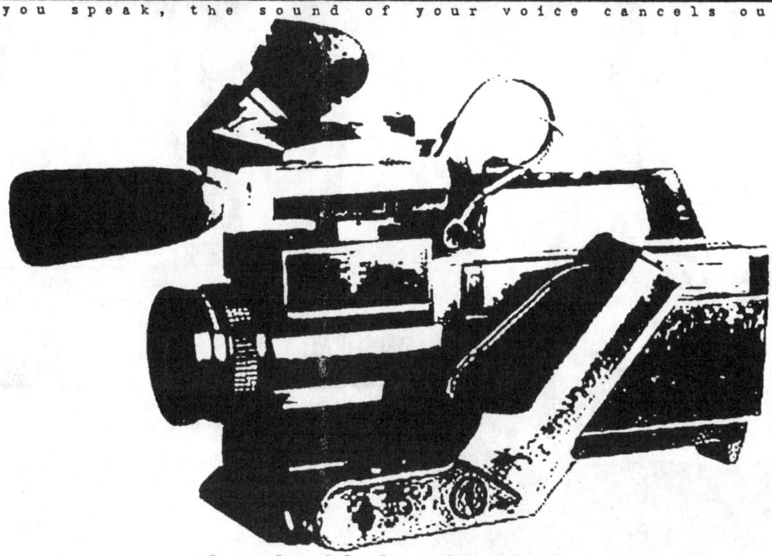

шйо шатсйеч шйо? шйо шатсйеч шйо? шйо шатсйеч уоъ?

With th e advent of the affordable **portable** video camera, multiple watch groups and activist sects have sprung up worldwide, operating in such hot spots as ***Eastern Europe,** the former **Soviet Union,** **N orthern Ireland,** and urban areas **across the** United States.

i r r i t a i n m e n t

villinokivic--

monday, dec 12.

4 students were killed yesterday in the latest clash between the USF and state police. the confrontation erupted when the police attempted to deter the students from publically airing amateur video footage of alleged human rights abuses by the police during last months demonstrations.

w h o   w a t c h e s   w h o ?   w h o   w a t c h e s   y o u ?

..clashes between British troops and pro-independence terrorists agan claimed the lives of several tourists. while such incidents are becoming commonplace, eyewitnesses say the tourists were specifically targeted by the troops because they were filming the demonstration. the families of the victims are outraged, and at this time, Scotland Yard has declined to comment. a search has uncovered no video cameras or video cassettes in the vicinity...

YOUR MIND IS A WEAPON.
USE IT.

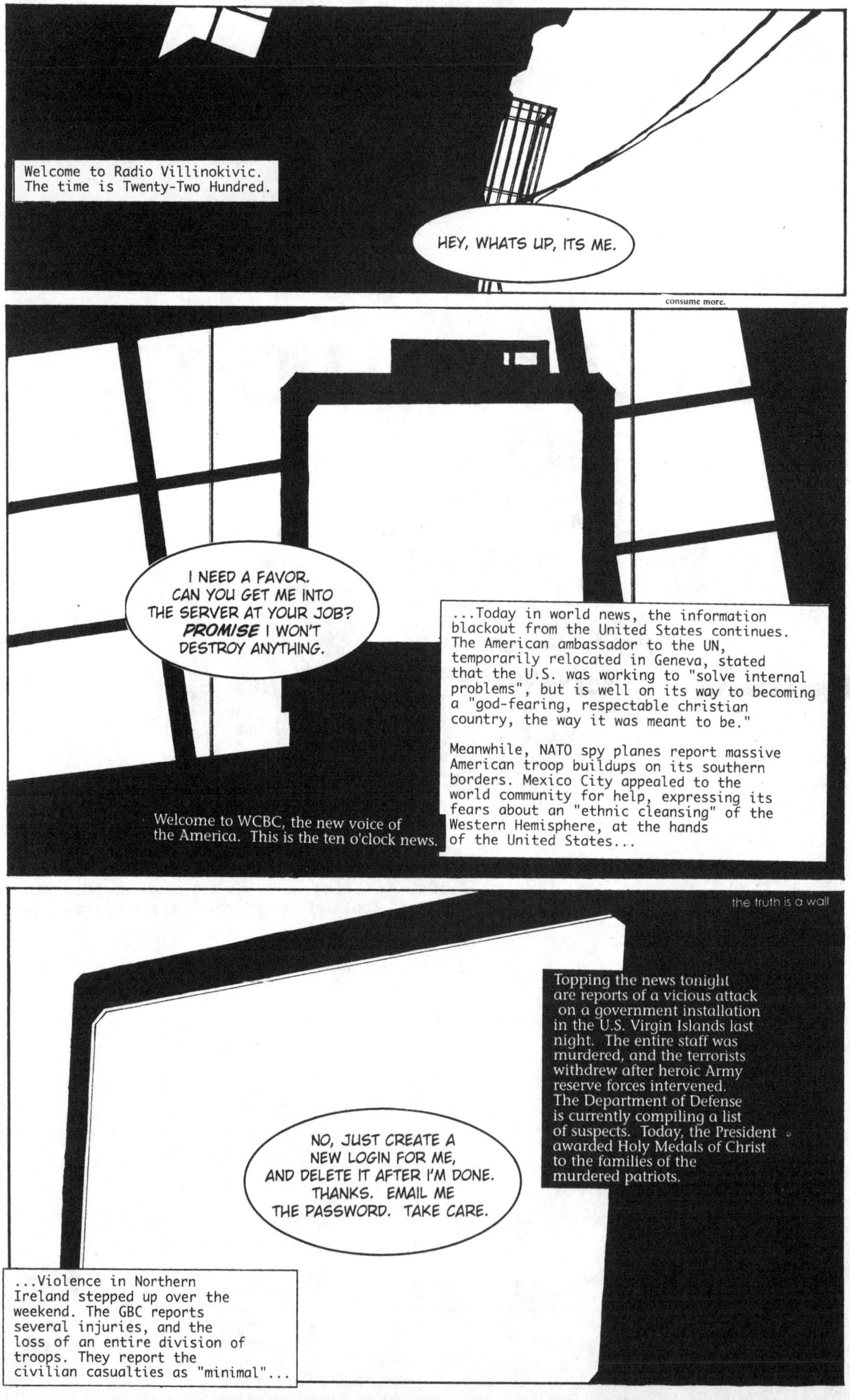

Welcome to Radio Villinokivic. The time is Twenty-Two Hundred.
HEY, WHATS UP, ITS ME.
consume more.
I NEED A FAVOR. CAN YOU GET ME INTO THE SERVER AT YOUR JOB? *PROMISE* I WON'T DESTROY ANYTHING.
...Today in world news, the information blackout from the United States continues. The American ambassador to the UN, temporarily relocated in Geneva, stated that the U.S. was working to "solve internal problems", but is well on its way to becoming a "god-fearing, respectable christian country, the way it was meant to be."
Meanwhile, NATO spy planes report massive American troop buildups on its southern borders. Mexico City appealed to the world community for help, expressing its fears about an "ethnic cleansing" of the Western Hemisphere, at the hands of the United States...
Welcome to WCBC, the new voice of the America. This is the ten o'clock news.
the truth is a wall
Topping the news tonight are reports of a vicious attack on a government installation in the U.S. Virgin Islands last night. The entire staff was murdered, and the terrorists withdrew after heroic Army reserve forces intervened. The Department of Defense is currently compiling a list of suspects. Today, the President awarded Holy Medals of Christ to the families of the murdered patriots.
NO, JUST CREATE A NEW LOGIN FOR ME, AND DELETE IT AFTER I'M DONE. THANKS. EMAIL ME THE PASSWORD. TAKE CARE.
...Violence in Northern Ireland stepped up over the weekend. The GBC reports several injuries, and the loss of an entire division of troops. They report the civilian casualties as "minimal"...

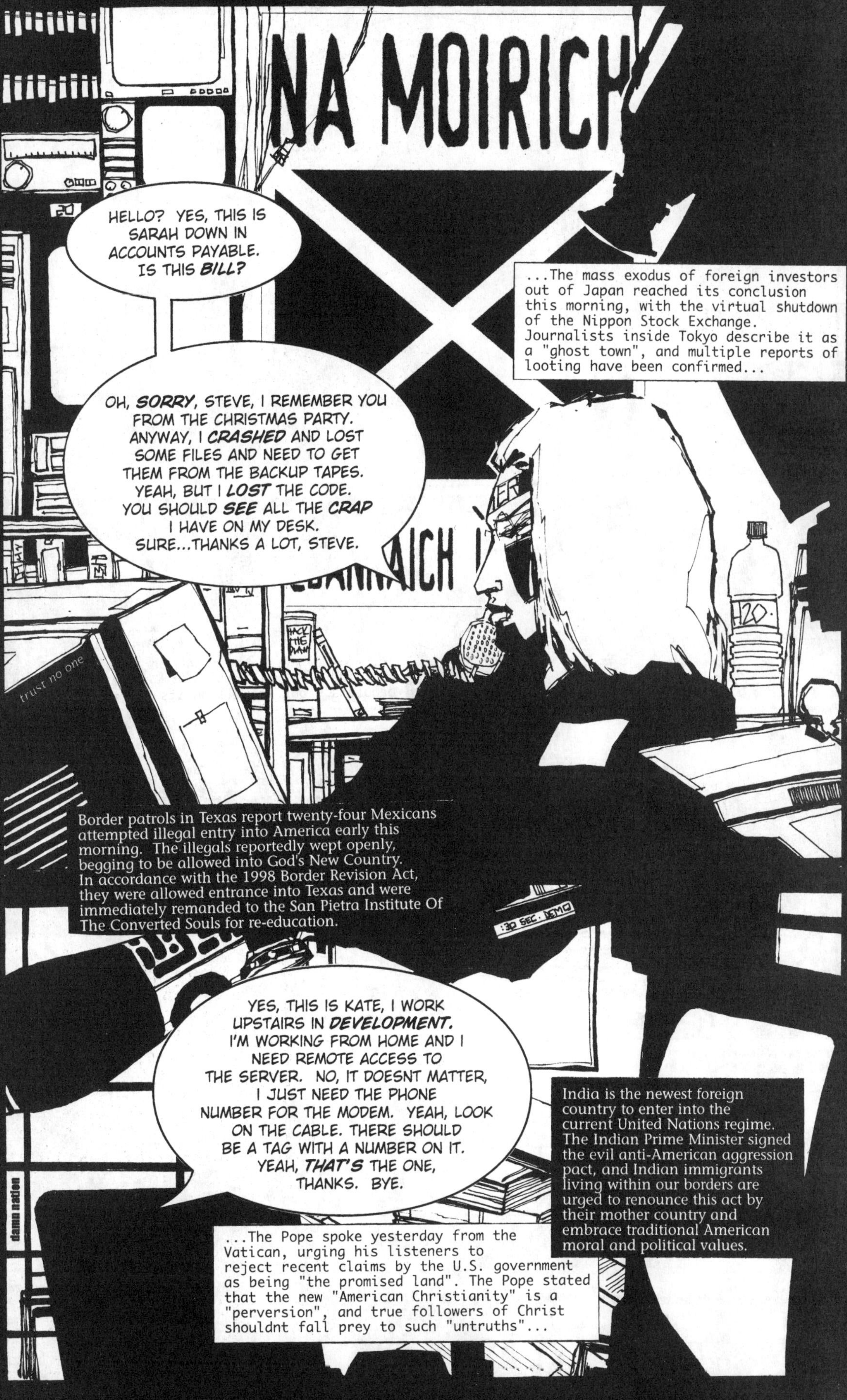
NA MOIRICH
HELLO? YES, THIS IS SARAH DOWN IN ACCOUNTS PAYABLE. IS THIS BILL?
...The mass exodus of foreign investors out of Japan reached its conclusion this morning, with the virtual shutdown of the Nippon Stock Exchange. Journalists inside Tokyo describe it as a "ghost town", and multiple reports of looting have been confirmed...
OH, SORRY, STEVE, I REMEMBER YOU FROM THE CHRISTMAS PARTY. ANYWAY, I CRASHED AND LOST SOME FILES AND NEED TO GET THEM FROM THE BACKUP TAPES. YEAH, BUT I LOST THE CODE. YOU SHOULD SEE ALL THE CRAP I HAVE ON MY DESK. SURE...THANKS A LOT, STEVE.
trust no one
H2O
Border patrols in Texas report twenty-four Mexicans attempted illegal entry into America early this morning. The illegals reportedly wept openly, begging to be allowed into God's New Country. In accordance with the 1998 Border Revision Act, they were allowed entrance into Texas and were immediately remanded to the San Pietra Institute Of The Converted Souls for re-education.
:30 SEC. DEMO
YES, THIS IS KATE, I WORK UPSTAIRS IN DEVELOPMENT. I'M WORKING FROM HOME AND I NEED REMOTE ACCESS TO THE SERVER. NO, IT DOESNT MATTER, I JUST NEED THE PHONE NUMBER FOR THE MODEM. YEAH, LOOK ON THE CABLE. THERE SHOULD BE A TAG WITH A NUMBER ON IT. YEAH, THAT'S THE ONE, THANKS. BYE.
India is the newest foreign country to enter into the current United Nations regime. The Indian Prime Minister signed the evil anti-American aggression pact, and Indian immigrants living within our borders are urged to renounce this act by their mother country and embrace traditional American moral and political values.
damn nation
...The Pope spoke yesterday from the Vatican, urging his listeners to reject recent claims by the U.S. government as being "the promised land". The Pope stated that the new "American Christianity" is a "perversion", and true followers of Christ shouldnt fall prey to such "untruths"...

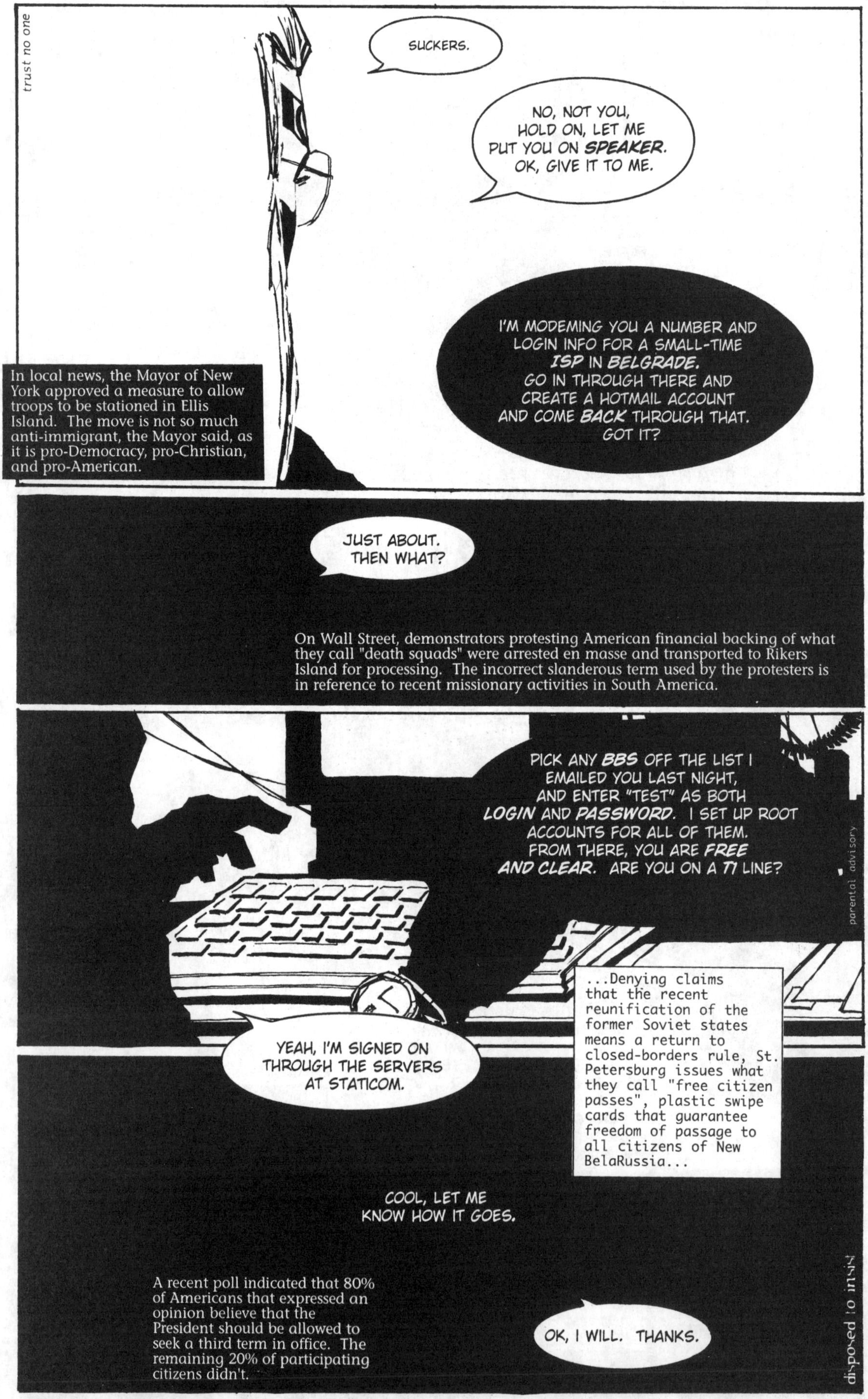
trust no one
SUCKERS.
NO, NOT YOU, HOLD ON, LET ME PUT YOU ON SPEAKER. OK, GIVE IT TO ME.
I'M MODEMING YOU A NUMBER AND LOGIN INFO FOR A SMALL-TIME ISP IN BELGRADE. GO IN THROUGH THERE AND CREATE A HOTMAIL ACCOUNT AND COME BACK THROUGH THAT. GOT IT?
In local news, the Mayor of New York approved a measure to allow troops to be stationed in Ellis Island. The move is not so much anti-immigrant, the Mayor said, as it is pro-Democracy, pro-Christian, and pro-American.
JUST ABOUT. THEN WHAT?
On Wall Street, demonstrators protesting American financial backing of what they call "death squads" were arrested en masse and transported to Rikers Island for processing. The incorrect slanderous term used by the protesters is in reference to recent missionary activities in South America.
PICK ANY BBS OFF THE LIST I EMAILED YOU LAST NIGHT, AND ENTER "TEST" AS BOTH LOGIN AND PASSWORD. I SET UP ROOT ACCOUNTS FOR ALL OF THEM. FROM THERE, YOU ARE FREE AND CLEAR. ARE YOU ON A T1 LINE?
parental advisory
YEAH, I'M SIGNED ON THROUGH THE SERVERS AT STATICOM.
...Denying claims that the recent reunification of the former Soviet states means a return to closed-borders rule, St. Petersburg issues what they call "free citizen passes", plastic swipe cards that guarantee freedom of passage to all citizens of New BelaRussia...
COOL, LET ME KNOW HOW IT GOES.
A recent poll indicated that 80% of Americans that expressed an opinion believe that the President should be allowed to seek a third term in office. The remaining 20% of participating citizens didn't.
OK, I WILL. THANKS.

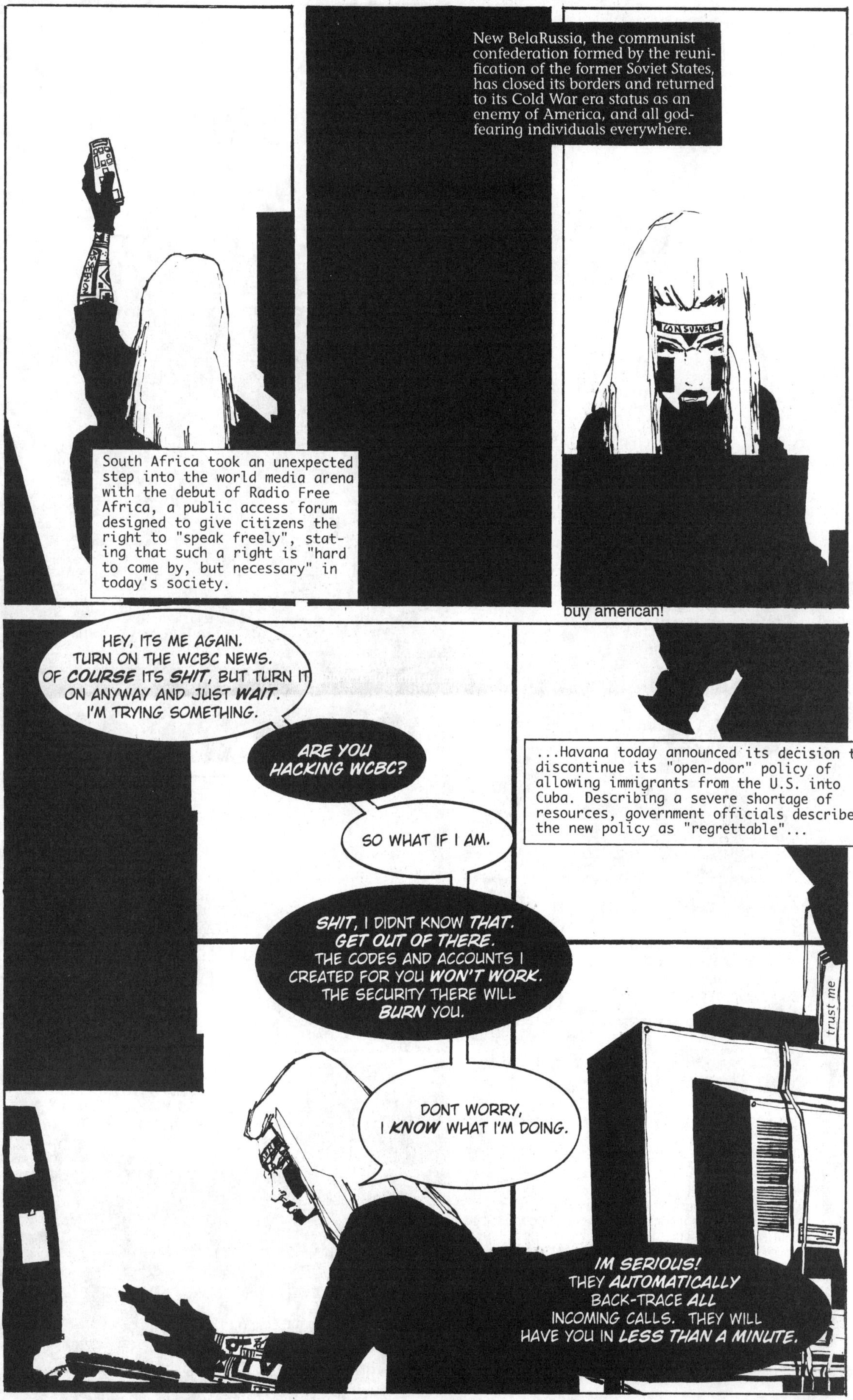

South Africa took an unexpected step into the world media arena with the debut of Radio Free Africa, a public access forum designed to give citizens the right to "speak freely", stating that such a right is "hard to come by, but necessary" in today's society.
New BelaRussia, the communist confederation formed by the reunification of the former Soviet States, has closed its borders and returned to its Cold War era status as an enemy of America, and all god-fearing individuals everywhere.
CONSUMER
buy american!
HEY, ITS ME AGAIN. TURN ON THE WCBC NEWS. OF COURSE ITS SHIT, BUT TURN IT ON ANYWAY AND JUST WAIT. I'M TRYING SOMETHING.
ARE YOU HACKING WCBC?
SO WHAT IF I AM.
...Havana today announced its decision to discontinue its "open-door" policy of allowing immigrants from the U.S. into Cuba. Describing a severe shortage of resources, government officials described the new policy as "regrettable"...
SHIT, I DIDNT KNOW THAT. GET OUT OF THERE. THE CODES AND ACCOUNTS I CREATED FOR YOU WON'T WORK. THE SECURITY THERE WILL BURN YOU.
trust me
DONT WORRY, I KNOW WHAT I'M DOING.
IM SERIOUS! THEY AUTOMATICALLY BACK-TRACE ALL INCOMING CALLS. THEY WILL HAVE YOU IN LESS THAN A MINUTE.

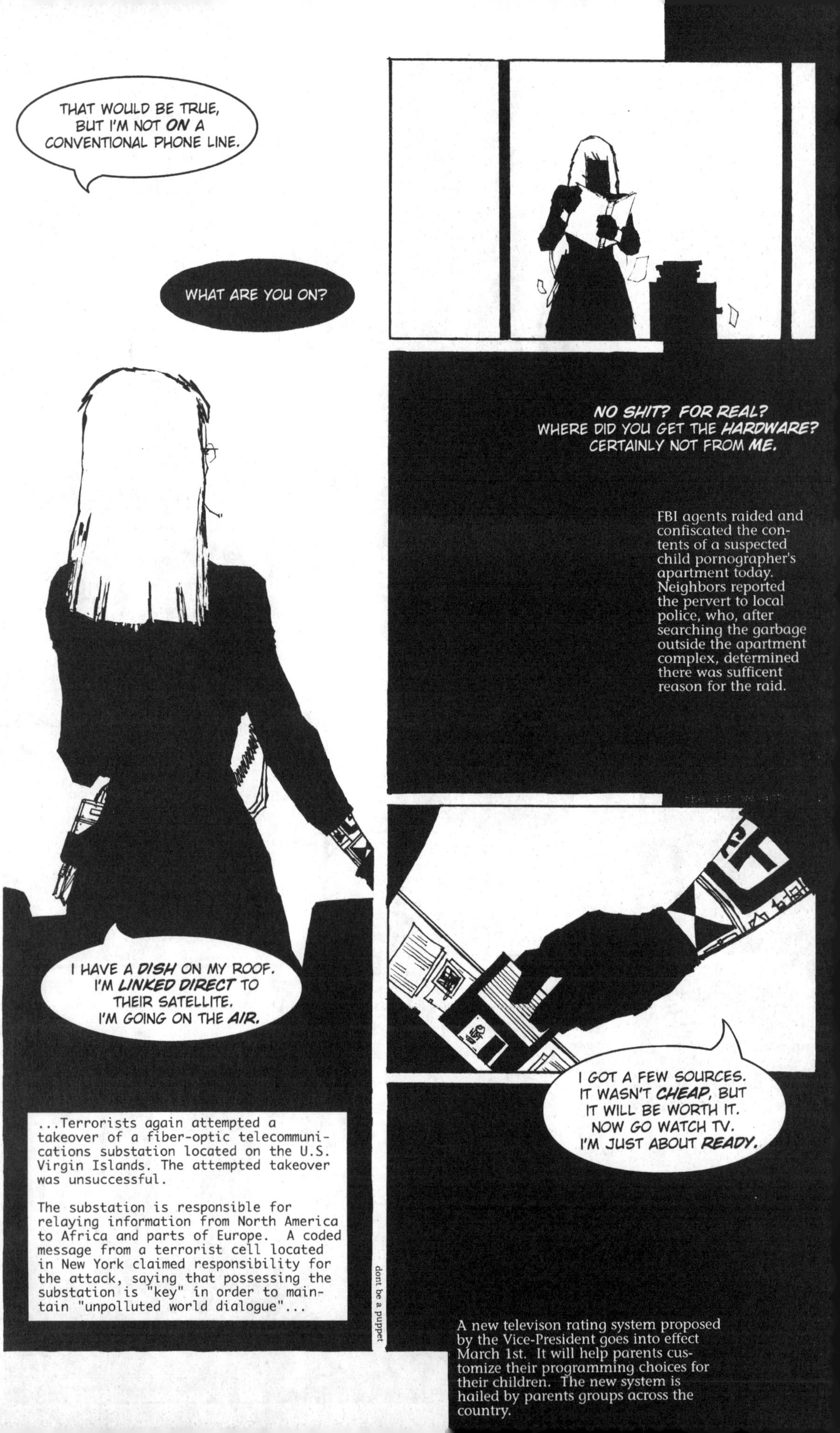
THAT WOULD BE TRUE, BUT I'M NOT ON A CONVENTIONAL PHONE LINE.
WHAT ARE YOU ON?
I HAVE A DISH ON MY ROOF. I'M LINKED DIRECT TO THEIR SATELLITE. I'M GOING ON THE AIR.
...Terrorists again attempted a takeover of a fiber-optic telecommunications substation located on the U.S. Virgin Islands. The attempted takeover was unsuccessful.
The substation is responsible for relaying information from North America to Africa and parts of Europe. A coded message from a terrorist cell located in New York claimed responsibility for the attack, saying that possessing the substation is "key" in order to maintain "unpolluted world dialogue"...
dont be a puppet
NO SHIT? FOR REAL? WHERE DID YOU GET THE HARDWARE? CERTAINLY NOT FROM ME.
FBI agents raided and confiscated the contents of a suspected child pornographer's apartment today. Neighbors reported the pervert to local police, who, after searching the garbage outside the apartment complex, determined there was sufficent reason for the raid.
I GOT A FEW SOURCES. IT WASN'T CHEAP, BUT IT WILL BE WORTH IT. NOW GO WATCH TV. I'M JUST ABOUT READY.
A new televison rating system proposed by the Vice-President goes into effect March 1st. It will help parents customize their programming choices for their children. The new system is hailed by parents groups across the country.

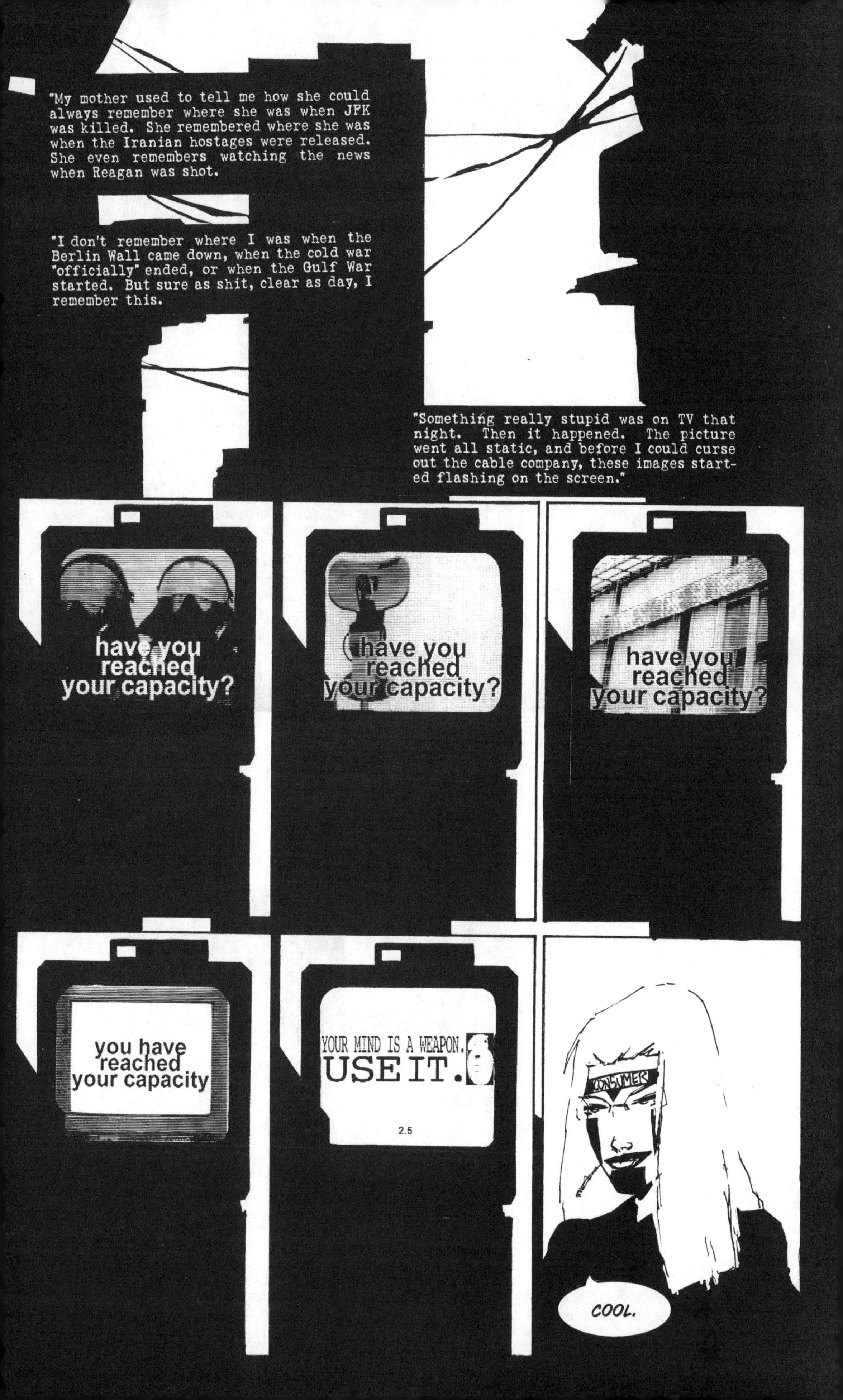
"My mother used to tell me how she could always remember where she was when JFK was killed. She remembered where she was when the Iranian hostages were released. She even remembers watching the news when Reagan was shot.
"I don't remember where I was when the Berlin Wall came down, when the cold war "officially" ended, or when the Gulf War started. But sure as shit, clear as day, I remember this.
"Something really stupid was on TV that night. Then it happened. The picture went all static, and before I could curse out the cable company, these images started flashing on the screen."
have you reached your capacity?
have you reached your capacity?
have you reached your capacity?
you have reached your capacity
YOUR MIND IS A WEAPON. USE IT.
2.5
CONSUMER
COOL.

"It was literally out of nowhere. Television had turned our brains to shit with its Top 100 Video Countdowns and reruns of Seinfeld. But when I saw those 3 seconds of broadcast, I knew something big was about to happen."

Welcome to Radio Villinokivic.   The time is Oh-Six Hundred. Good Morning.

Watch groups in Berlin last night reported what appeared to be 4 seconds of illegal broadcast on WCBC television. Normal programming was interrupted by a series of images and phrases. The source of the broadcast is unknown, although experts believe it was an electronic break-in originating on American soil.

Strangely, there has been no report of this incident on any American news sources.

CONTINUED...

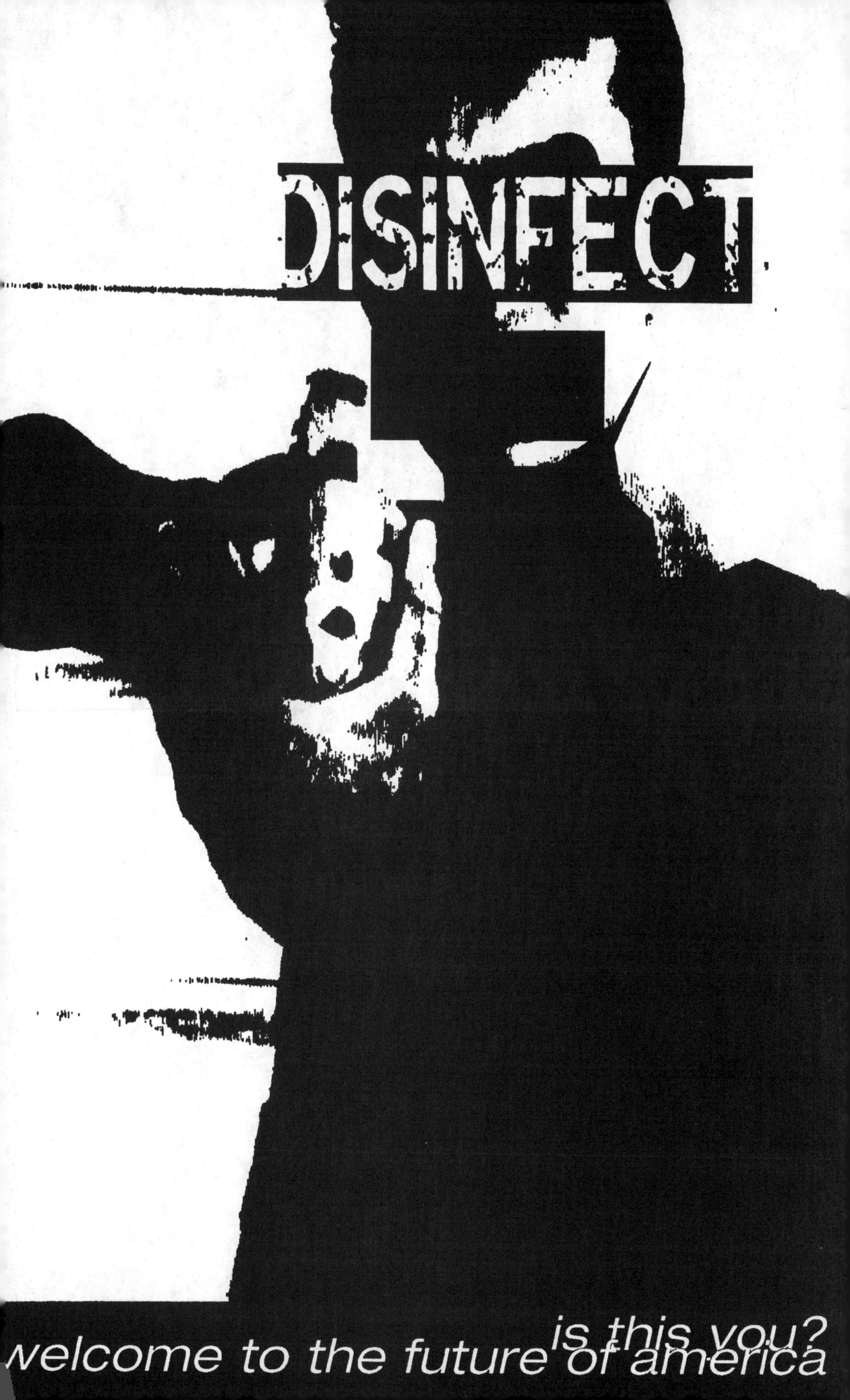
DISINFECT
is this you?
welcome to the future of america

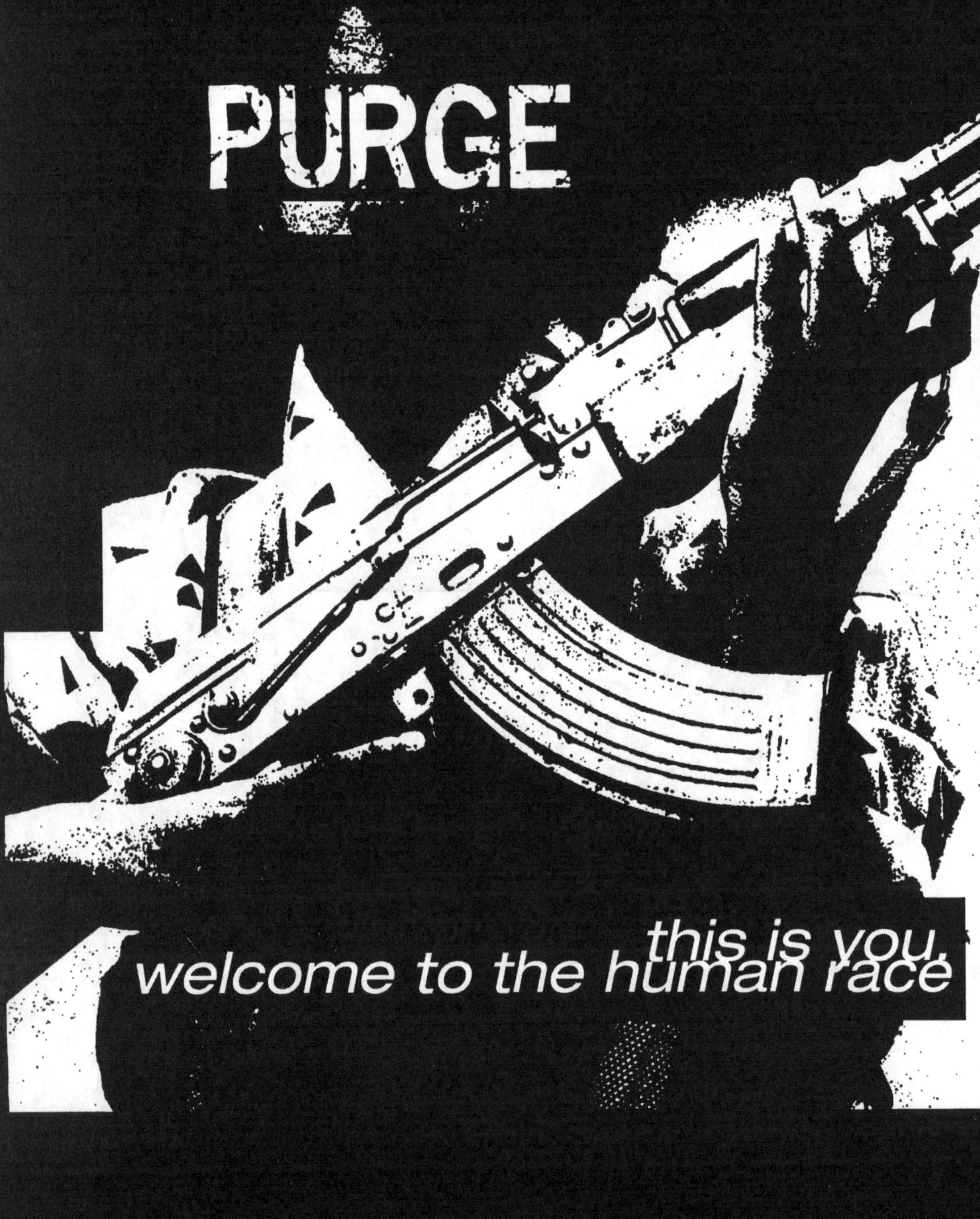
PURGE
this is you,
welcome to the human race

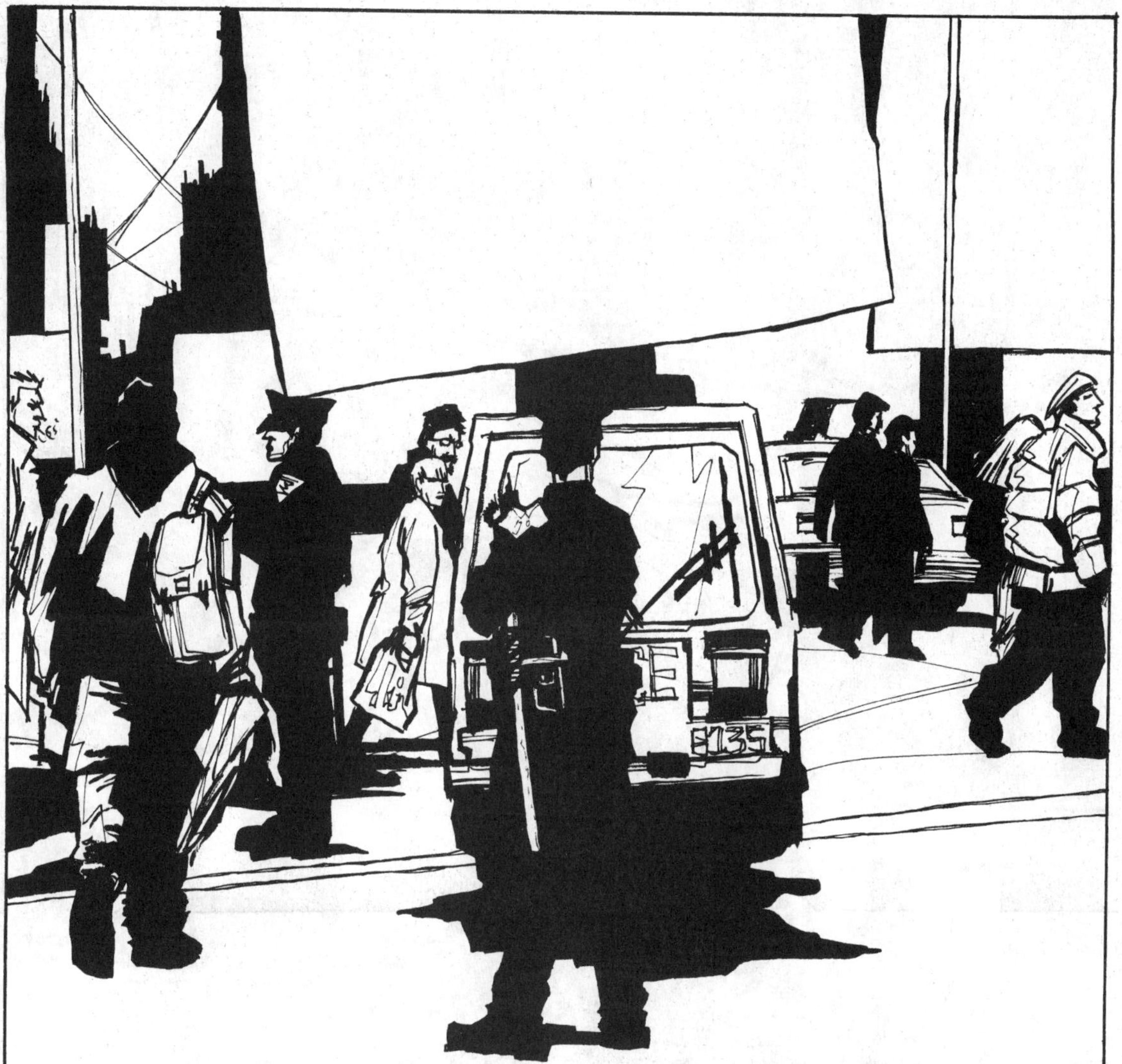

I remember Jennie 2.5 from way back, during the protests.
Well, if you can call them protests.

I'm old enough to remember demonstrating against the Gulf Wars, and the human rights violations in China. But these 'Free the Media' protests were little more than over-enthusiastic college students showing off, making noise, going through the actions.

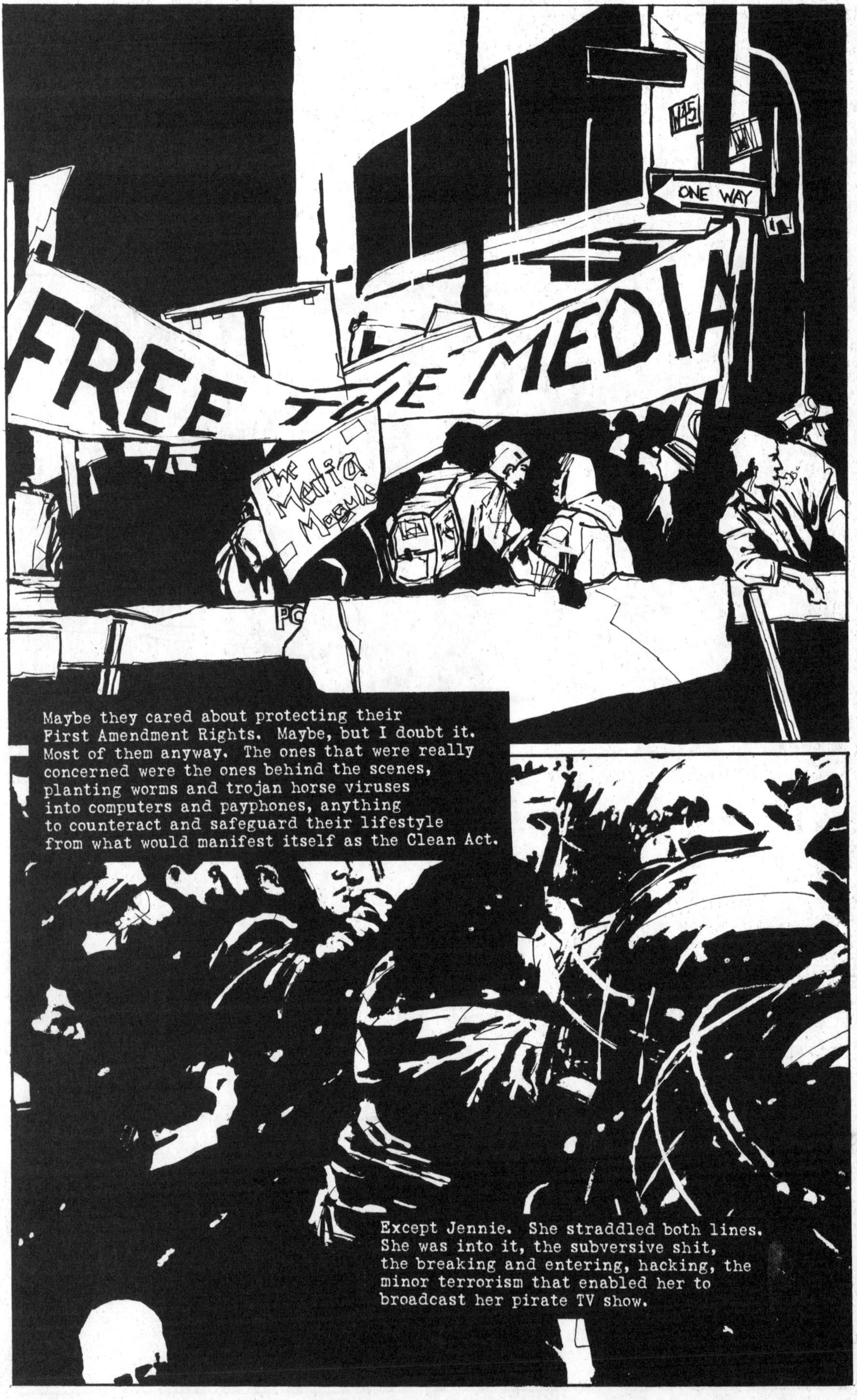
ONE WAY
FREE THE MEDIA
The Media Moguls
Maybe they cared about protecting their First Amendment Rights. Maybe, but I doubt it. Most of them anyway. The ones that were really concerned were the ones behind the scenes, planting worms and trojan horse viruses into computers and payphones, anything to counteract and safeguard their lifestyle from what would manifest itself as the Clean Act.
Except Jennie. She straddled both lines. She was into it, the subversive shit, the breaking and entering, hacking, the minor terrorism that enabled her to broadcast her pirate TV show.

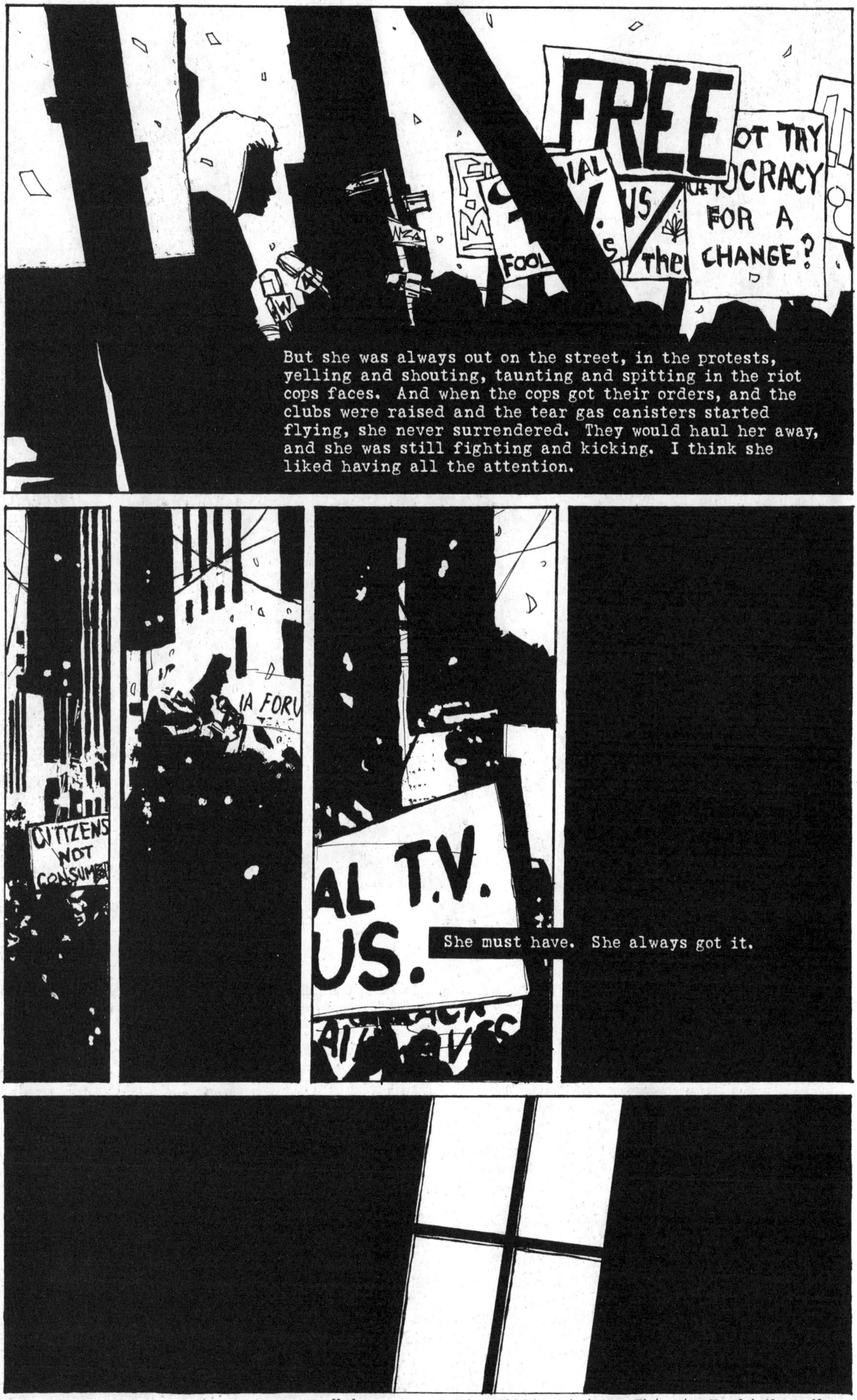
FREE
OT TRY
OCRACY
FOR A
CHANGE?
But she was always out on the street, in the protests, yelling and shouting, taunting and spitting in the riot cops faces. And when the cops got their orders, and the clubs were raised and the tear gas canisters started flying, she never surrendered. They would haul her away, and she was still fighting and kicking. I think she liked having all the attention.
CITIZENS
NOT
AL T.V.
US.
She must have. She always got it.

Welcome to Radio Villinokivic. This is World News Now.

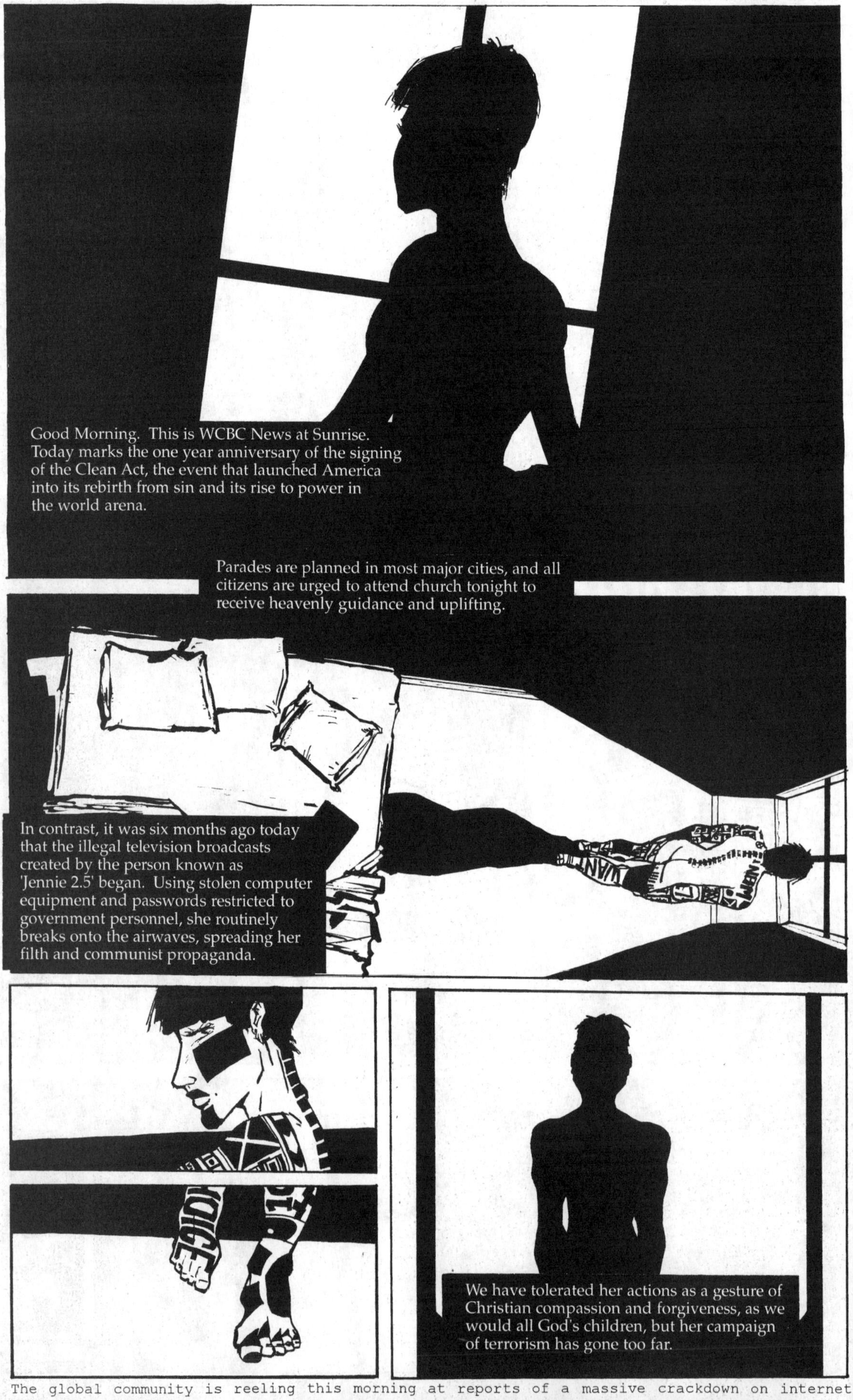

Good Morning. This is WCBC News at Sunrise. Today marks the one year anniversary of the signing of the Clean Act, the event that launched America into its rebirth from sin and its rise to power in the world arena.
Parades are planned in most major cities, and all citizens are urged to attend church tonight to receive heavenly guidance and uplifting.
In contrast, it was six months ago today that the illegal television broadcasts created by the person known as 'Jennie 2.5' began. Using stolen computer equipment and passwords restricted to government personnel, she routinely breaks onto the airwaves, spreading her filth and communist propaganda.
We have tolerated her actions as a gesture of Christian compassion and forgiveness, as we would all God's children, but her campaign of terrorism has gone too far.

The global community is reeling this morning at reports of a massive crackdown on internet

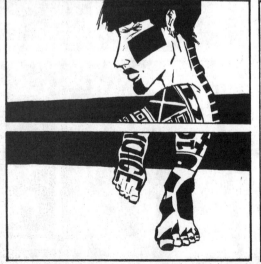

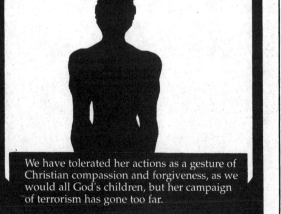

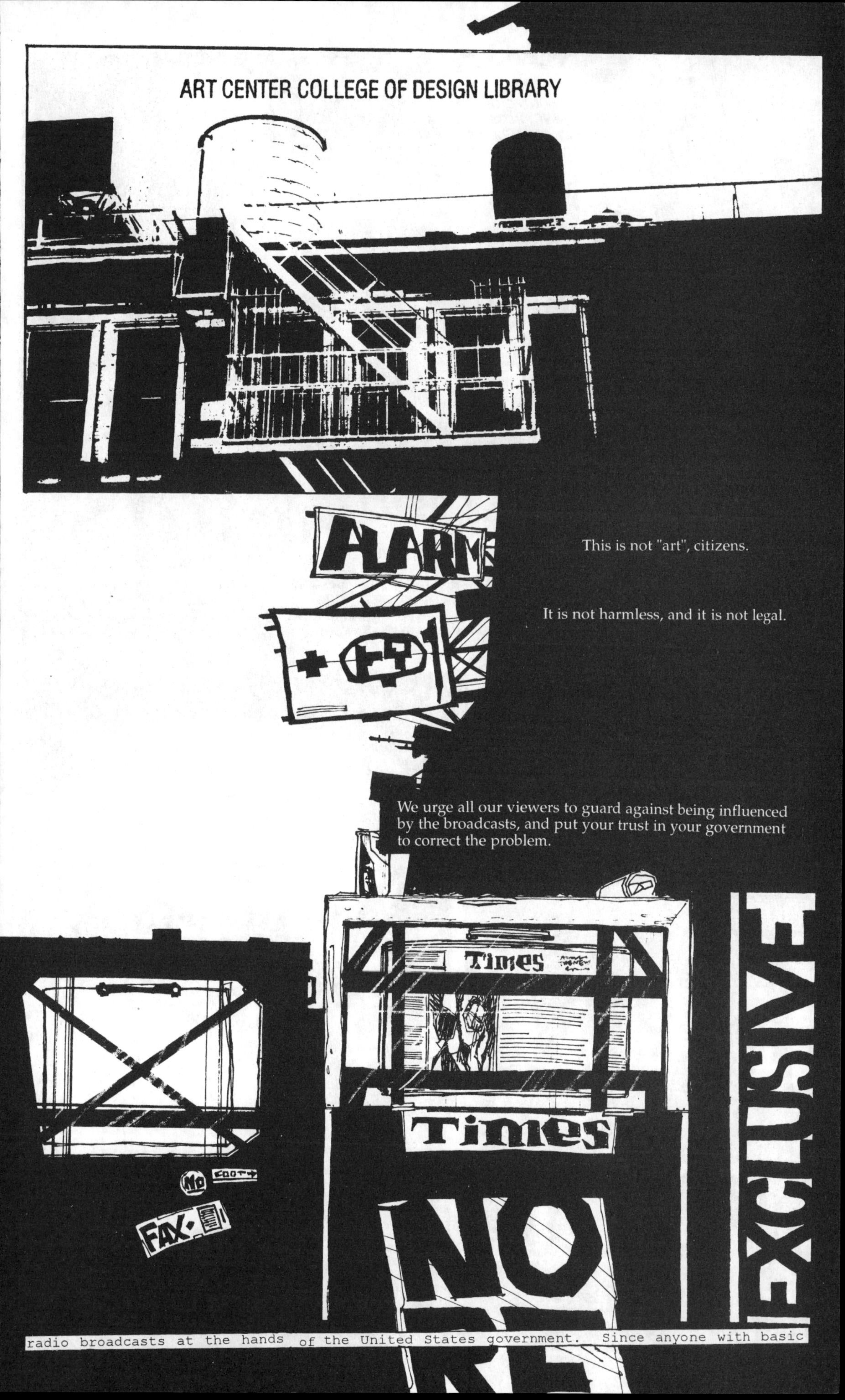
ALARM
This is not "art", citizens.
It is not harmless, and it is not legal.
We urge all our viewers to guard against being influenced by the broadcasts, and put your trust in your government to correct the problem.
Times
Times
NO
FAX

radio broadcasts at the hands of the United States government. Since anyone with basic

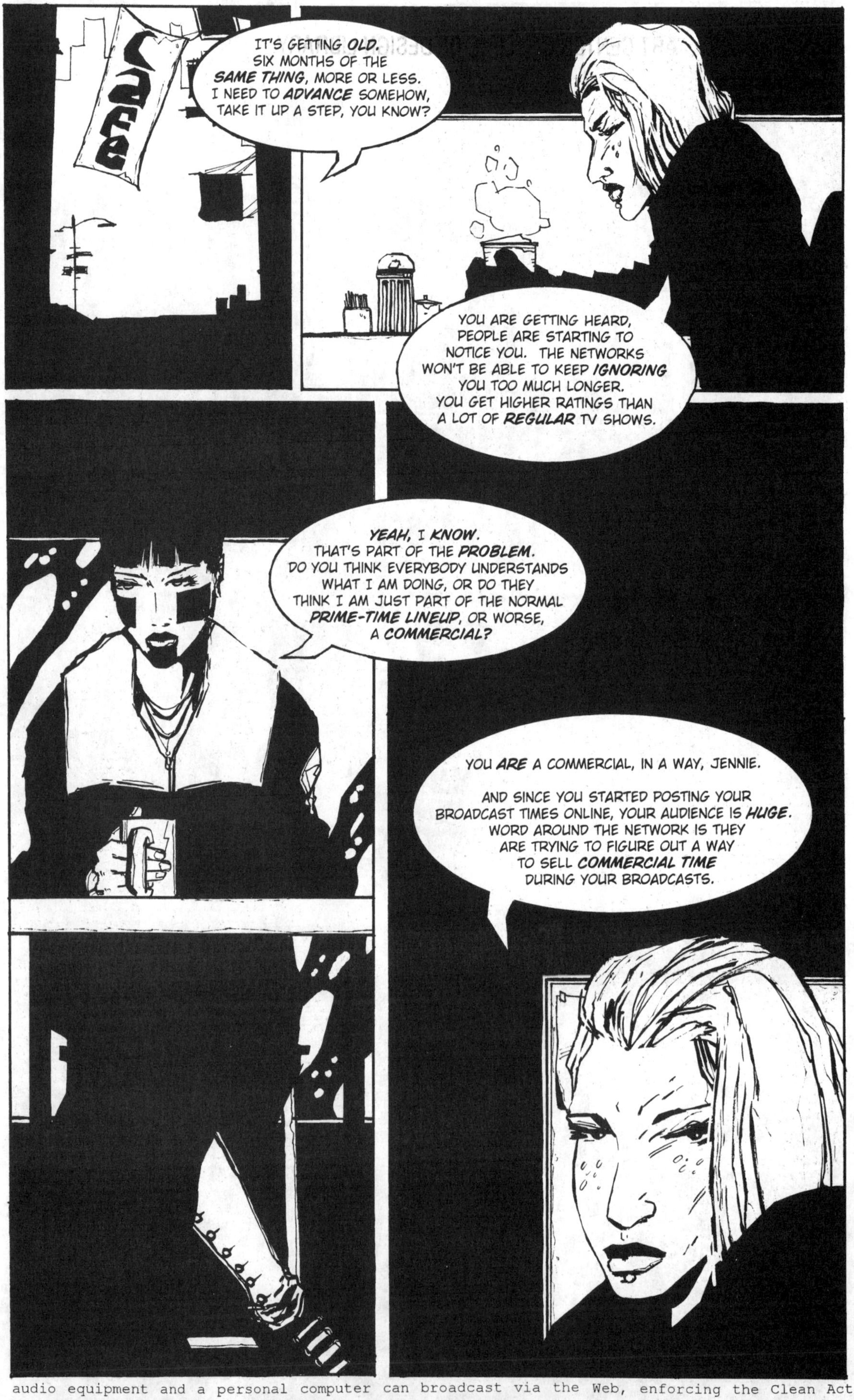
IT'S GETTING OLD. SIX MONTHS OF THE SAME THING, MORE OR LESS. I NEED TO ADVANCE SOMEHOW, TAKE IT UP A STEP, YOU KNOW?
YOU ARE GETTING HEARD, PEOPLE ARE STARTING TO NOTICE YOU. THE NETWORKS WON'T BE ABLE TO KEEP IGNORING YOU TOO MUCH LONGER. YOU GET HIGHER RATINGS THAN A LOT OF REGULAR TV SHOWS.
YEAH, I KNOW. THAT'S PART OF THE PROBLEM. DO YOU THINK EVERYBODY UNDERSTANDS WHAT I AM DOING, OR DO THEY THINK I AM JUST PART OF THE NORMAL PRIME-TIME LINEUP, OR WORSE, A COMMERCIAL?
YOU ARE A COMMERCIAL, IN A WAY, JENNIE.
AND SINCE YOU STARTED POSTING YOUR BROADCAST TIMES ONLINE, YOUR AUDIENCE IS HUGE. WORD AROUND THE NETWORK IS THEY ARE TRYING TO FIGURE OUT A WAY TO SELL COMMERCIAL TIME DURING YOUR BROADCASTS.

audio equipment and a personal computer can broadcast via the Web, enforcing the Clean Act

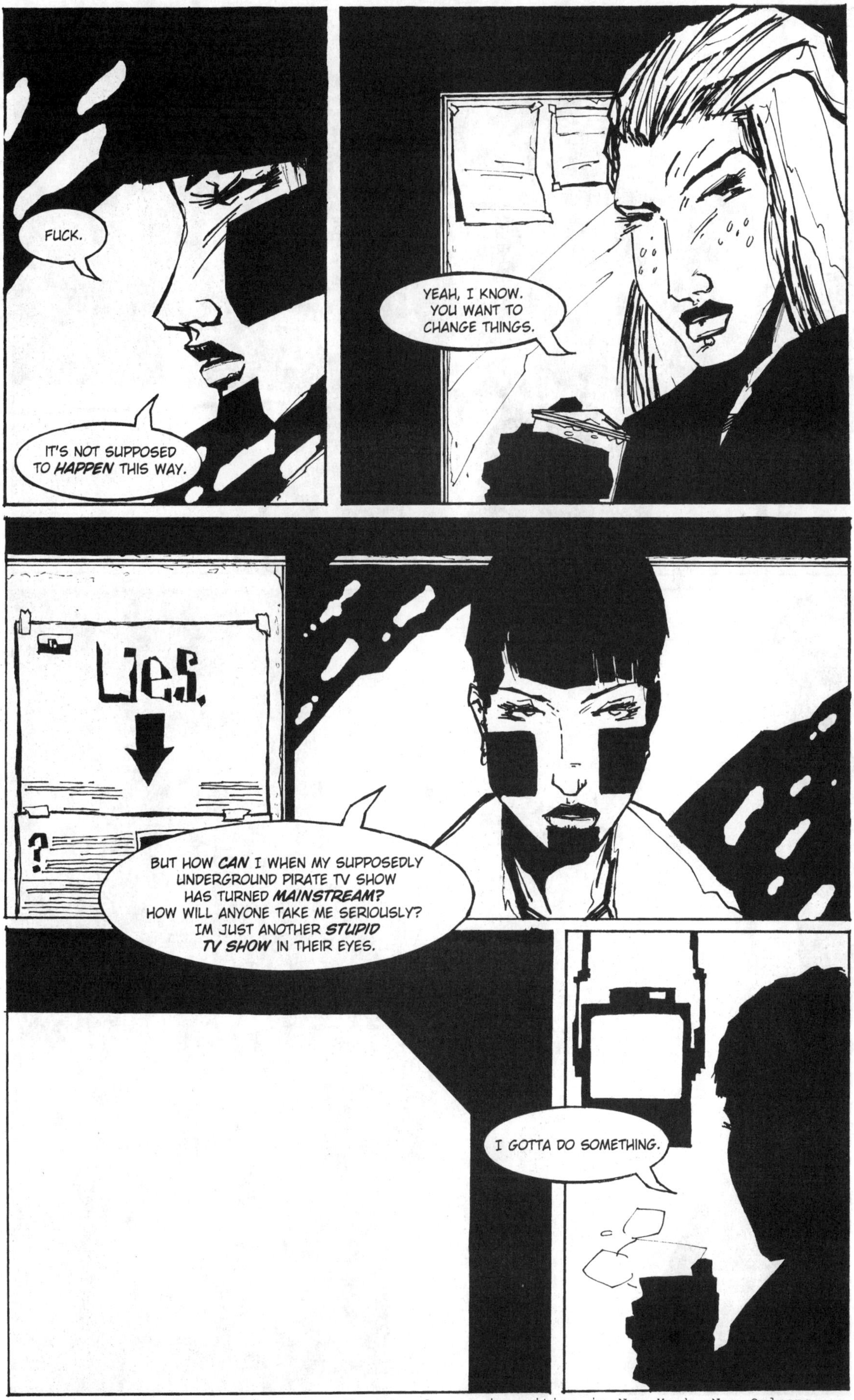
FUCK.
IT'S NOT SUPPOSED TO HAPPEN THIS WAY.
YEAH, I KNOW. YOU WANT TO CHANGE THINGS.
BUT HOW CAN I WHEN MY SUPPOSEDLY UNDERGROUND PIRATE TV SHOW HAS TURNED MAINSTREAM? HOW WILL ANYONE TAKE ME SERIOUSLY? IM JUST ANOTHER STUPID TV SHOW IN THEIR EYES.
I GOTTA DO SOMETHING.

has proved difficult in this area. Reports from universities in New York, New Orleans,

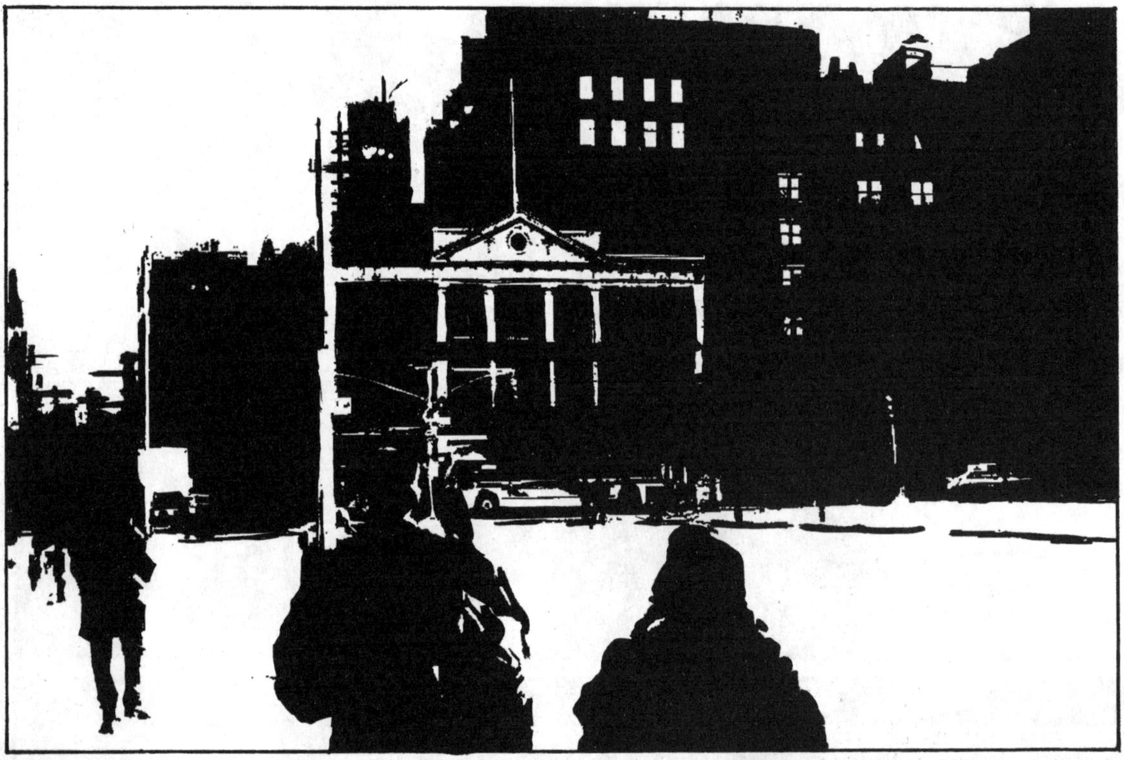

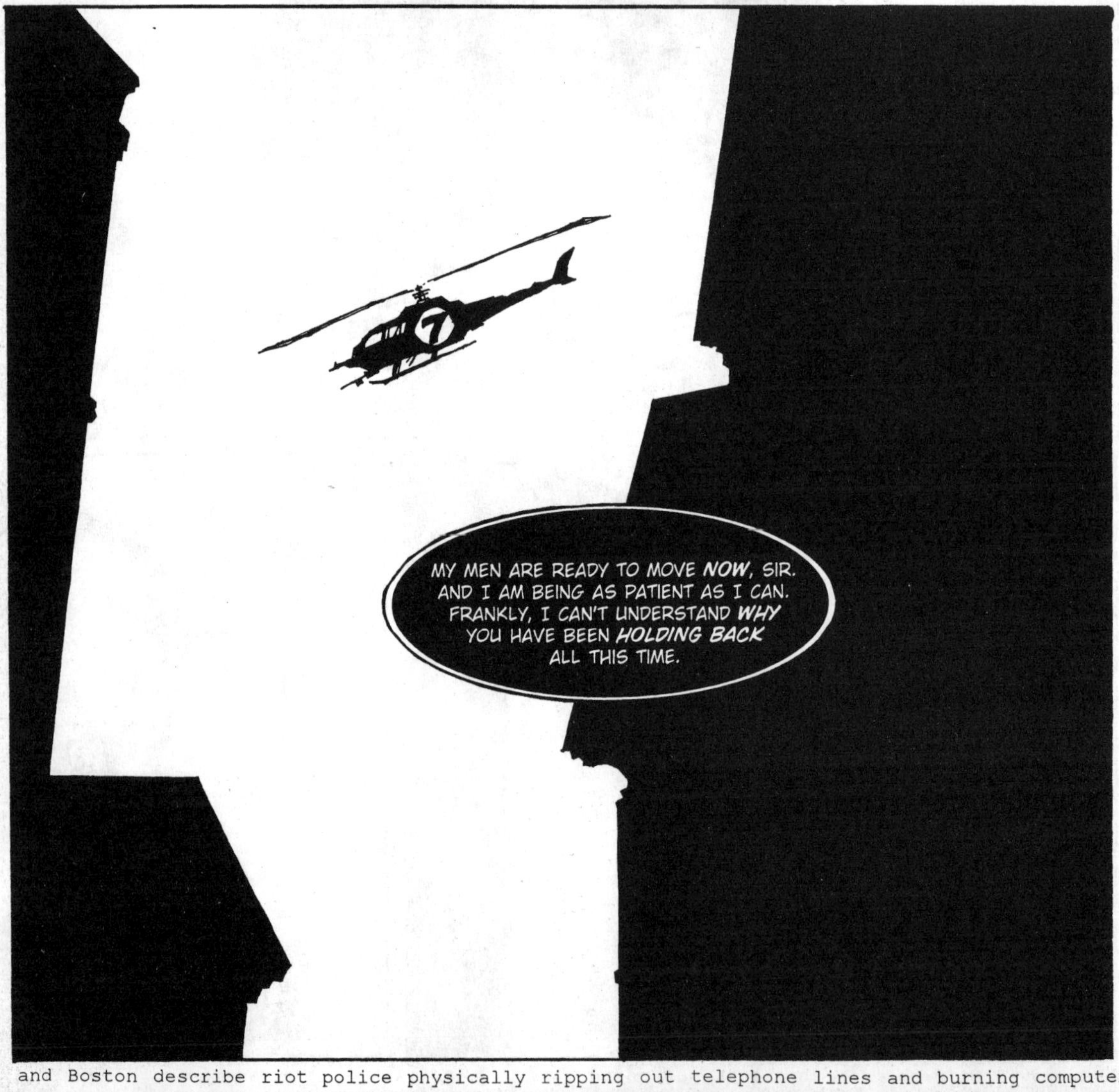
MY MEN ARE READY TO MOVE NOW, SIR. AND I AM BEING AS PATIENT AS I CAN. FRANKLY, I CAN'T UNDERSTAND WHY YOU HAVE BEEN HOLDING BACK ALL THIS TIME.

and Boston describe riot police physically ripping out telephone lines and burning computer

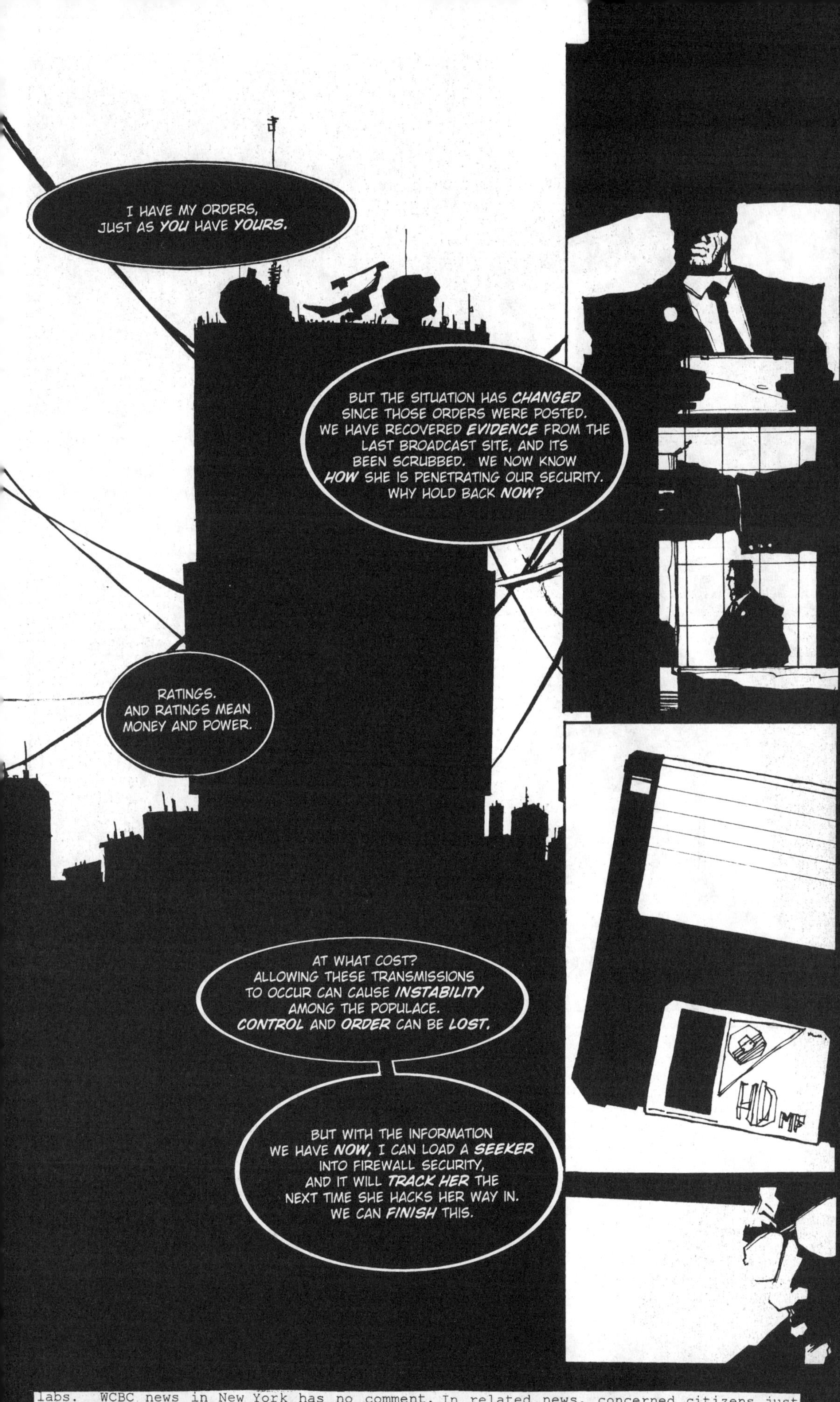
I HAVE MY ORDERS, JUST AS YOU HAVE YOURS.
BUT THE SITUATION HAS CHANGED SINCE THOSE ORDERS WERE POSTED. WE HAVE RECOVERED EVIDENCE FROM THE LAST BROADCAST SITE, AND ITS BEEN SCRUBBED. WE NOW KNOW HOW SHE IS PENETRATING OUR SECURITY. WHY HOLD BACK NOW?
RATINGS. AND RATINGS MEAN MONEY AND POWER.
AT WHAT COST? ALLOWING THESE TRANSMISSIONS TO OCCUR CAN CAUSE INSTABILITY AMONG THE POPULACE. CONTROL AND ORDER CAN BE LOST.
BUT WITH THE INFORMATION WE HAVE NOW, I CAN LOAD A SEEKER INTO FIREWALL SECURITY, AND IT WILL TRACK HER THE NEXT TIME SHE HACKS HER WAY IN. WE CAN FINISH THIS.
HD MF

labs. WCBC news in New York has no comment. In related news, concerned citizens just

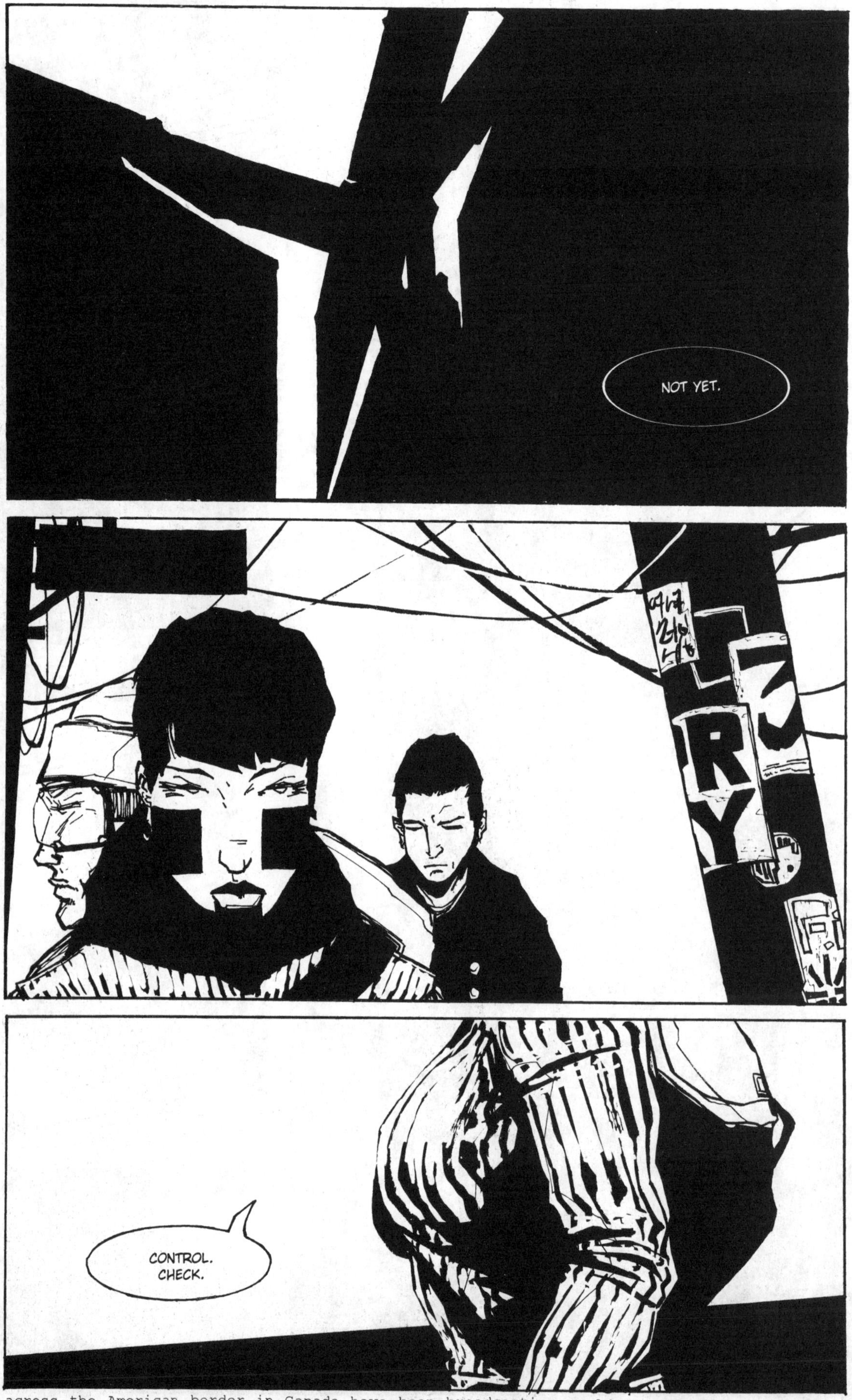
NOT YET.
CONTROL. CHECK.

across the American border in Canada have been broadcasting world news feeds over public

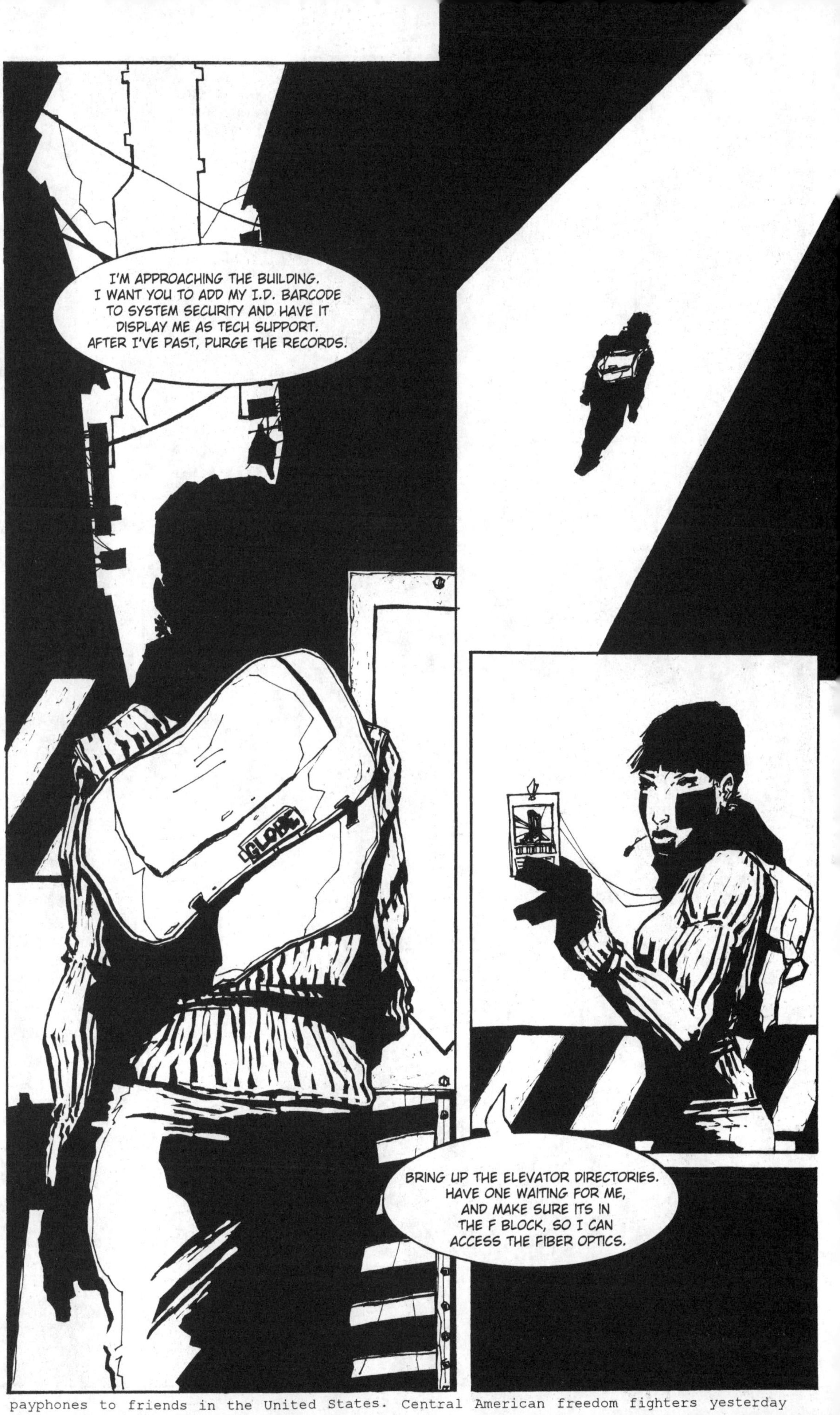
I'M APPROACHING THE BUILDING. I WANT YOU TO ADD MY I.D. BARCODE TO SYSTEM SECURITY AND HAVE IT DISPLAY ME AS TECH SUPPORT. AFTER I'VE PAST, PURGE THE RECORDS.
GLOBE
BRING UP THE ELEVATOR DIRECTORIES. HAVE ONE WAITING FOR ME, AND MAKE SURE ITS IN THE F BLOCK, SO I CAN ACCESS THE FIBER OPTICS.

payphones to friends in the United States. Central American freedom fighters yesterday

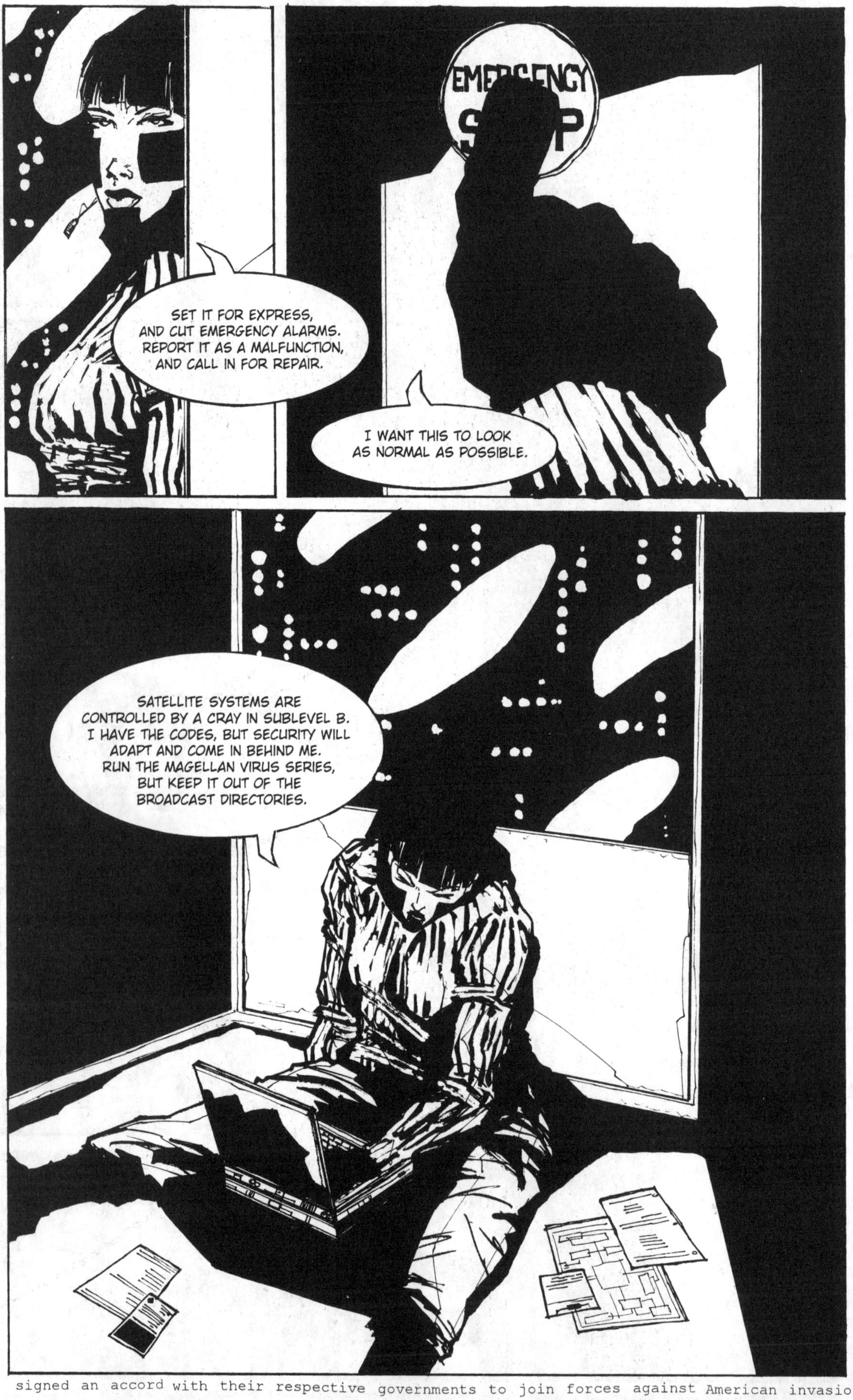
EMERGENCY
SET IT FOR EXPRESS, AND CUT EMERGENCY ALARMS. REPORT IT AS A MALFUNCTION, AND CALL IN FOR REPAIR.
I WANT THIS TO LOOK AS NORMAL AS POSSIBLE.
SATELLITE SYSTEMS ARE CONTROLLED BY A CRAY IN SUBLEVEL B. I HAVE THE CODES, BUT SECURITY WILL ADAPT AND COME IN BEHIND ME. RUN THE MAGELLAN VIRUS SERIES, BUT KEEP IT OUT OF THE BROADCAST DIRECTORIES.

signed an accord with their respective governments to join forces against American invasion

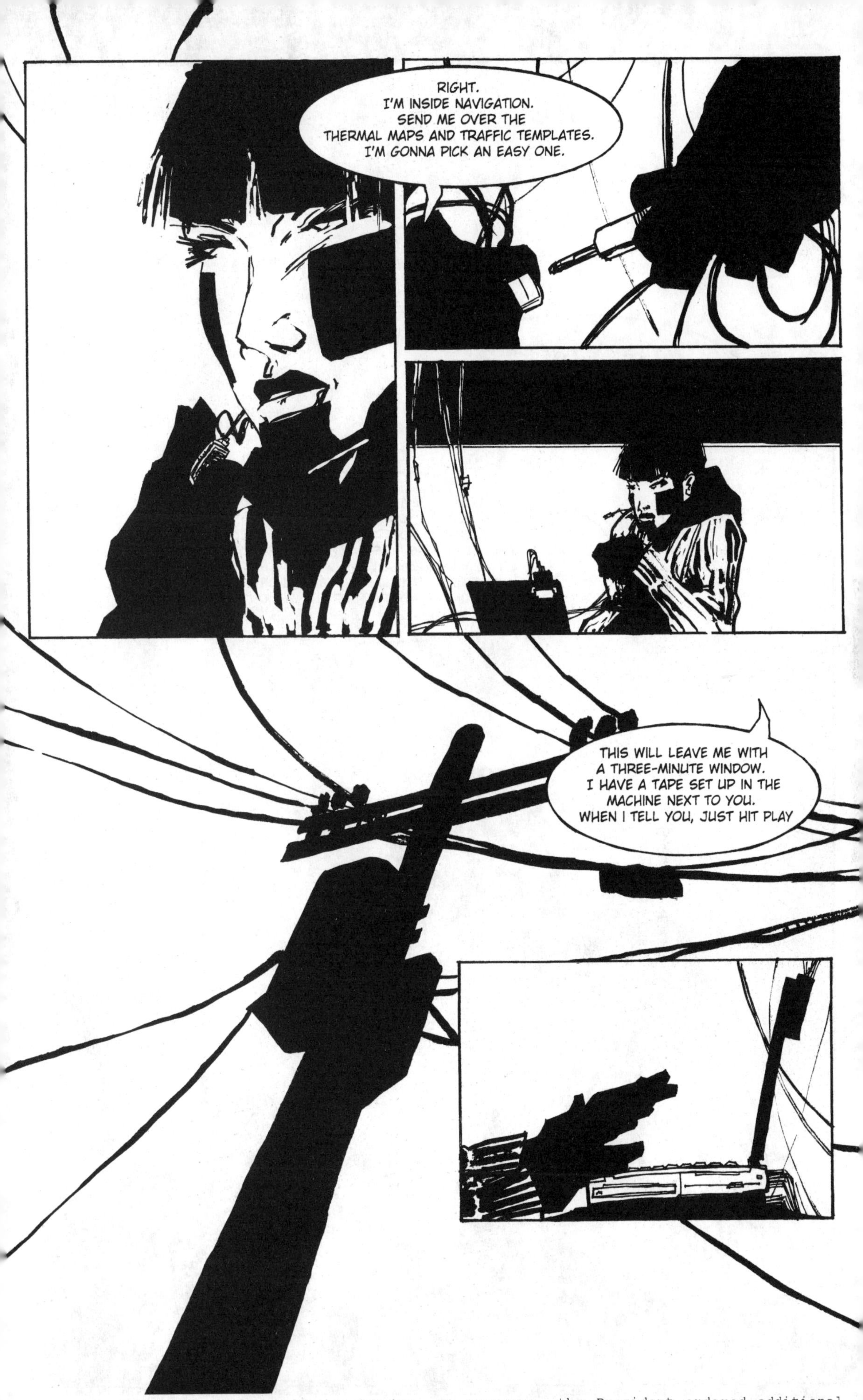
RIGHT.
I'M INSIDE NAVIGATION.
SEND ME OVER THE
THERMAL MAPS AND TRAFFIC TEMPLATES.
I'M GONNA PICK AN EASY ONE.
THIS WILL LEAVE ME WITH
A THREE-MINUTE WINDOW.
I HAVE A TAPE SET UP IN THE
MACHINE NEXT TO YOU.
WHEN I TELL YOU, JUST HIT PLAY

forces poised at the Texas/Mexico border. In response, the President ordered additional

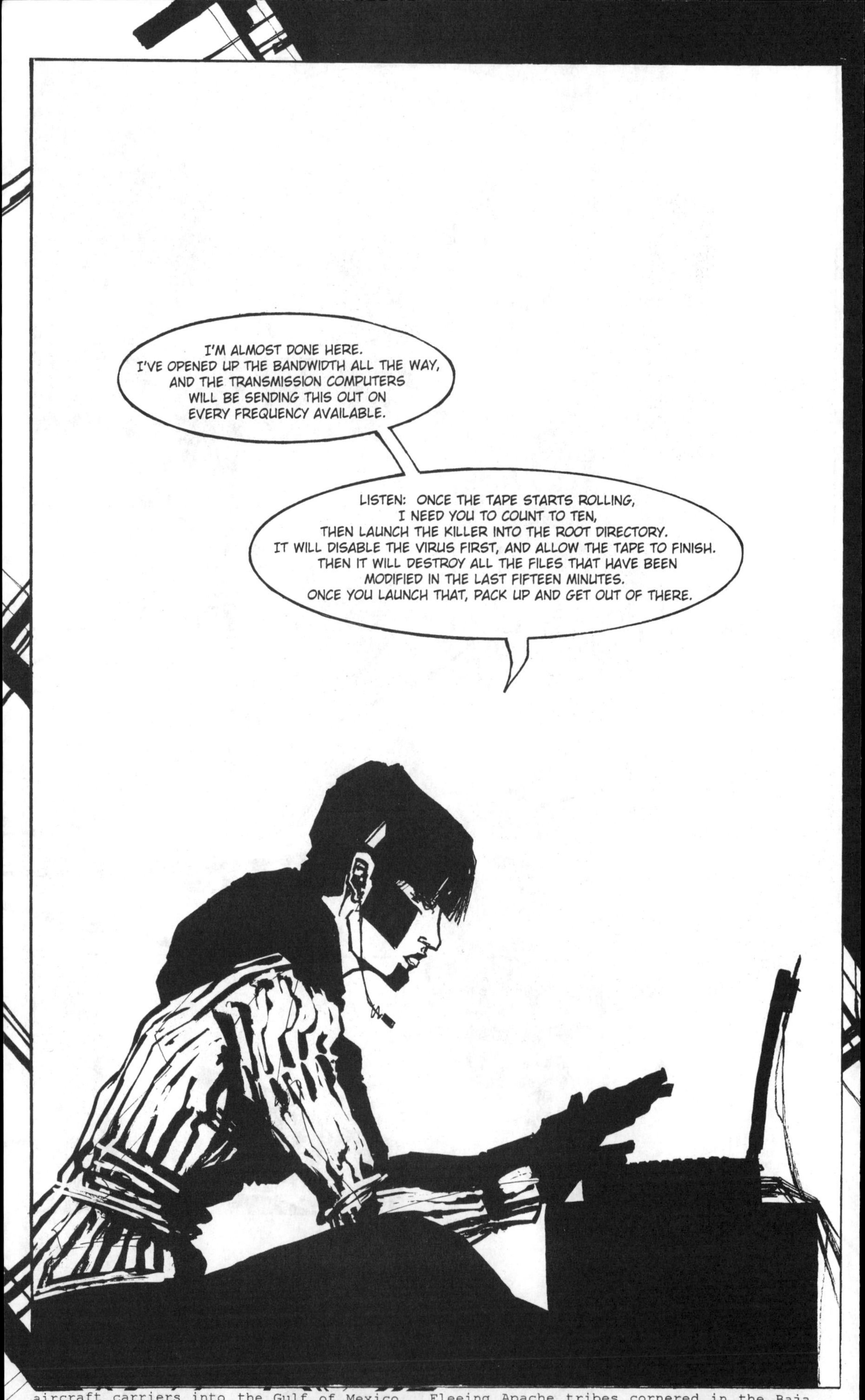
I'M ALMOST DONE HERE. I'VE OPENED UP THE BANDWIDTH ALL THE WAY, AND THE TRANSMISSION COMPUTERS WILL BE SENDING THIS OUT ON EVERY FREQUENCY AVAILABLE.
LISTEN: ONCE THE TAPE STARTS ROLLING, I NEED YOU TO COUNT TO TEN, THEN LAUNCH THE KILLER INTO THE ROOT DIRECTORY. IT WILL DISABLE THE VIRUS FIRST, AND ALLOW THE TAPE TO FINISH. THEN IT WILL DESTROY ALL THE FILES THAT HAVE BEEN MODIFIED IN THE LAST FIFTEEN MINUTES. ONCE YOU LAUNCH THAT, PACK UP AND GET OUT OF THERE.

aircraft carriers into the Gulf of Mexico. Fleeing Apache tribes cornered in the Baja

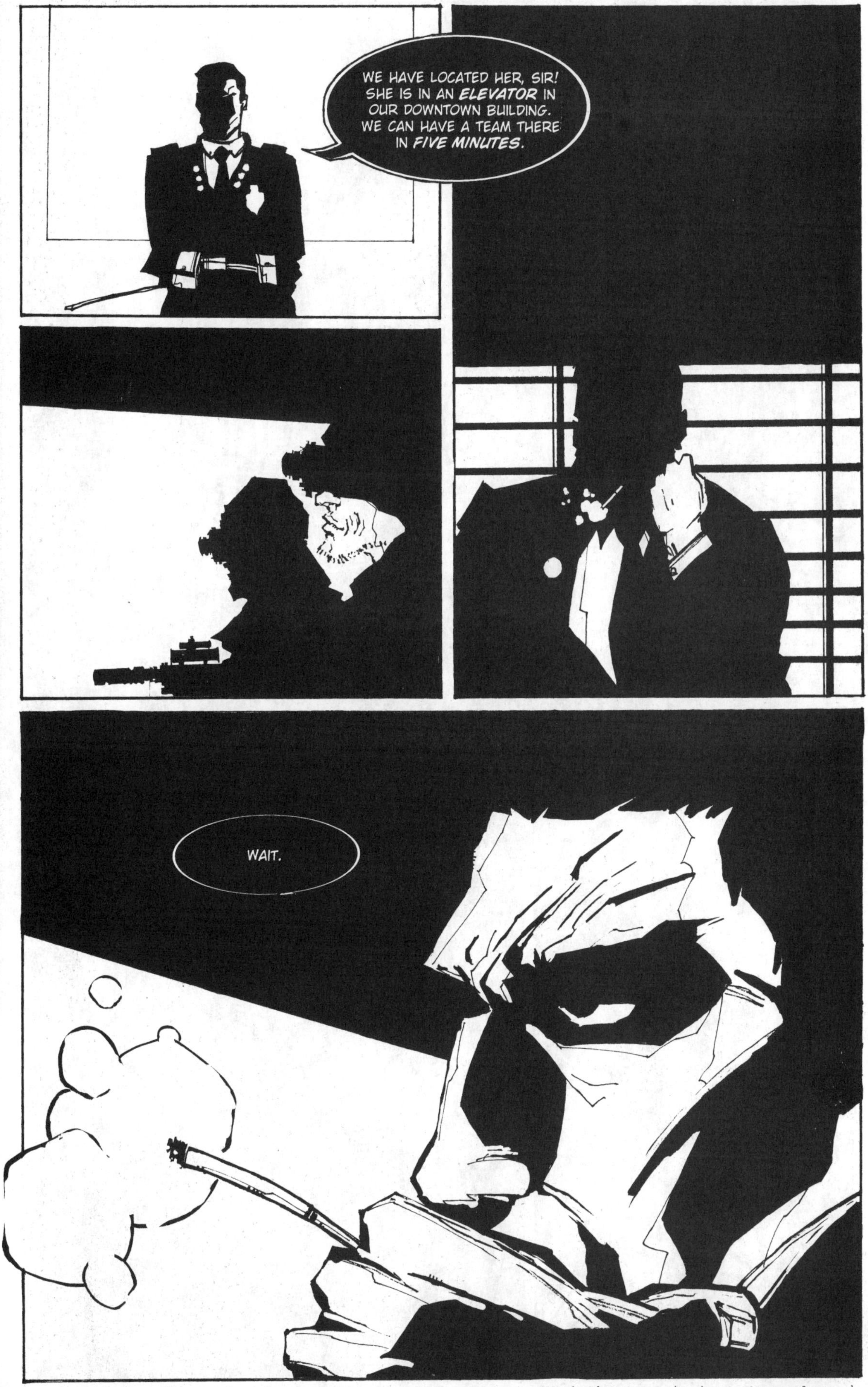
WE HAVE LOCATED HER, SIR! SHE IS IN AN *ELEVATOR* IN OUR DOWNTOWN BUILDING. WE CAN HAVE A TEAM THERE IN *FIVE MINUTES*.
WAIT.

Peninsula have stopped and seem determined to make a stand there. Britain today released

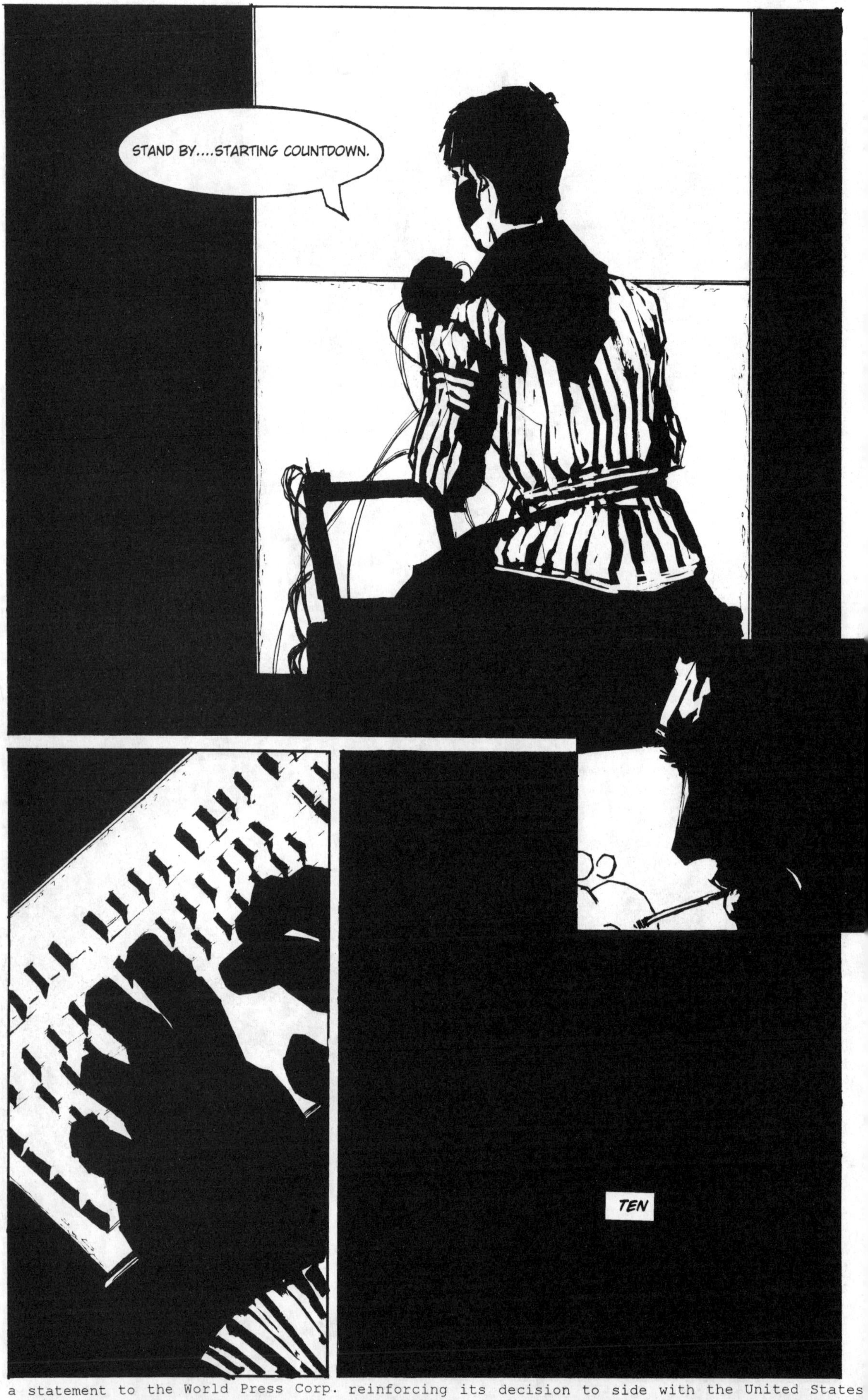
STAND BY....STARTING COUNTDOWN.
TEN

a statement to the World Press Corp. reinforcing its decision to side with the United States

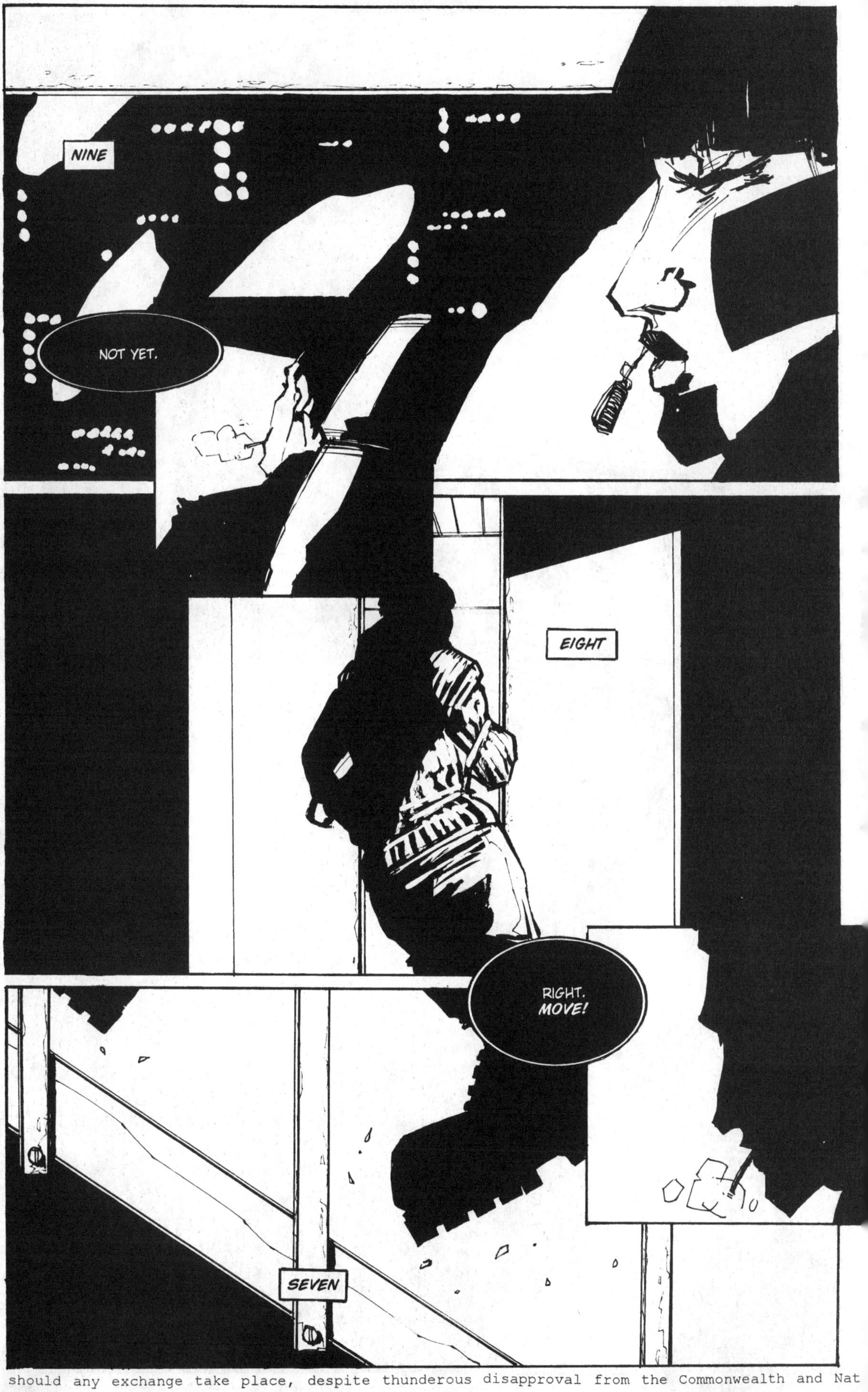
NINE
NOT YET.
EIGHT
RIGHT.
MOVE!
SEVEN

should any exchange take place, despite thunderous disapproval from the Commonwealth and Nat

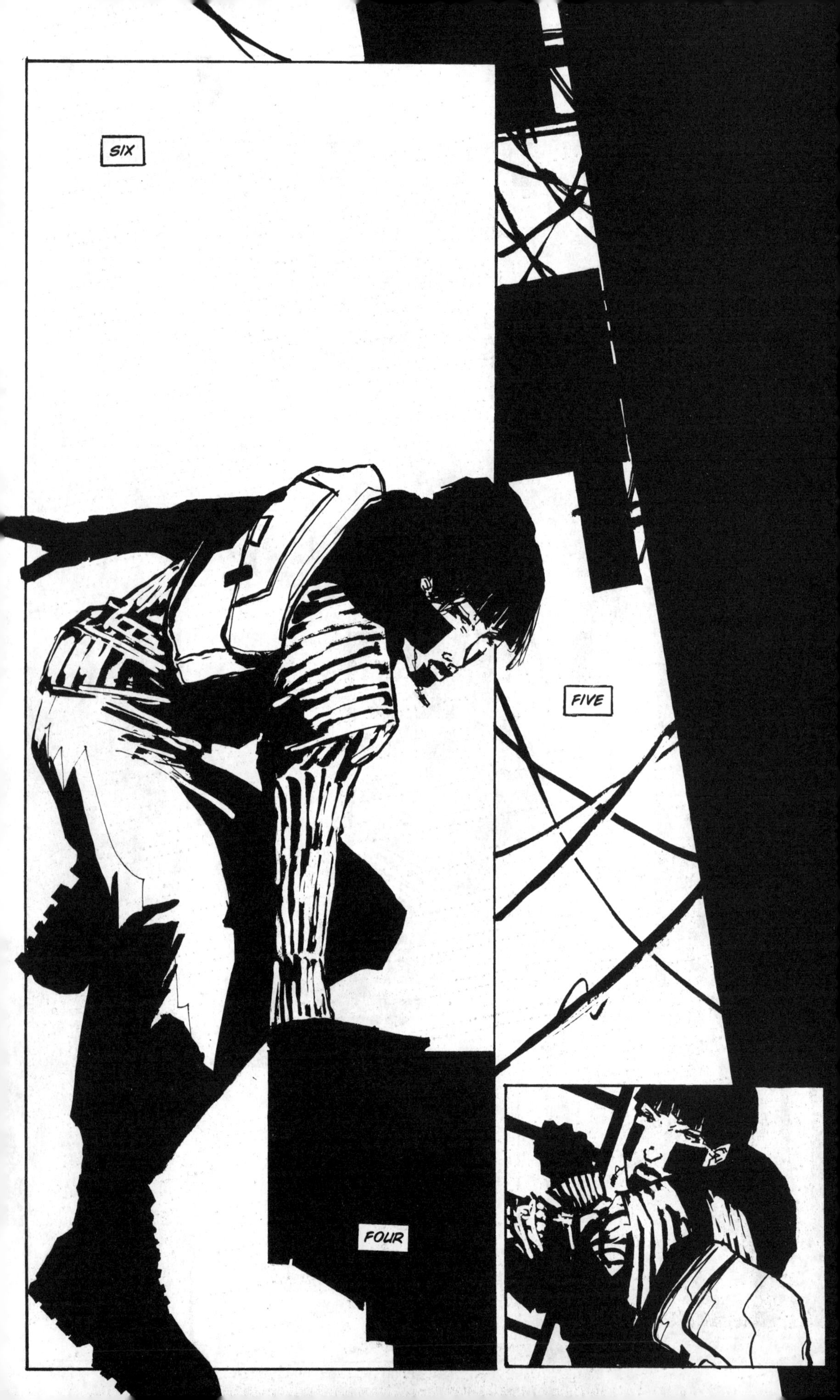

SIX
FIVE
FOUR

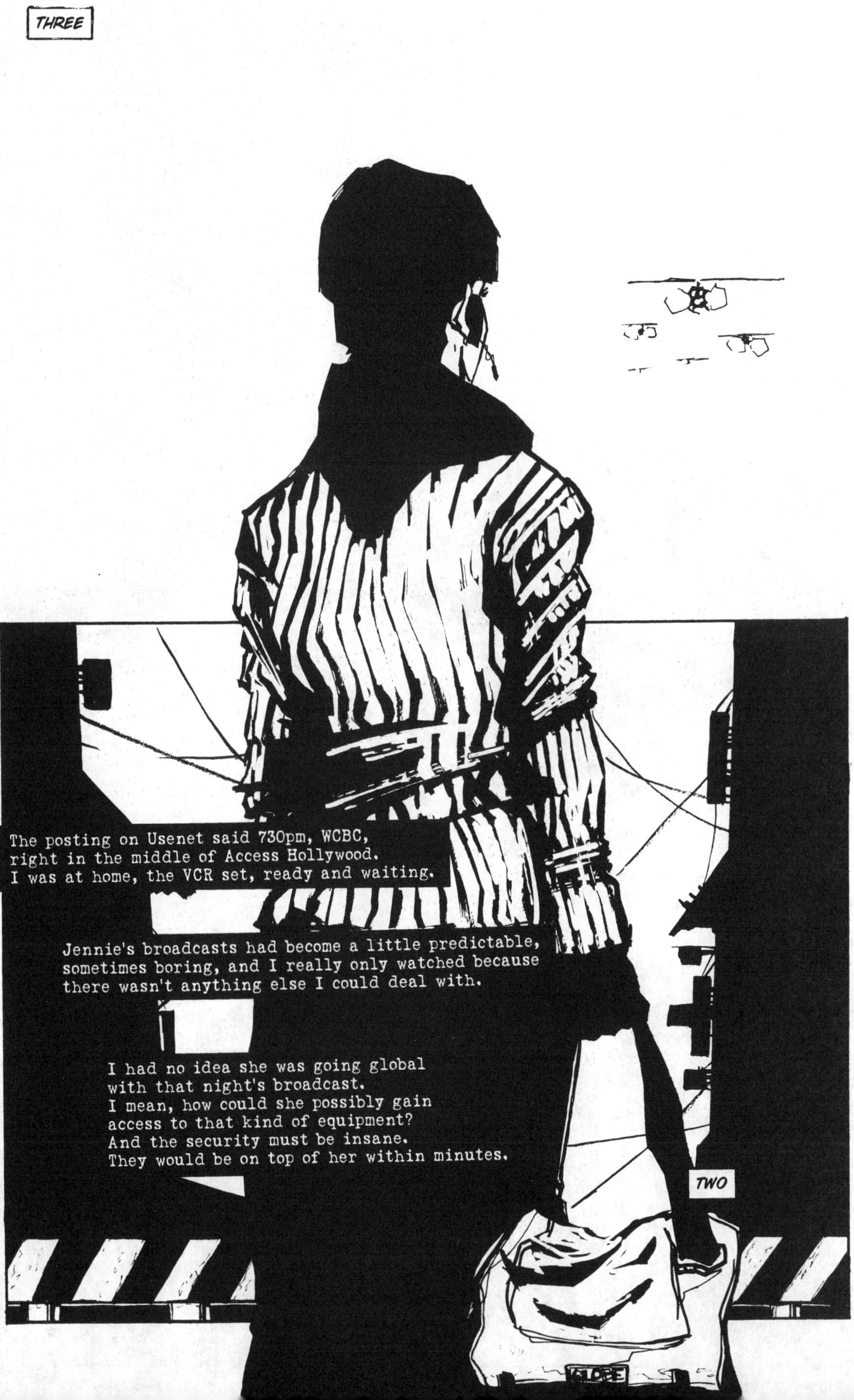
THREE
The posting on Usenet said 730pm, WCBC, right in the middle of Access Hollywood. I was at home, the VCR set, ready and waiting.
Jennie's broadcasts had become a little predictable, sometimes boring, and I really only watched because there wasn't anything else I could deal with.
I had no idea she was going global with that night's broadcast. I mean, how could she possibly gain access to that kind of equipment? And the security must be insane. They would be on top of her within minutes.
TWO

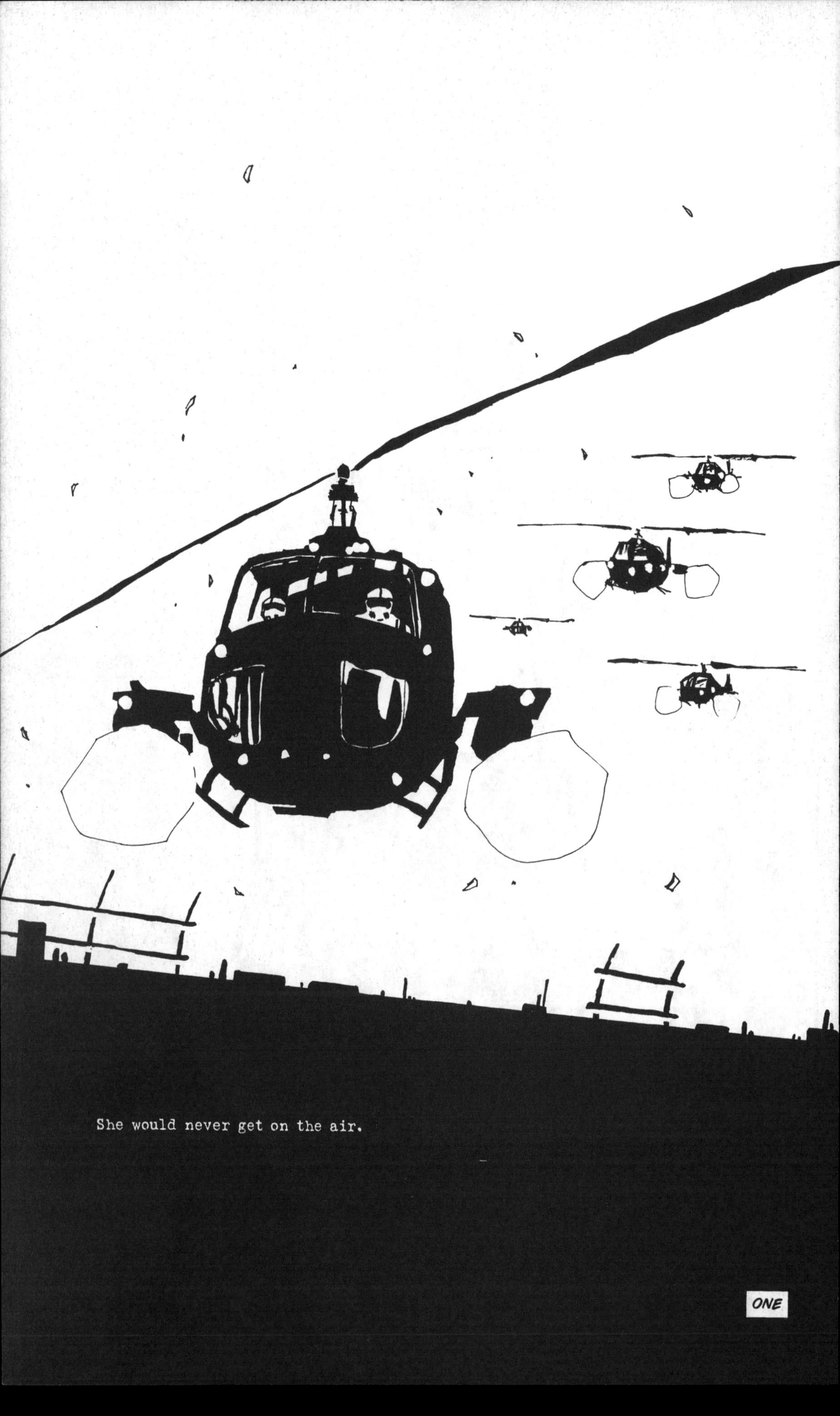
She would never get on the air.

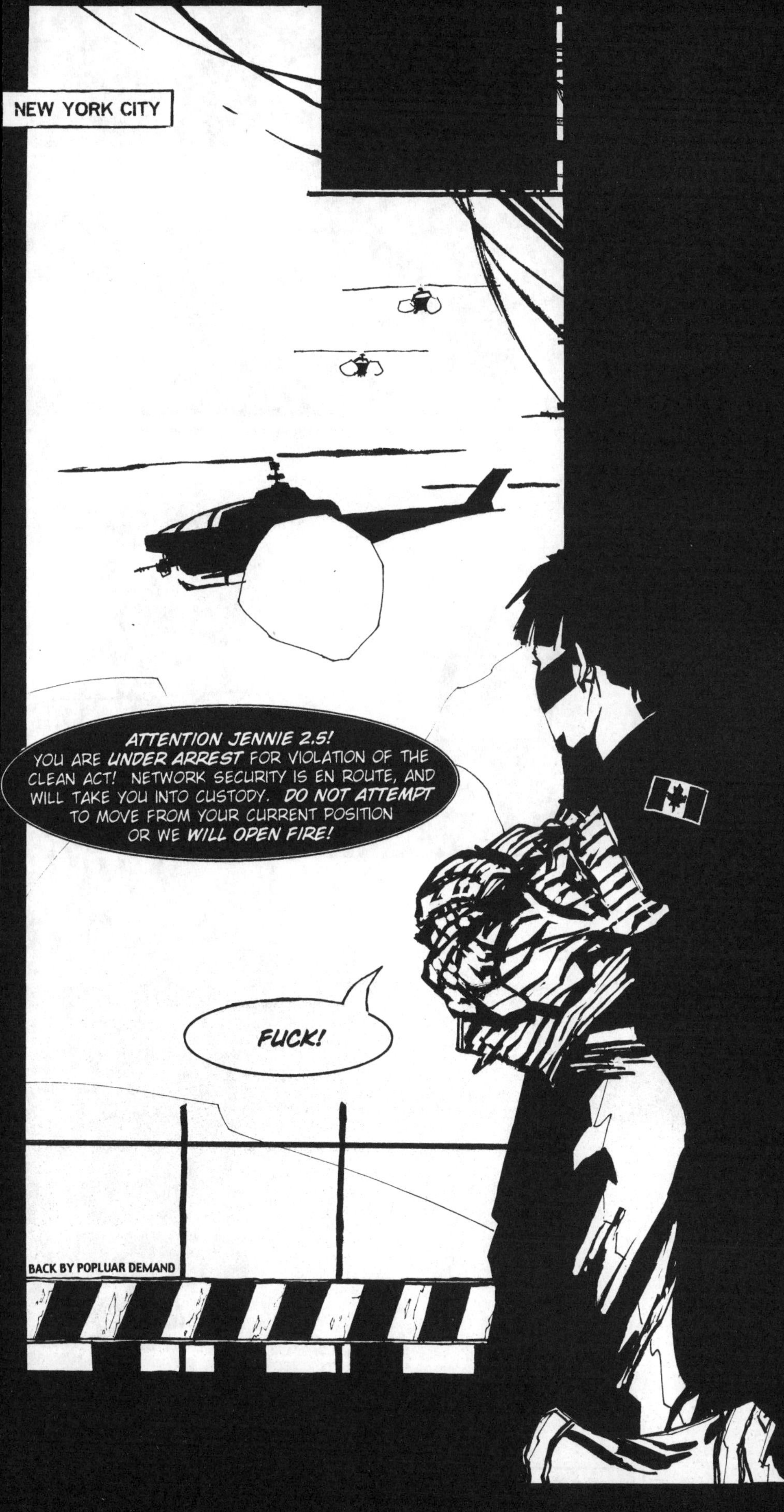
NEW YORK CITY
ATTENTION JENNIE 2.5! YOU ARE UNDER ARREST FOR VIOLATION OF THE CLEAN ACT! NETWORK SECURITY IS EN ROUTE, AND WILL TAKE YOU INTO CUSTODY. DO NOT ATTEMPT TO MOVE FROM YOUR CURRENT POSITION OR WE WILL OPEN FIRE!
FUCK!
BACK BY POPLUAR DEMAND

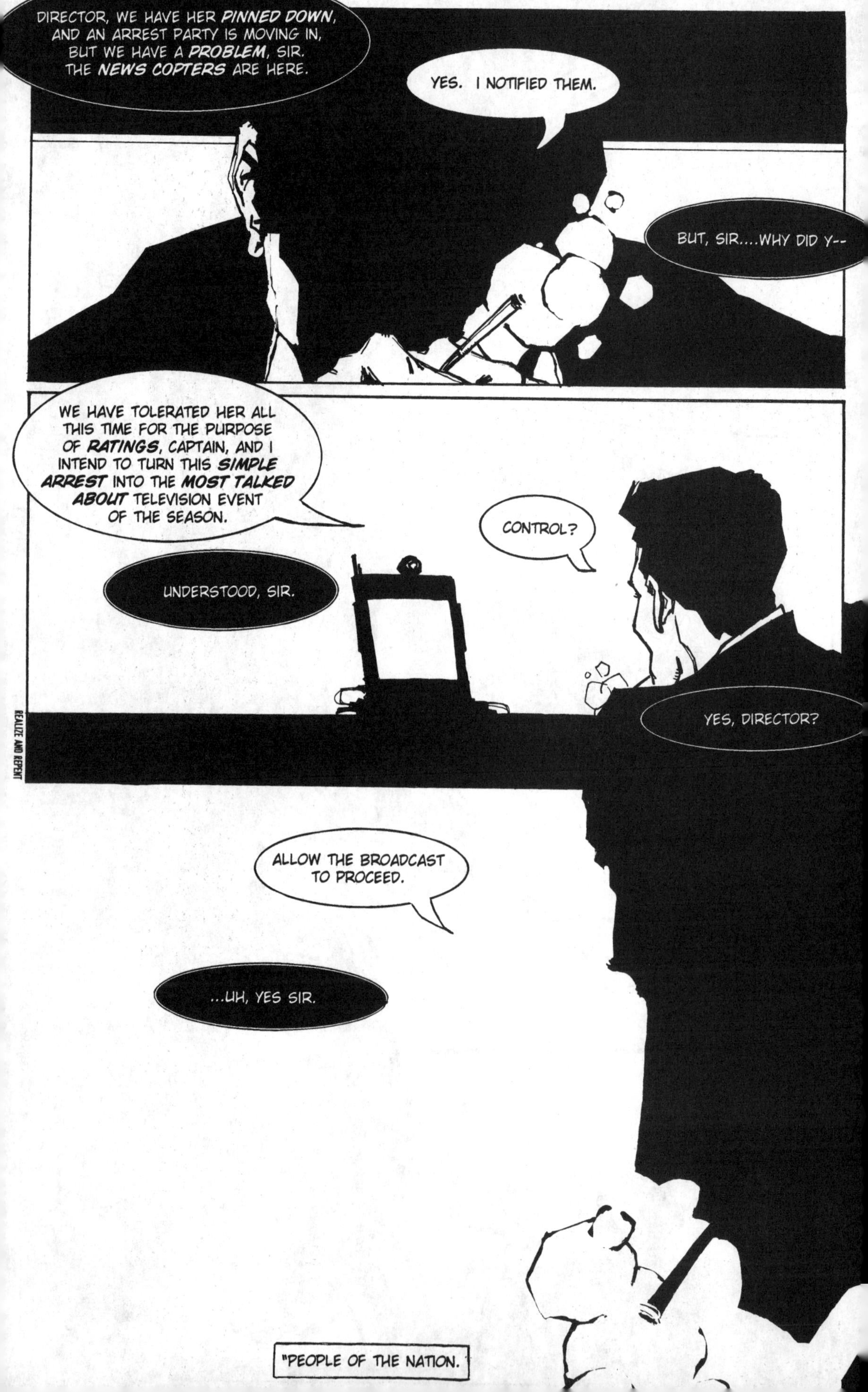
DIRECTOR, WE HAVE HER PINNED DOWN, AND AN ARREST PARTY IS MOVING IN, BUT WE HAVE A PROBLEM, SIR. THE NEWS COPTERS ARE HERE.
YES. I NOTIFIED THEM.
BUT, SIR....WHY DID Y--
WE HAVE TOLERATED HER ALL THIS TIME FOR THE PURPOSE OF RATINGS, CAPTAIN, AND I INTEND TO TURN THIS SIMPLE ARREST INTO THE MOST TALKED ABOUT TELEVISION EVENT OF THE SEASON.
UNDERSTOOD, SIR.
CONTROL?
YES, DIRECTOR?
ALLOW THE BROADCAST TO PROCEED.
...UH, YES SIR.
"PEOPLE OF THE NATION.

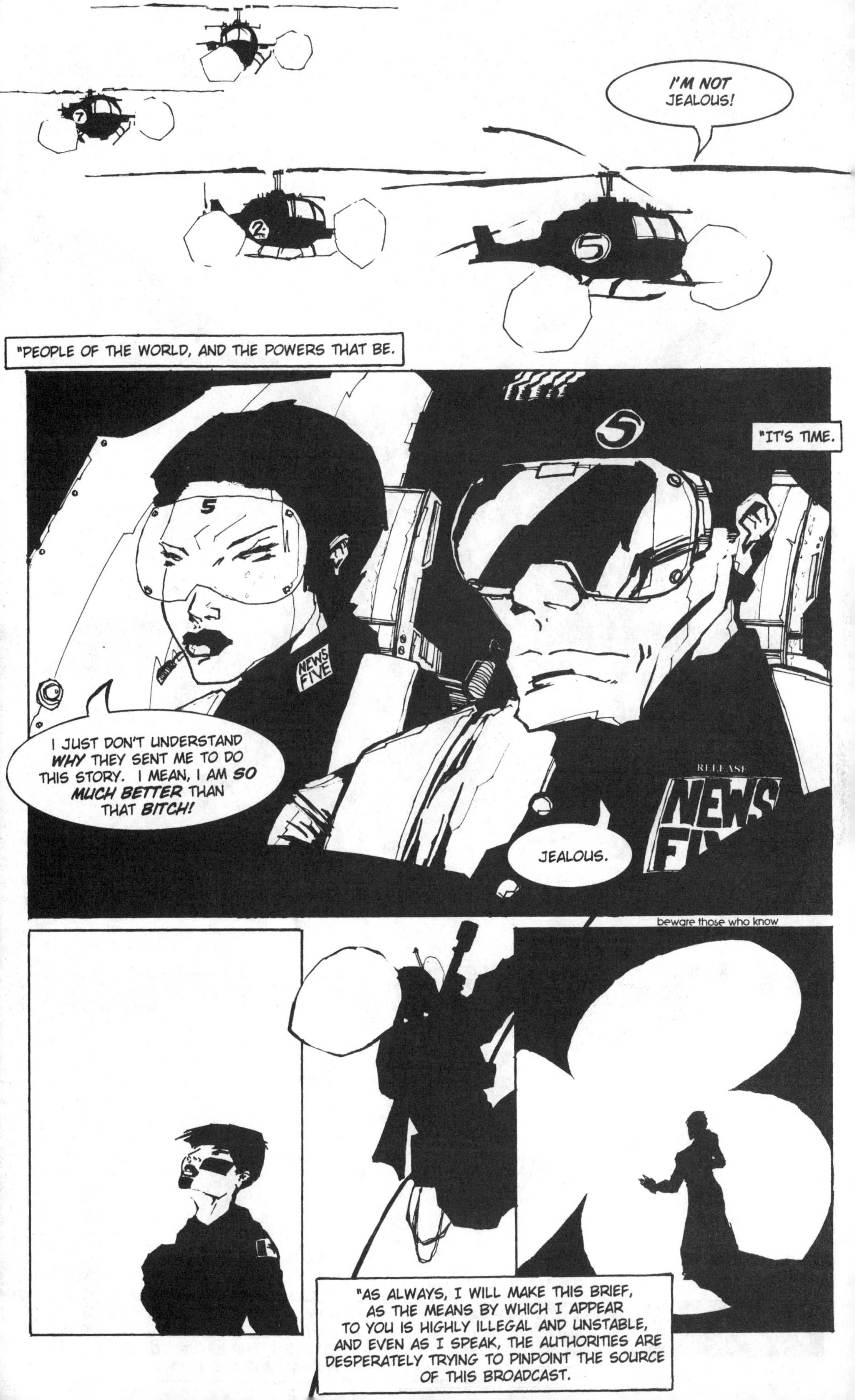
I'M NOT JEALOUS!
"PEOPLE OF THE WORLD, AND THE POWERS THAT BE.
"IT'S TIME.
I JUST DON'T UNDERSTAND WHY THEY SENT ME TO DO THIS STORY. I MEAN, I AM SO MUCH BETTER THAN THAT BITCH!
RELEASE
NEWS FIVE
JEALOUS.
beware those who know
"AS ALWAYS, I WILL MAKE THIS BRIEF, AS THE MEANS BY WHICH I APPEAR TO YOU IS HIGHLY ILLEGAL AND UNSTABLE, AND EVEN AS I SPEAK, THE AUTHORITIES ARE DESPERATELY TRYING TO PINPOINT THE SOURCE OF THIS BROADCAST.

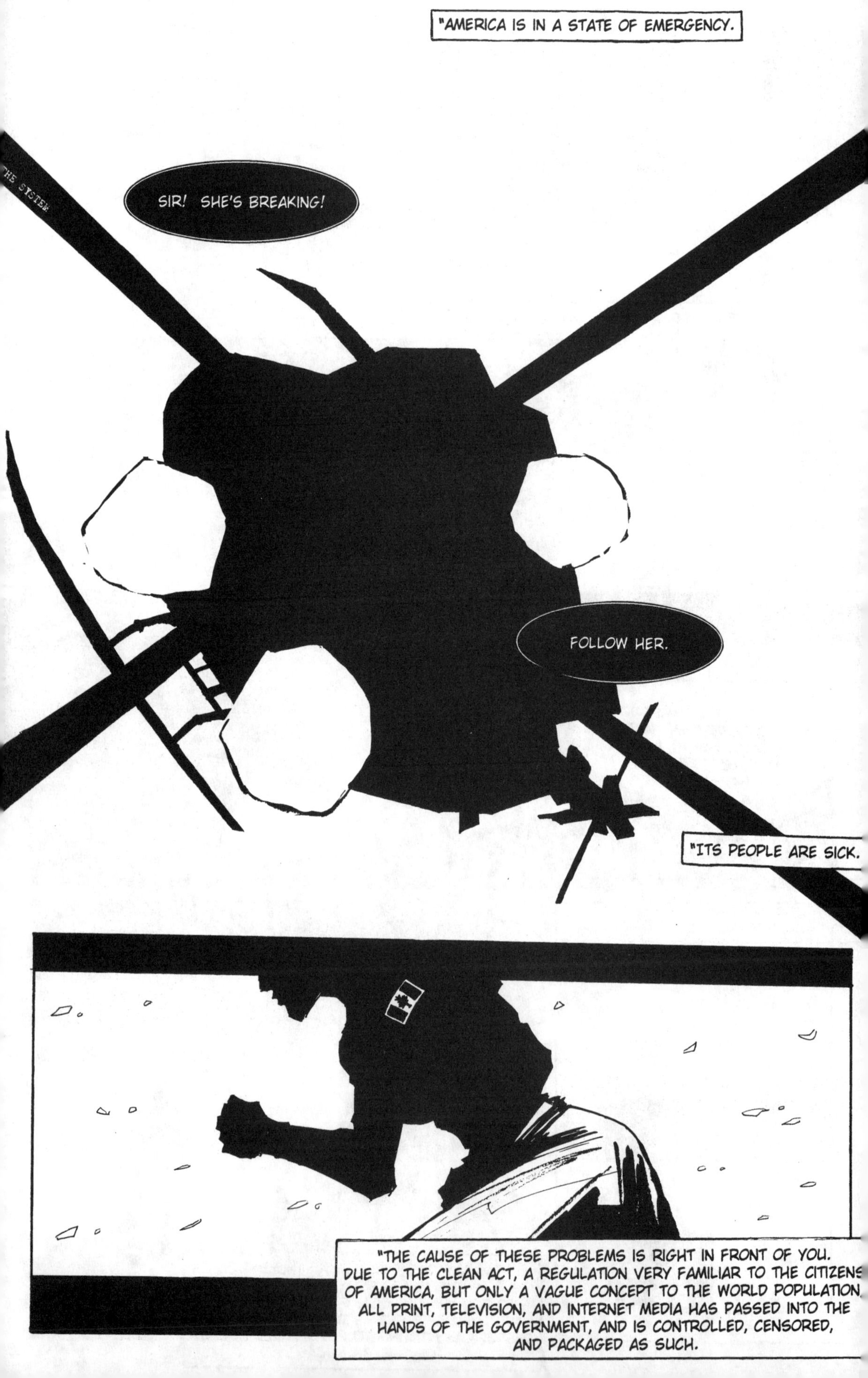
"AMERICA IS IN A STATE OF EMERGENCY.
SIR! SHE'S BREAKING!
FOLLOW HER.
"ITS PEOPLE ARE SICK.
"THE CAUSE OF THESE PROBLEMS IS RIGHT IN FRONT OF YOU. DUE TO THE CLEAN ACT, A REGULATION VERY FAMILIAR TO THE CITIZENS OF AMERICA, BUT ONLY A VAGUE CONCEPT TO THE WORLD POPULATION, ALL PRINT, TELEVISION, AND INTERNET MEDIA HAS PASSED INTO THE HANDS OF THE GOVERNMENT, AND IS CONTROLLED, CENSORED, AND PACKAGED AS SUCH.

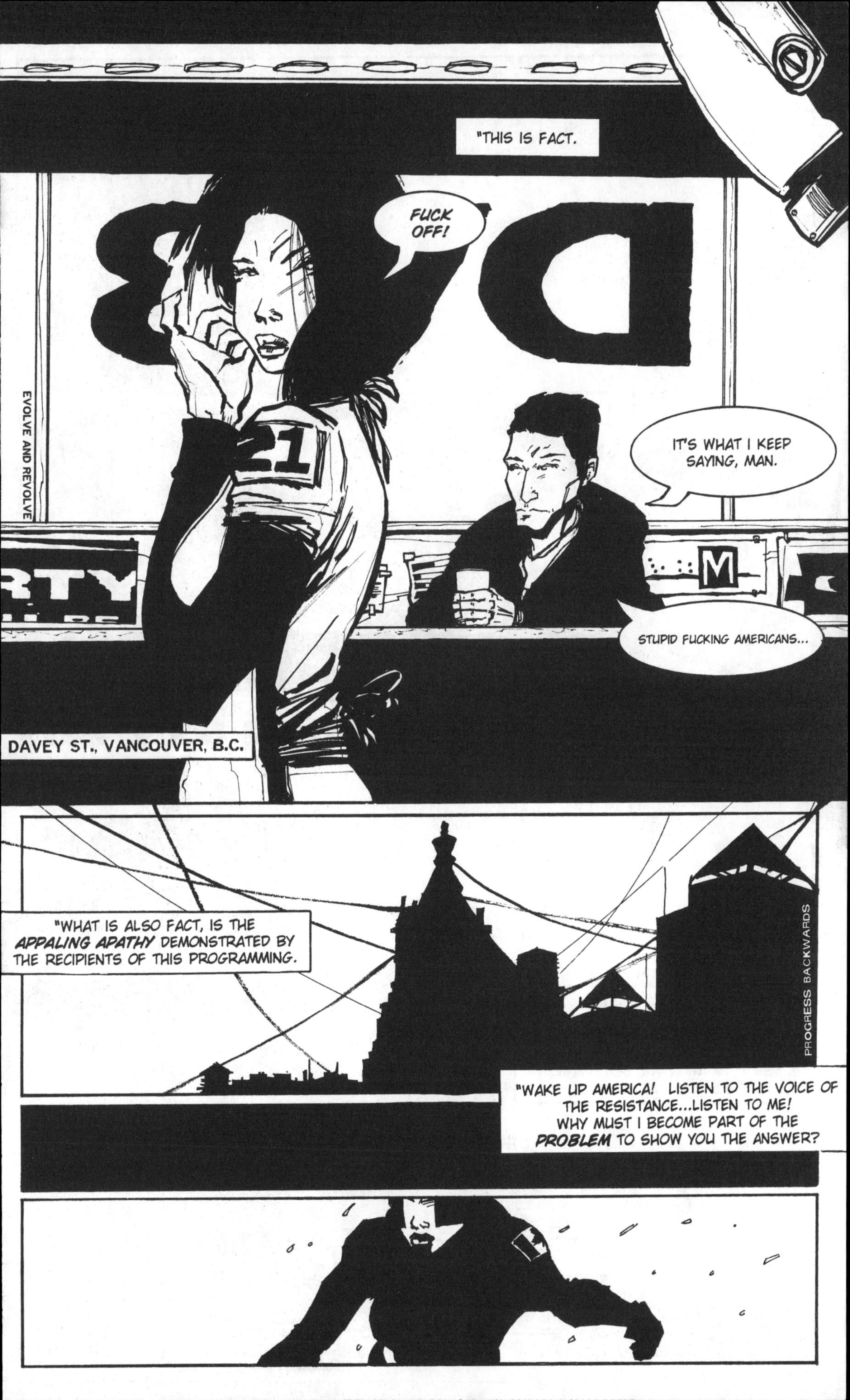
"THIS IS FACT.
FUCK OFF!
IT'S WHAT I KEEP SAYING, MAN.
STUPID FUCKING AMERICANS...
DAVEY ST., VANCOUVER, B.C.
EVOLVE AND REVOLVE
"WHAT IS ALSO FACT, IS THE *APPALING APATHY* DEMONSTRATED BY THE RECIPIENTS OF THIS PROGRAMMING.
PROGRESS BACKWARDS
"WAKE UP AMERICA! LISTEN TO THE VOICE OF THE RESISTANCE...LISTEN TO ME! WHY MUST I BECOME PART OF THE *PROBLEM* TO SHOW YOU THE ANSWER?

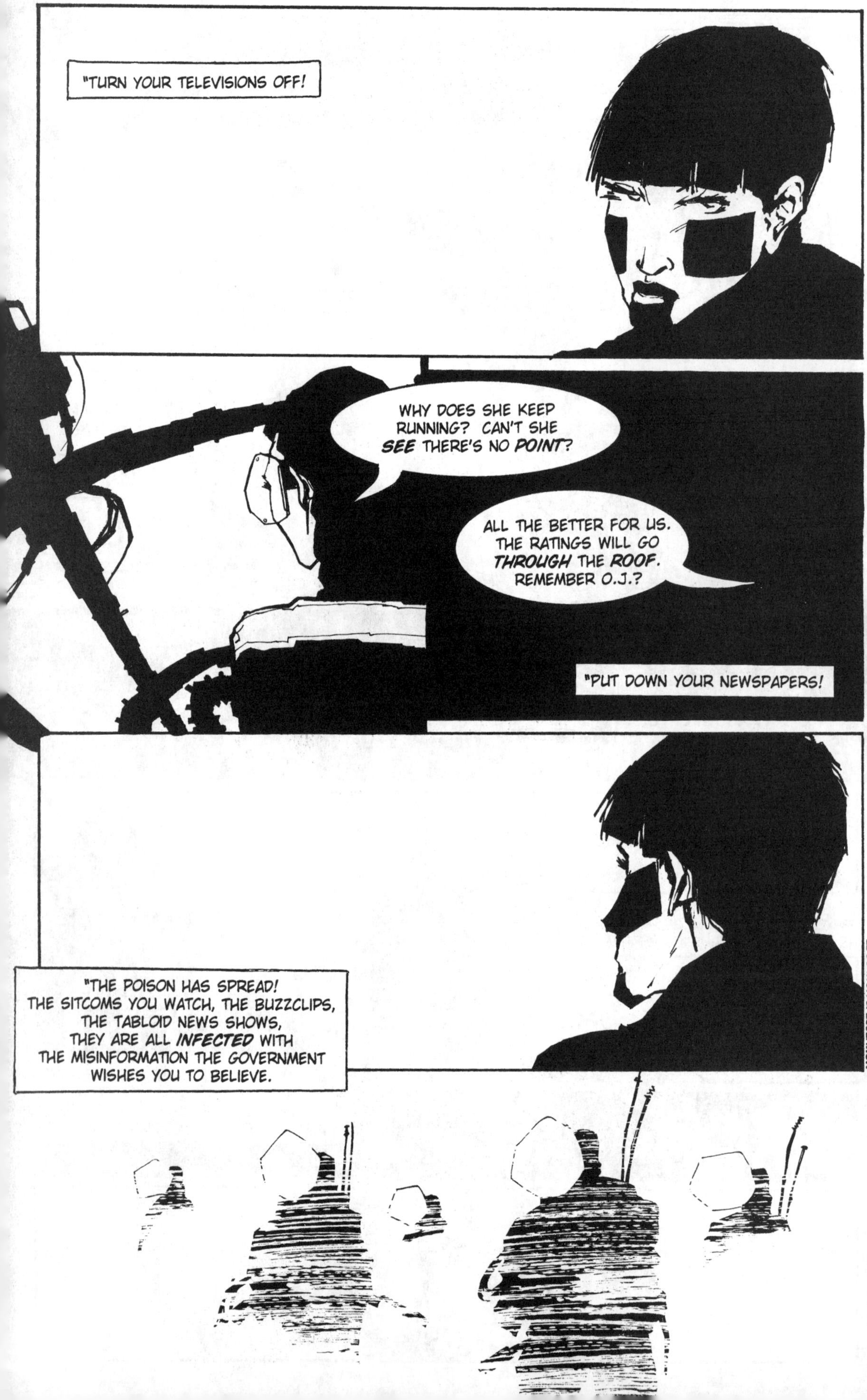
"TURN YOUR TELEVISIONS OFF!
WHY DOES SHE KEEP RUNNING? CAN'T SHE *SEE* THERE'S NO *POINT*?
ALL THE BETTER FOR US. THE RATINGS WILL GO *THROUGH* THE *ROOF*. REMEMBER O.J.?
"PUT DOWN YOUR NEWSPAPERS!
"THE POISON HAS SPREAD! THE SITCOMS YOU WATCH, THE BUZZCLIPS, THE TABLOID NEWS SHOWS, THEY ARE ALL *INFECTED* WITH THE MISINFORMATION THE GOVERNMENT WISHES YOU TO BELIEVE.

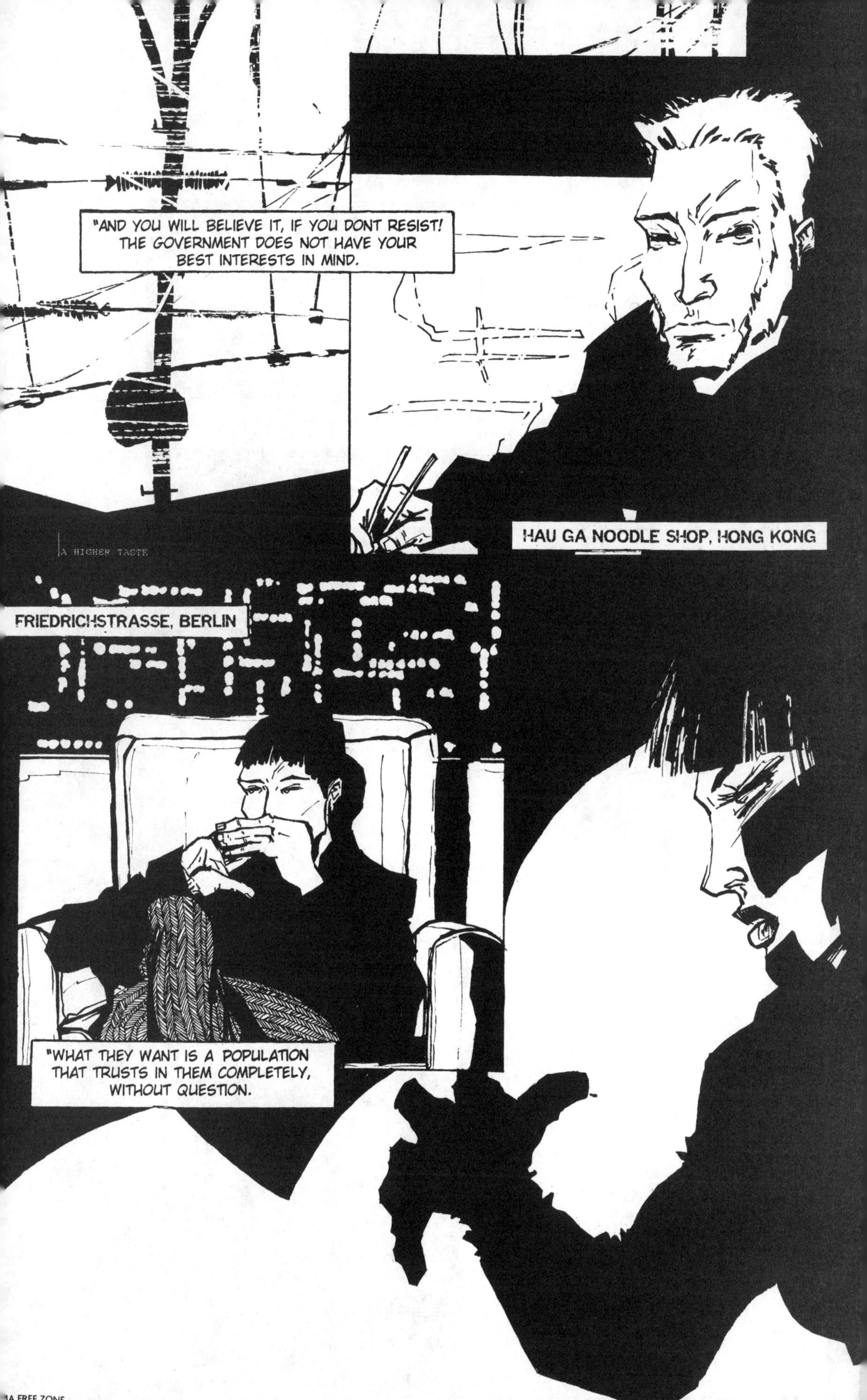
"AND YOU WILL BELIEVE IT, IF YOU DONT RESIST! THE GOVERNMENT DOES NOT HAVE YOUR BEST INTERESTS IN MIND.
HAU GA NOODLE SHOP, HONG KONG
A HIGHER TASTE
FRIEDRICHSTRASSE, BERLIN
"WHAT THEY WANT IS A POPULATION THAT TRUSTS IN THEM COMPLETELY, WITHOUT QUESTION.

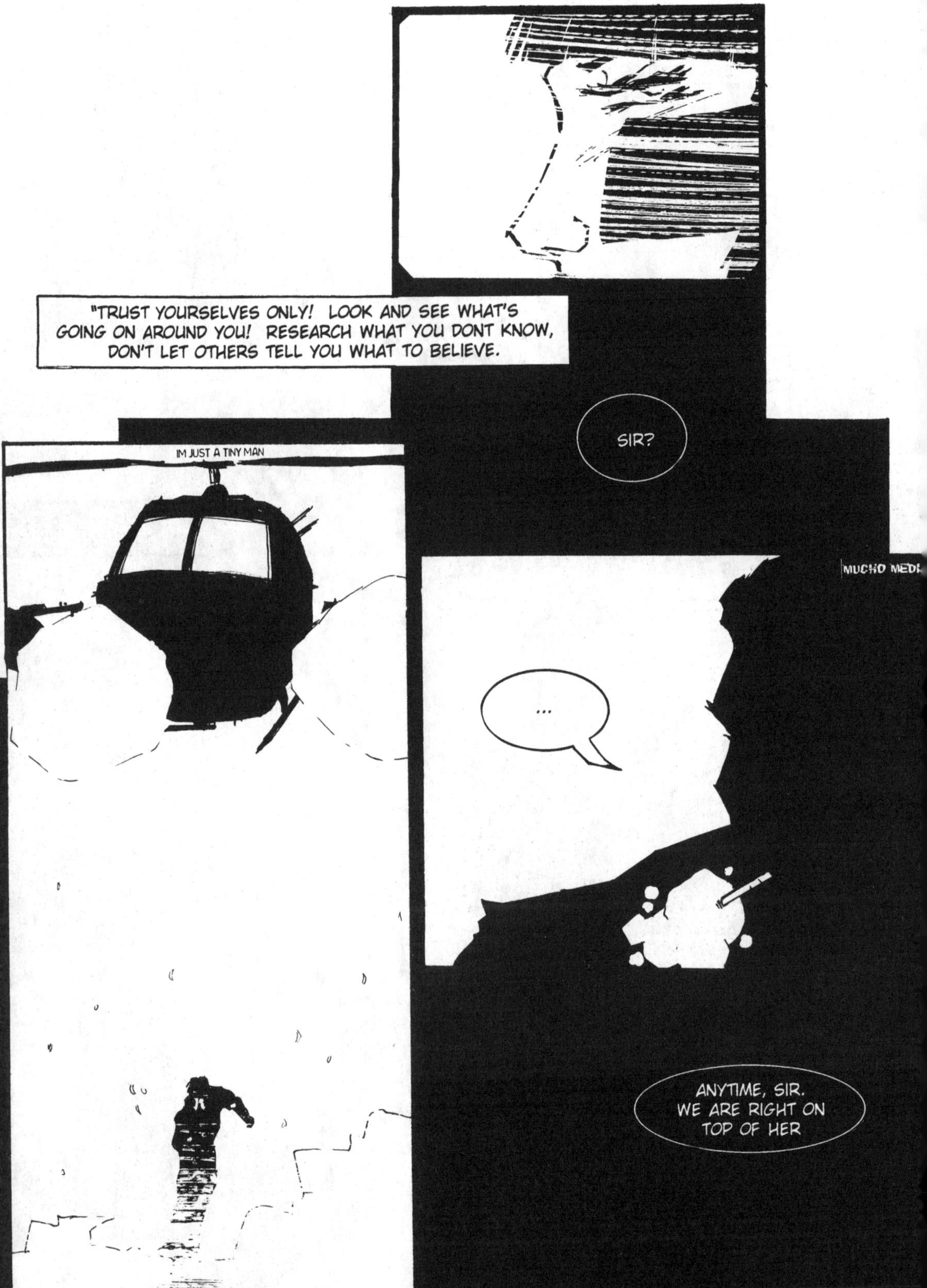
"TRUST YOURSELVES ONLY! LOOK AND SEE WHAT'S GOING ON AROUND YOU! RESEARCH WHAT YOU DONT KNOW, DON'T LET OTHERS TELL YOU WHAT TO BELIEVE.
SIR?
IM JUST A TINY MAN
MUCHO MEDI
...
ANYTIME, SIR. WE ARE RIGHT ON TOP OF HER

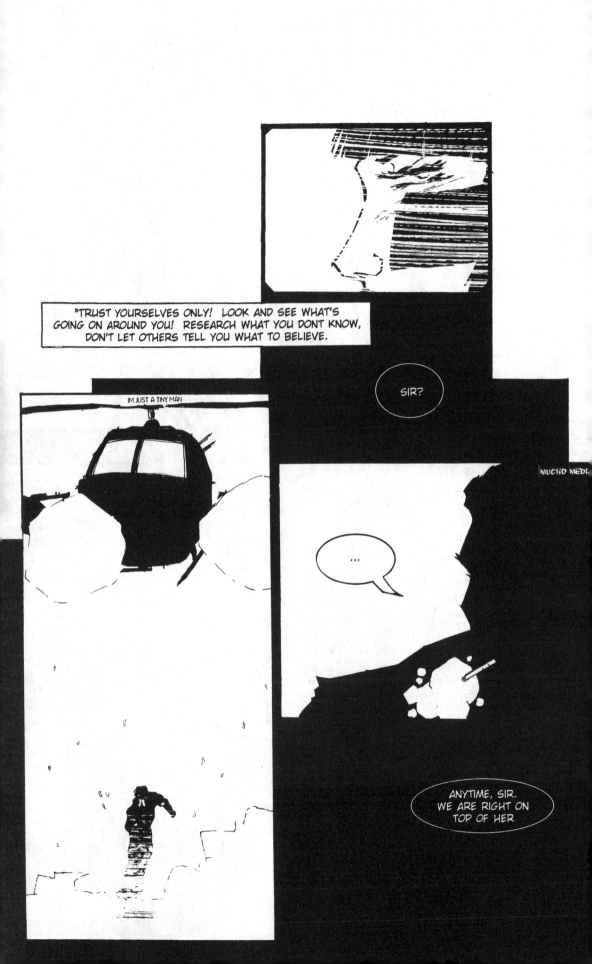

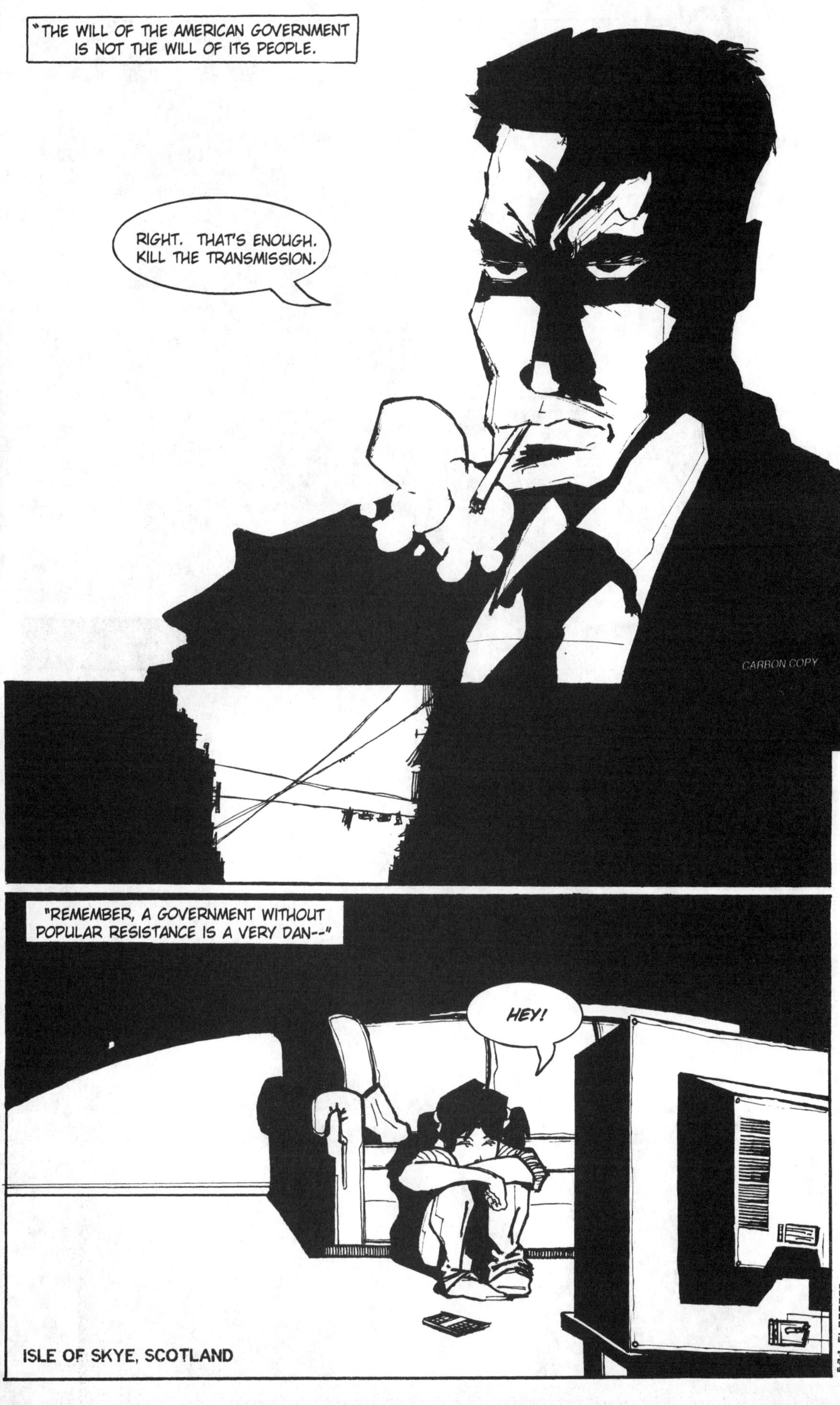
"THE WILL OF THE AMERICAN GOVERNMENT IS NOT THE WILL OF ITS PEOPLE.
RIGHT. THAT'S ENOUGH. KILL THE TRANSMISSION.
"REMEMBER, A GOVERNMENT WITHOUT POPULAR RESISTANCE IS A VERY DAN--"
HEY!
ISLE OF SKYE, SCOTLAND

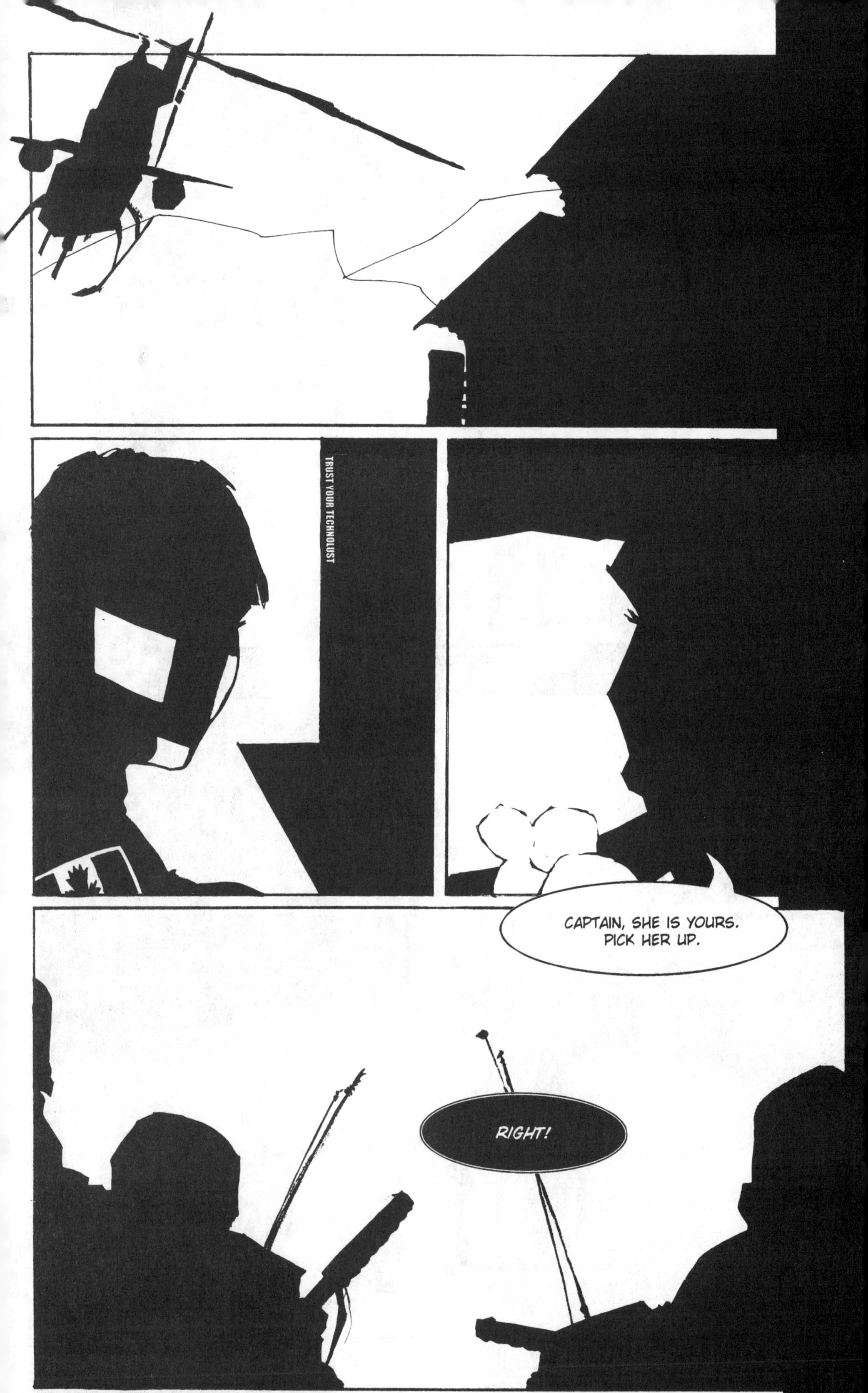
TRUST YOUR TECHNOLUST
CAPTAIN, SHE IS YOURS. PICK HER UP.
RIGHT!

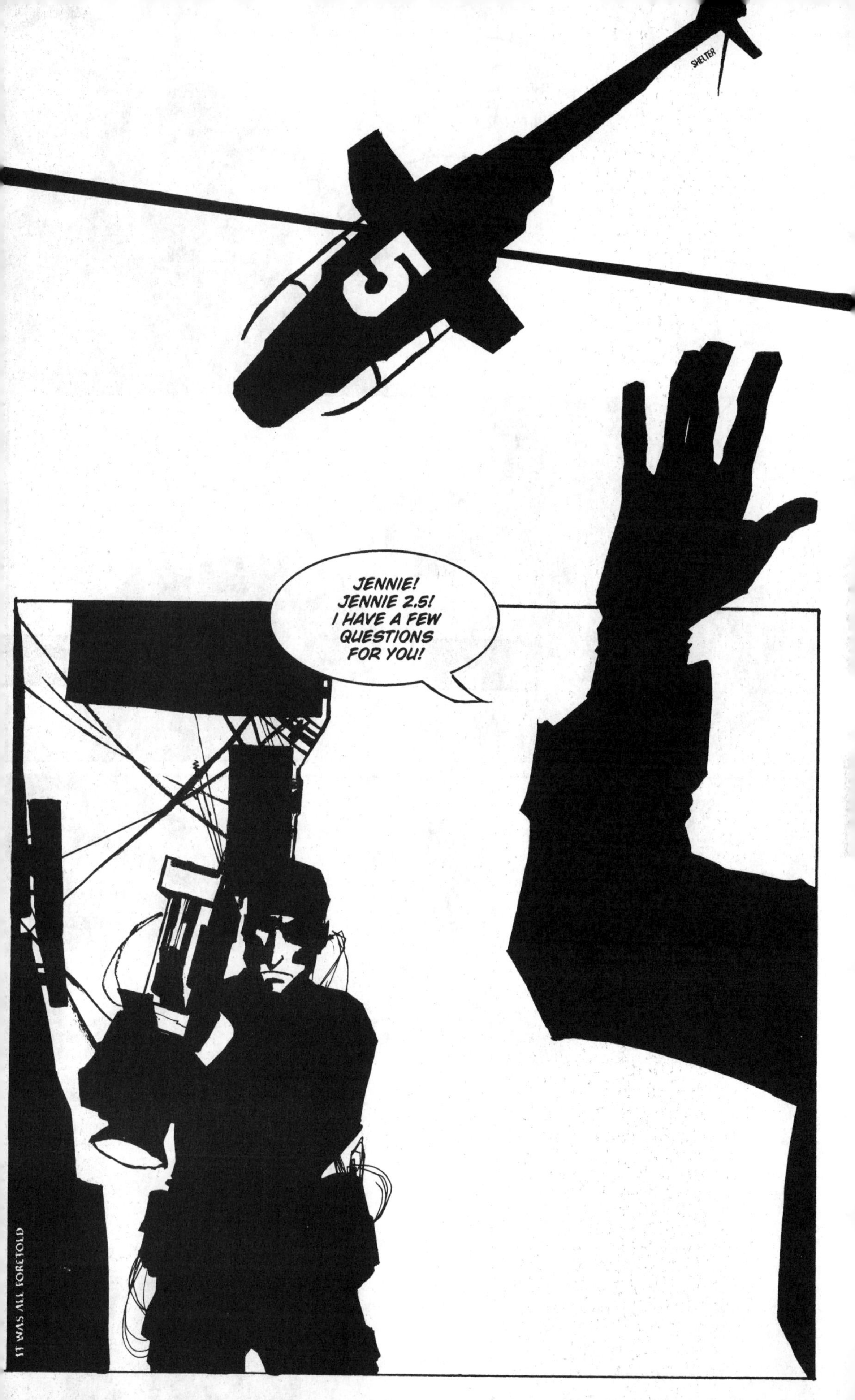
SHELTER
5
JENNIE! JENNIE 2.5! I HAVE A FEW QUESTIONS FOR YOU!

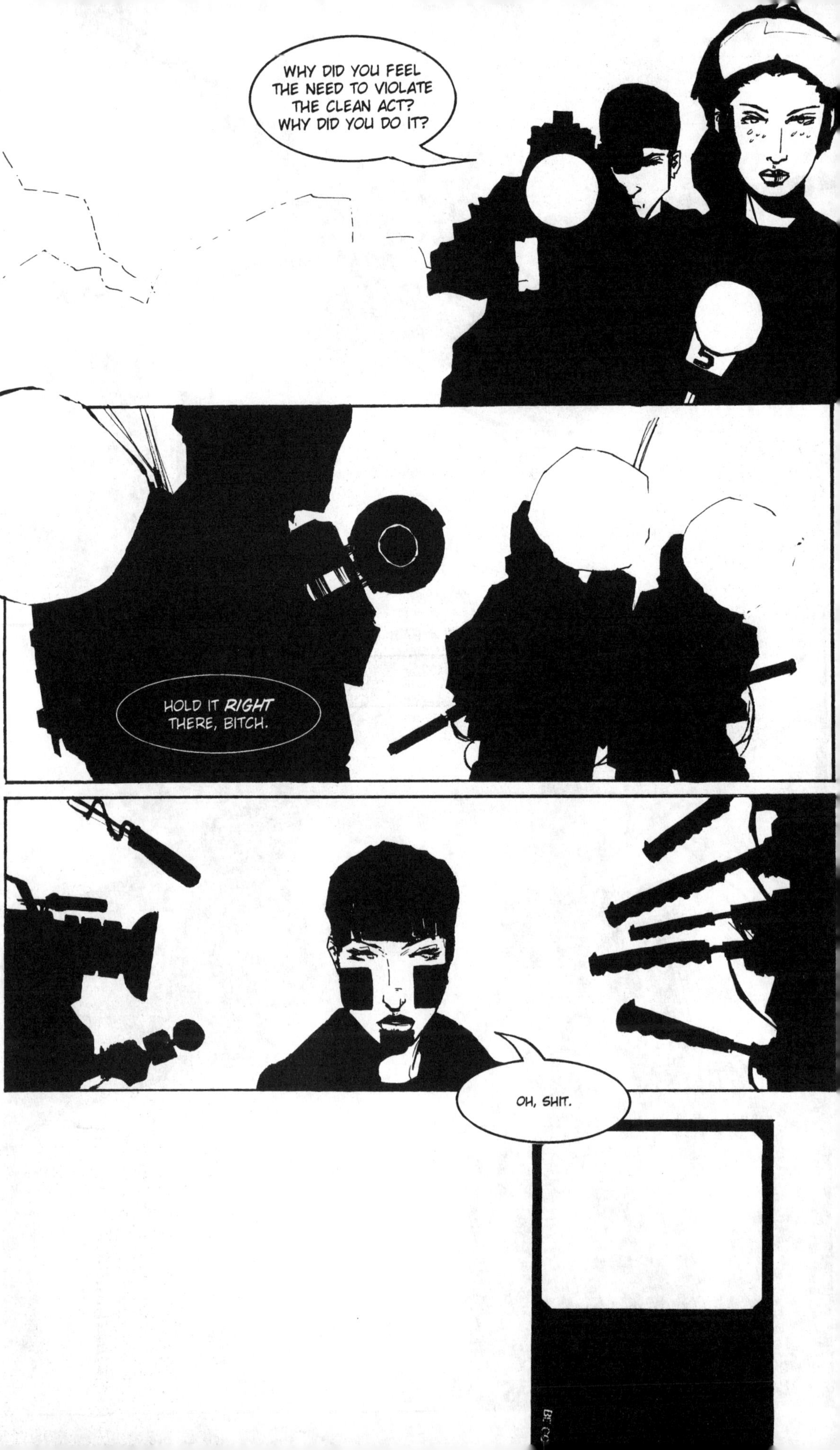
WHY DID YOU FEEL THE NEED TO VIOLATE THE CLEAN ACT? WHY DID YOU DO IT?
HOLD IT *RIGHT* THERE, BITCH.
OH, SHIT.

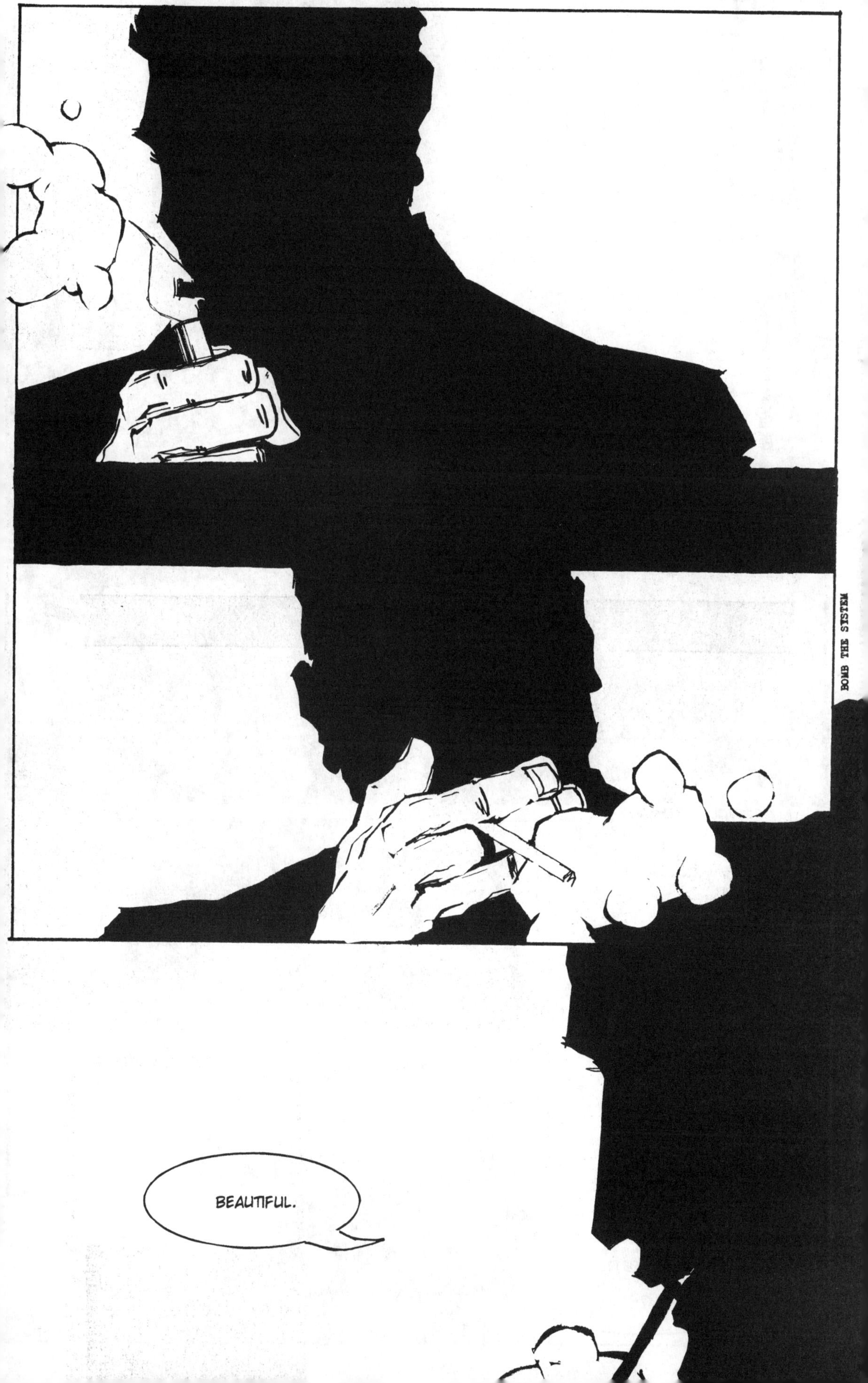
BEAUTIFUL.

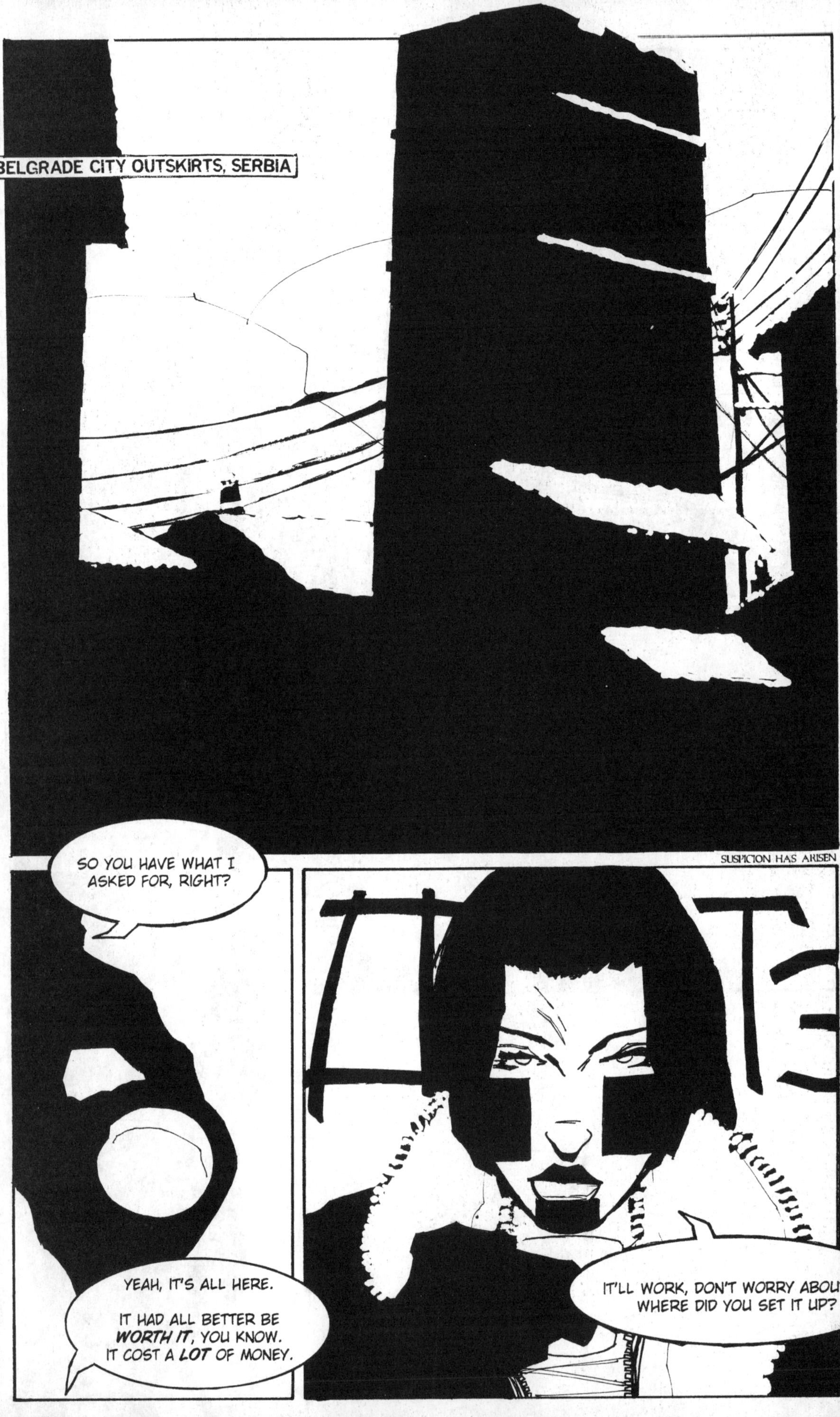
BELGRADE CITY OUTSKIRTS, SERBIA
SO YOU HAVE WHAT I ASKED FOR, RIGHT?
YEAH, IT'S ALL HERE.
IT HAD ALL BETTER BE **WORTH IT**, YOU KNOW. IT COST A **LOT** OF MONEY.
IT'LL WORK, DON'T WORRY ABOUT WHERE DID YOU SET IT UP?

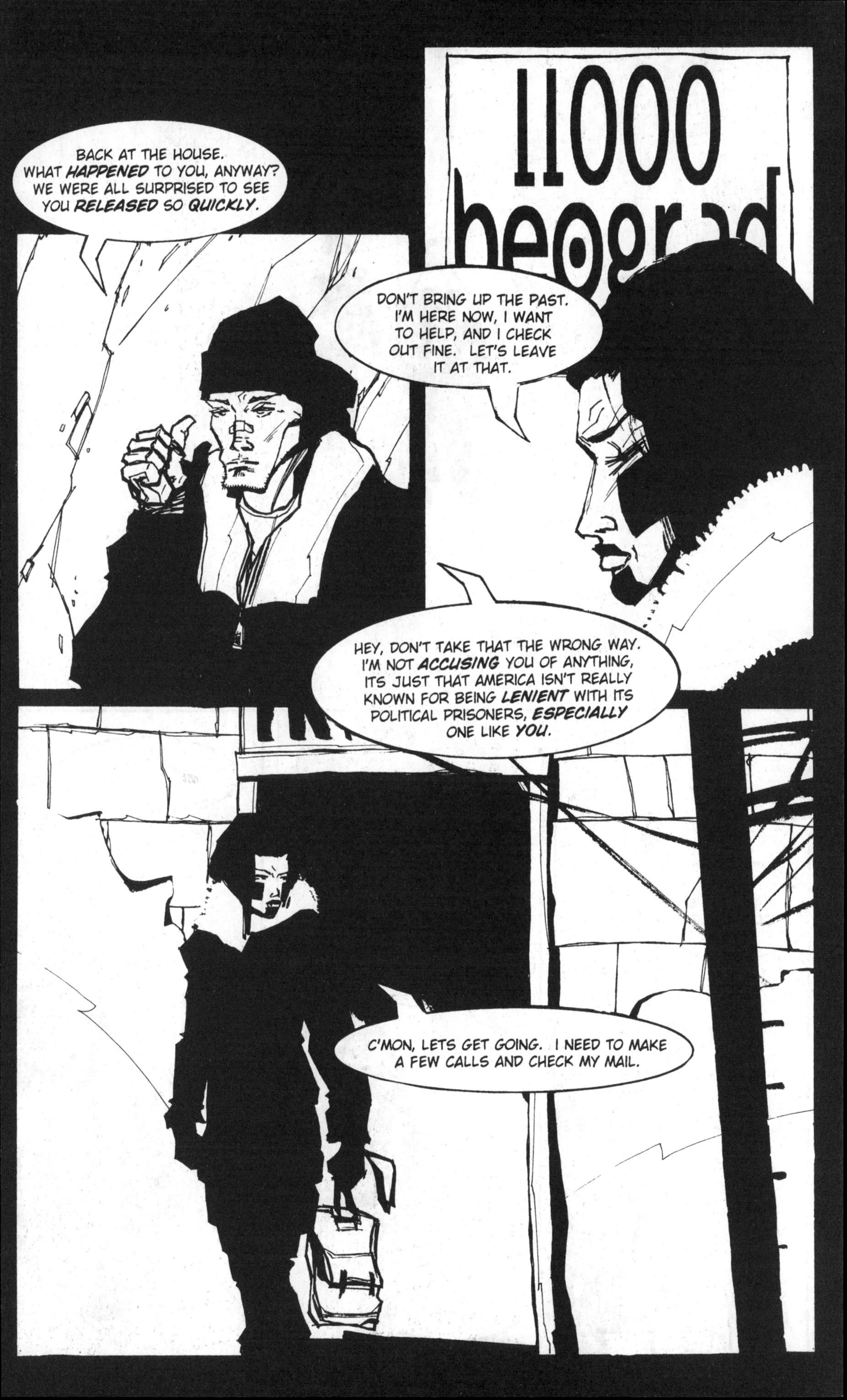
BACK AT THE HOUSE. WHAT HAPPENED TO YOU, ANYWAY? WE WERE ALL SURPRISED TO SEE YOU RELEASED SO QUICKLY.
11000 beograd
DON'T BRING UP THE PAST. I'M HERE NOW, I WANT TO HELP, AND I CHECK OUT FINE. LET'S LEAVE IT AT THAT.
HEY, DON'T TAKE THAT THE WRONG WAY. I'M NOT ACCUSING YOU OF ANYTHING, ITS JUST THAT AMERICA ISN'T REALLY KNOWN FOR BEING LENIENT WITH ITS POLITICAL PRISONERS, ESPECIALLY ONE LIKE YOU.
C'MON, LETS GET GOING. I NEED TO MAKE A FEW CALLS AND CHECK MY MAIL.

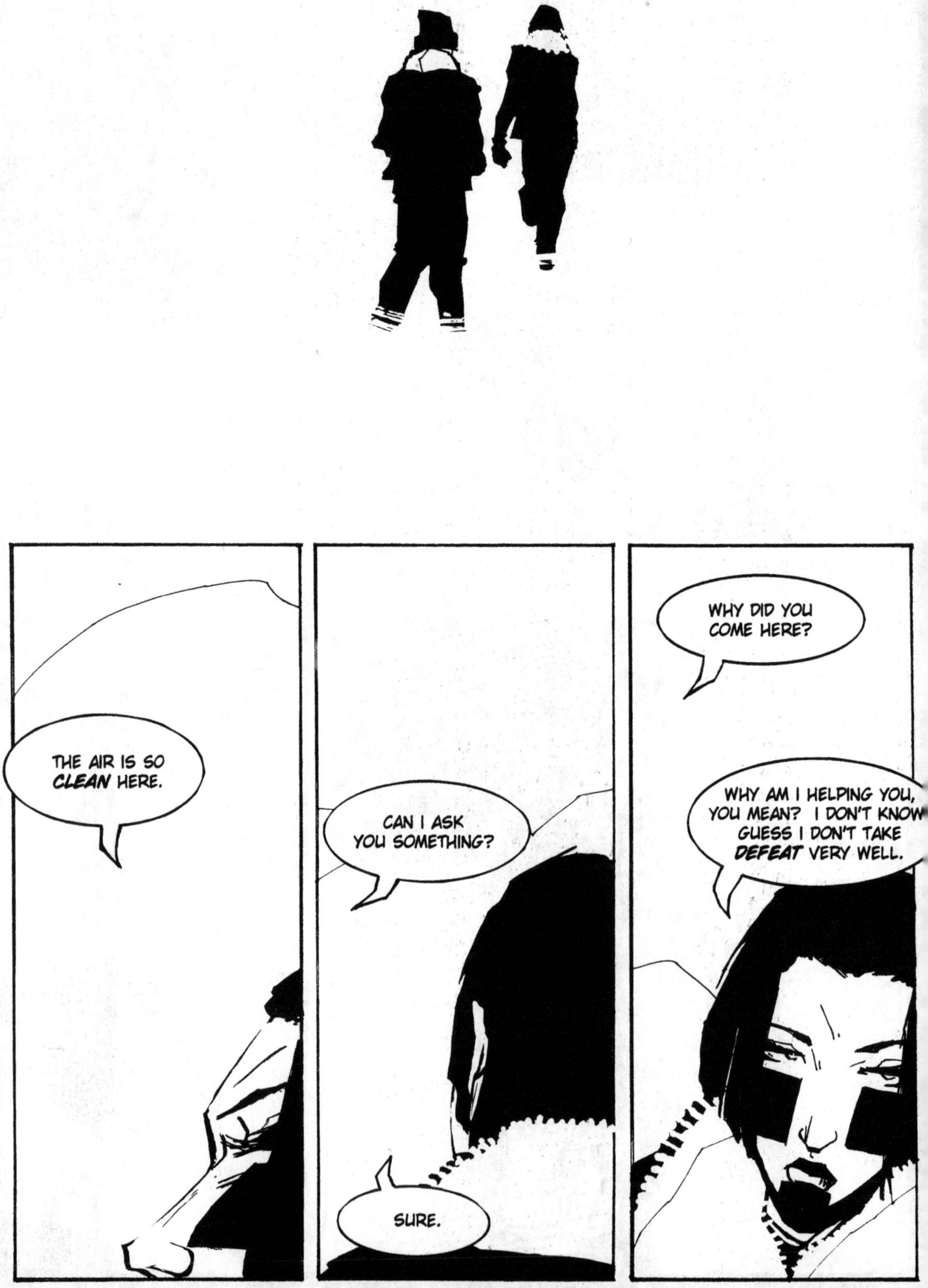
THE AIR IS SO CLEAN HERE.
CAN I ASK YOU SOMETHING?
SURE.
WHY DID YOU COME HERE?
WHY AM I HELPING YOU, YOU MEAN? I DON'T KNOW GUESS I DON'T TAKE DEFEAT VERY WELL.

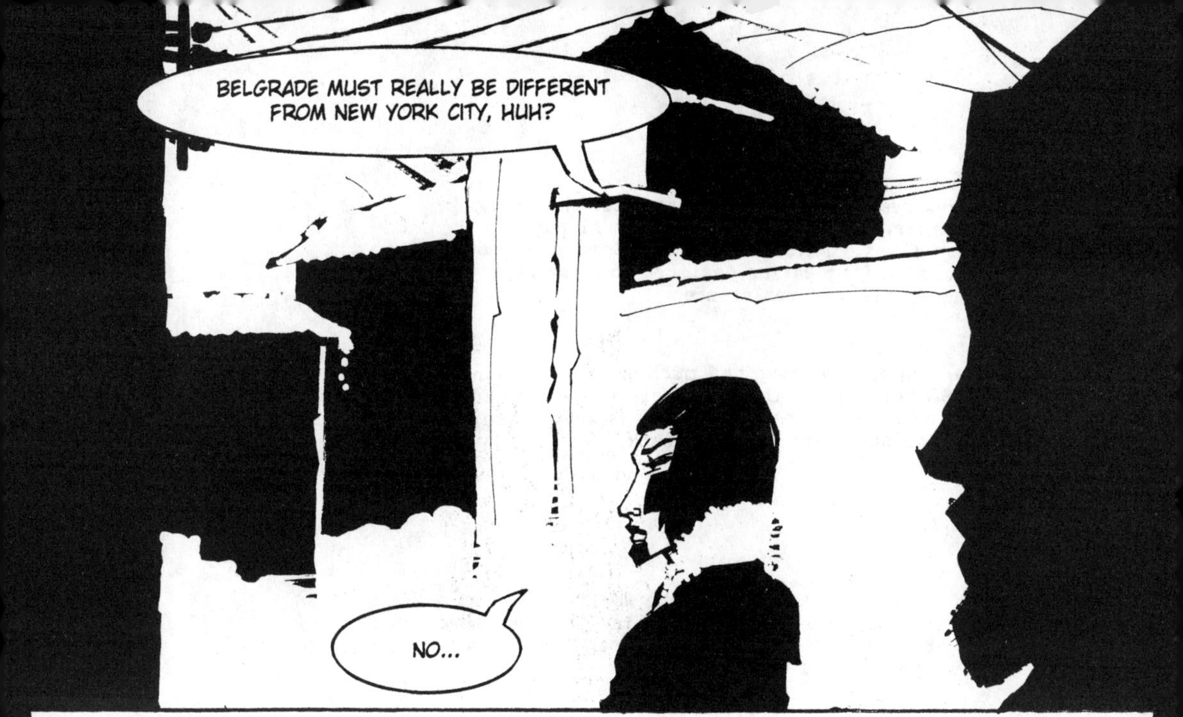
BELGRADE MUST REALLY BE DIFFERENT FROM NEW YORK CITY, HUH?
NO...

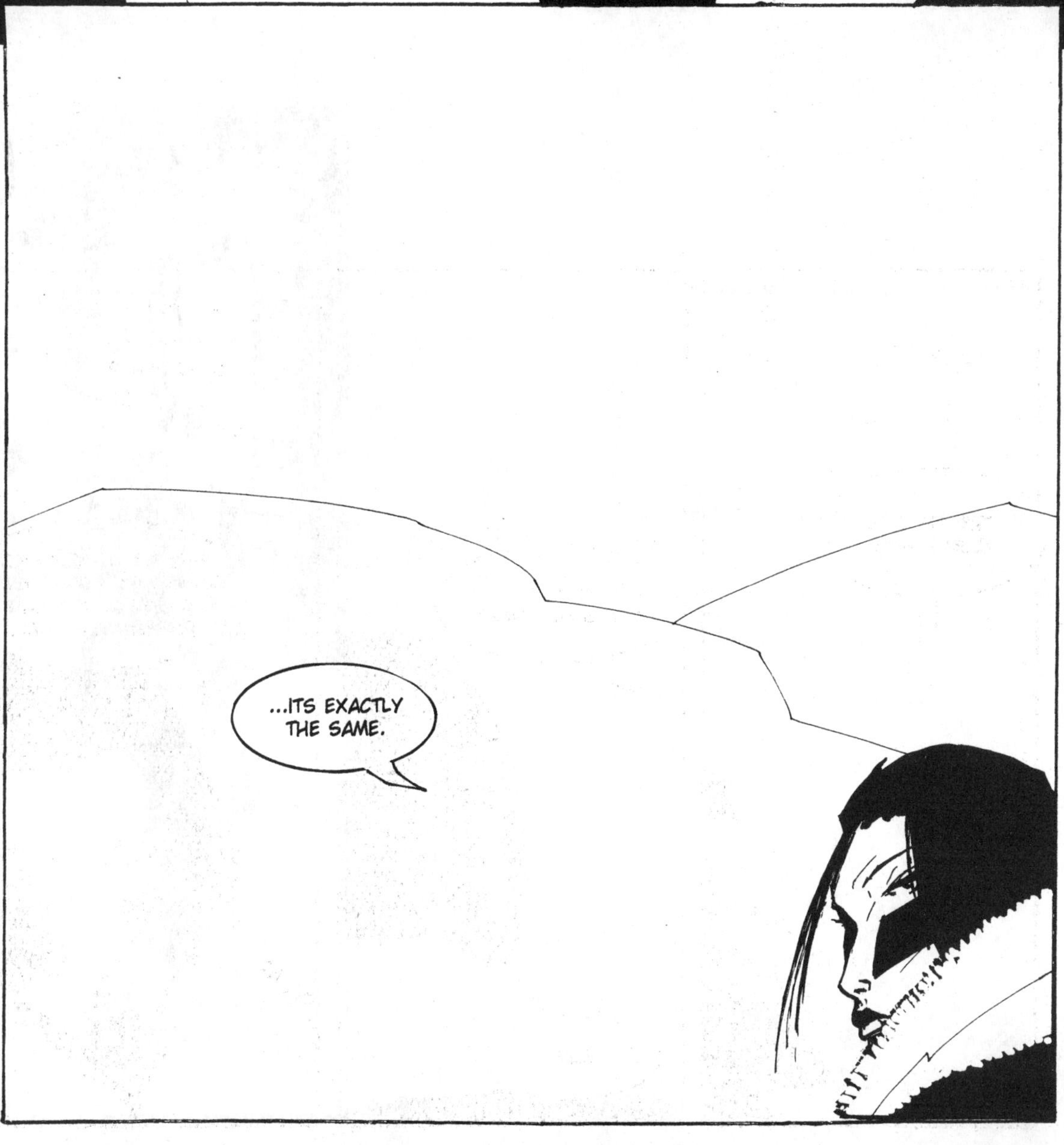
...ITS EXACTLY THE SAME.

In the end, nothing really changed. TV was still the same,
so were the newspapers. The Clean Act was still firmly in
place, and Jennie 2.5 was dismissed as a fad. Some even thought
it was all a government fabrication designed to boost ratings and
to demonstrate the futility of resistance.

But she was real. She may not have had much of an effect on the
general population, but she did inspire a select few who made
efforts to follow in her footsteps. Rumor had it she had relocated
to Eastern Europe and was planning a comeback.

I knew Jennie 2.5 personally, and I knew she wouldnt give up.
This would prove to be only the first chapter in what would become
close to a decade of work spent fighting the Clean Act,
and its various reincarnations and copycats.

But for now, life went on as before.

And people seemed to like that just fine.

THE END.

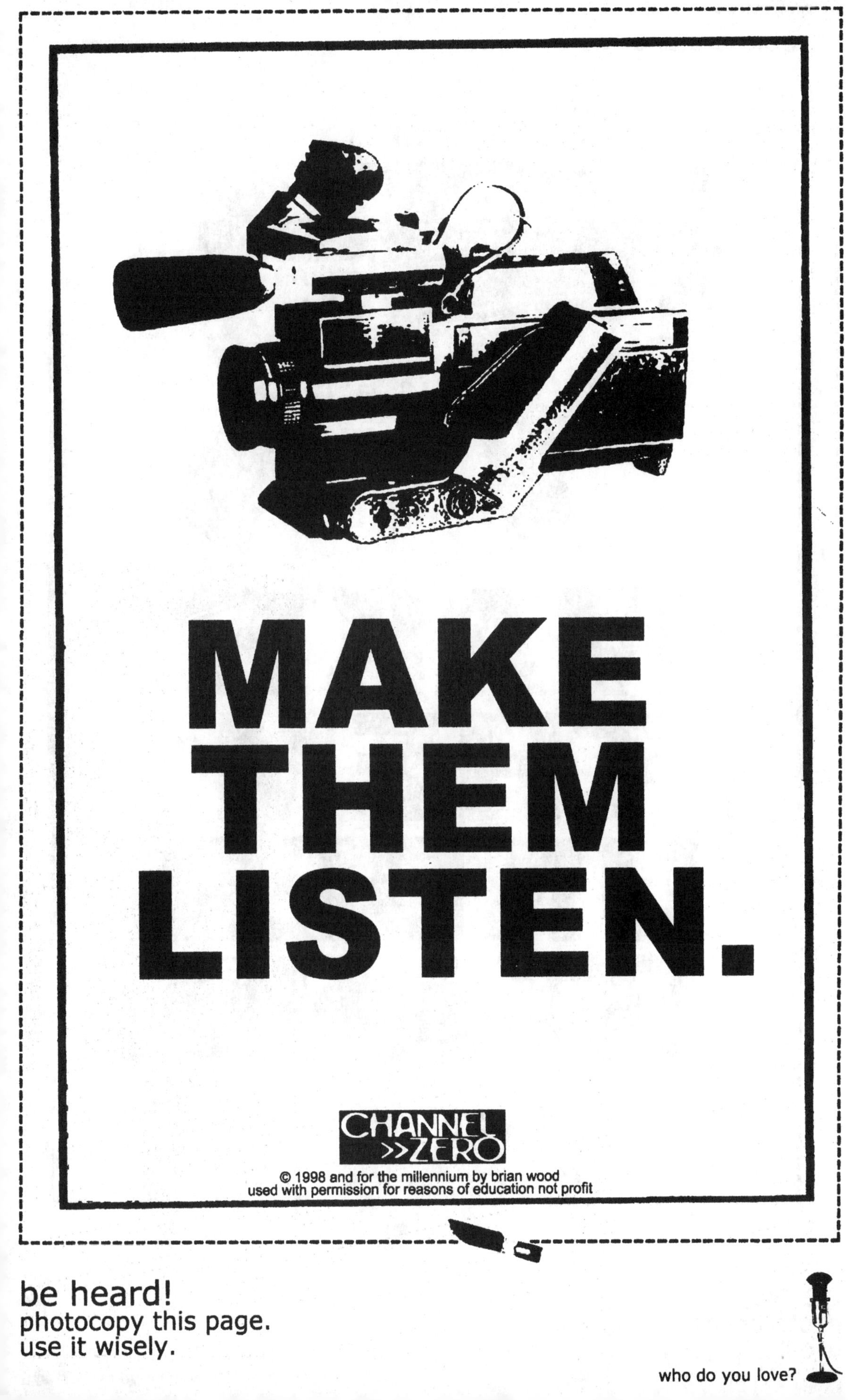

MAKE THEM LISTEN.

CHANNEL >>ZERO

be heard!
photocopy this page.
use it wisely.

who do you love?

MAKE THEM UNDER STAND.

CHANNEL >>ZERO

© 1998 and for the millennium by brian wood
used with permission for reasons of education not profit

be heard!
photocopy this page.
use it everywhere.

who do you love?

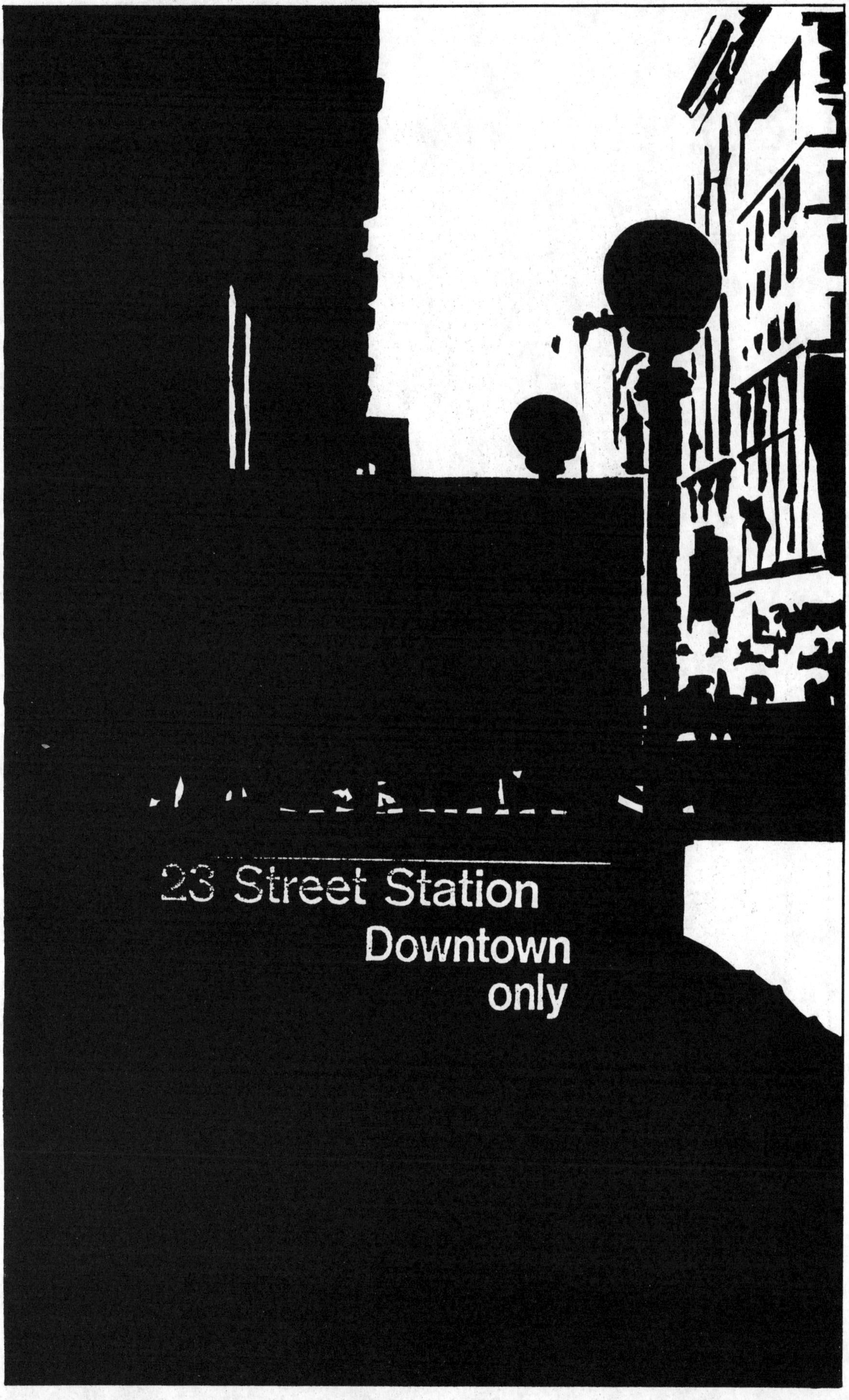
23 Street Station
Downtown
only

>>FILTER

"I wasn't wit' it, but just that very minute...
it occured to me
The suckers had authority."

- Chuck D

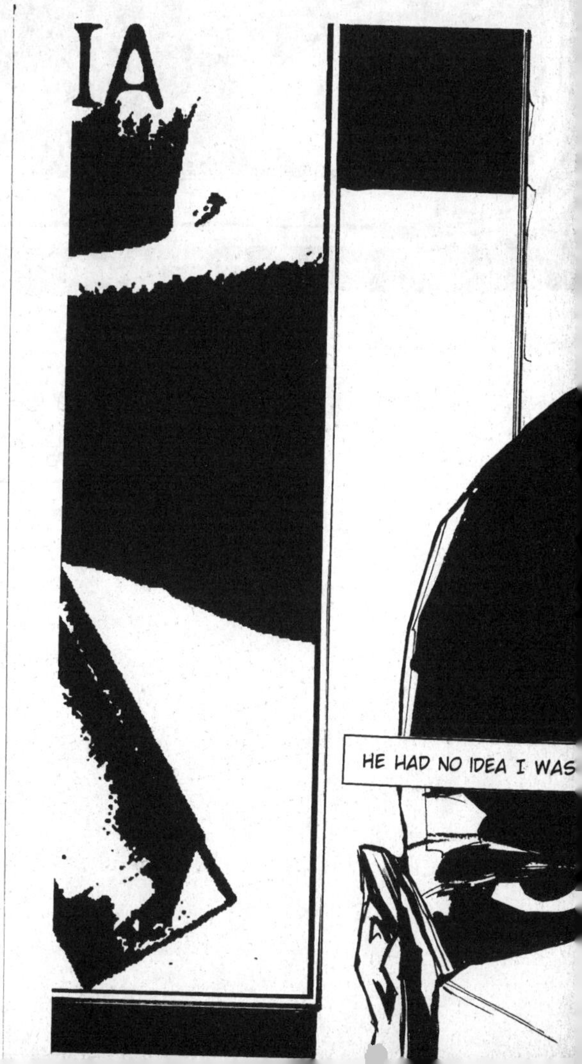
IA
HE HAD NO IDEA I WAS

I DID IT BECAUSE IT WAS MY JOB AS A ***CLEANER*** AND MY ***DUTY*** AS A CITIZEN. THAT'S ***CITIZEN*** WITH A CAPITAL ***"C"***. LET'S NOT FORGET THE ***BULLSHIT IMPORTANCE*** PLACED UPON US BY THOSE WHO WOULD HAVE US TO THEIR BIDDING.

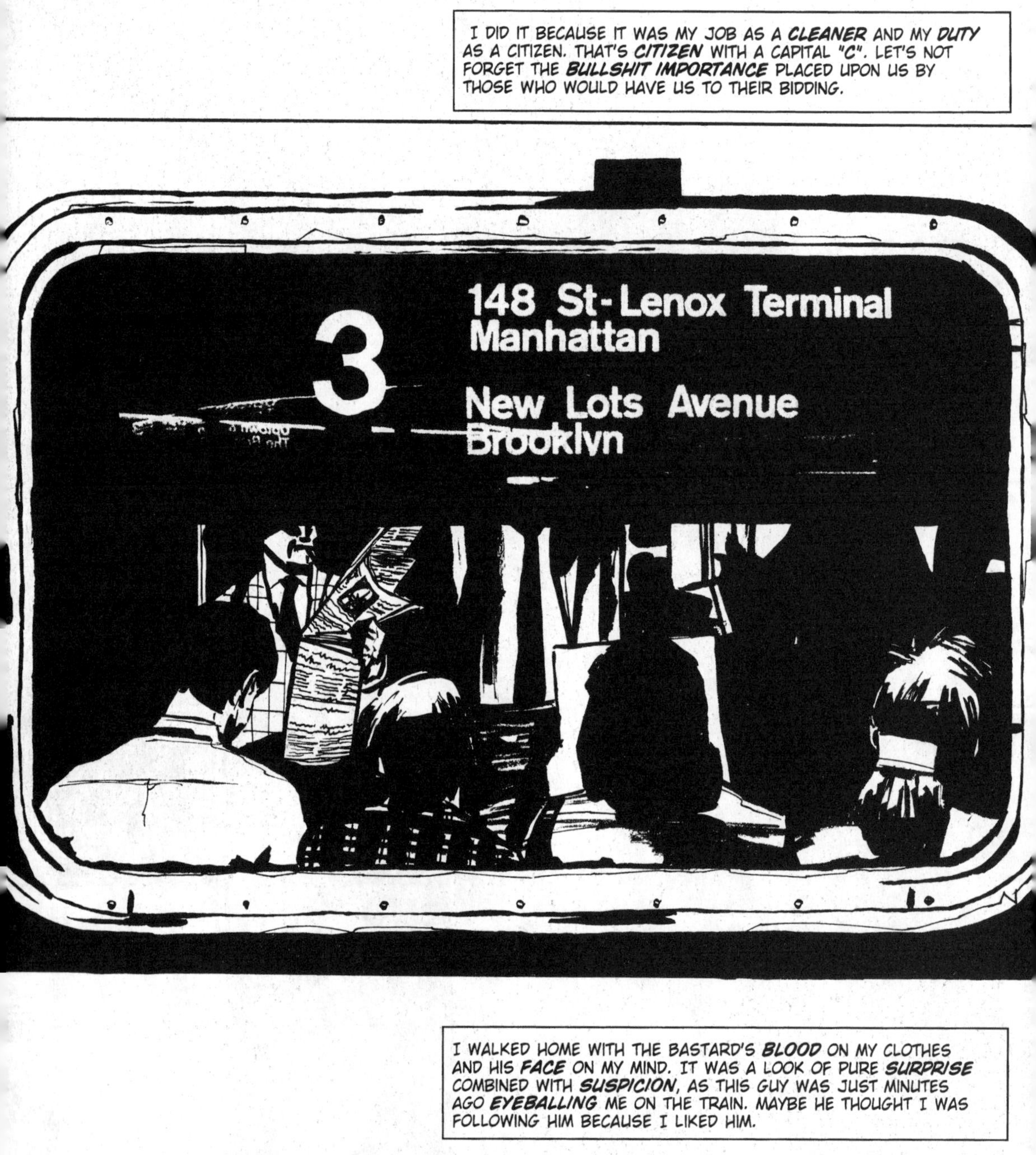
3
148 St-Lenox Terminal
Manhattan
New Lots Avenue
Brooklyn

I WALKED HOME WITH THE BASTARD'S ***BLOOD*** ON MY CLOTHES AND HIS ***FACE*** ON MY MIND. IT WAS A LOOK OF PURE ***SURPRISE*** COMBINED WITH ***SUSPICION***, AS THIS GUY WAS JUST MINUTES AGO ***EYEBALLING*** ME ON THE TRAIN. MAYBE HE THOUGHT I WAS FOLLOWING HIM BECAUSE I LIKED HIM.

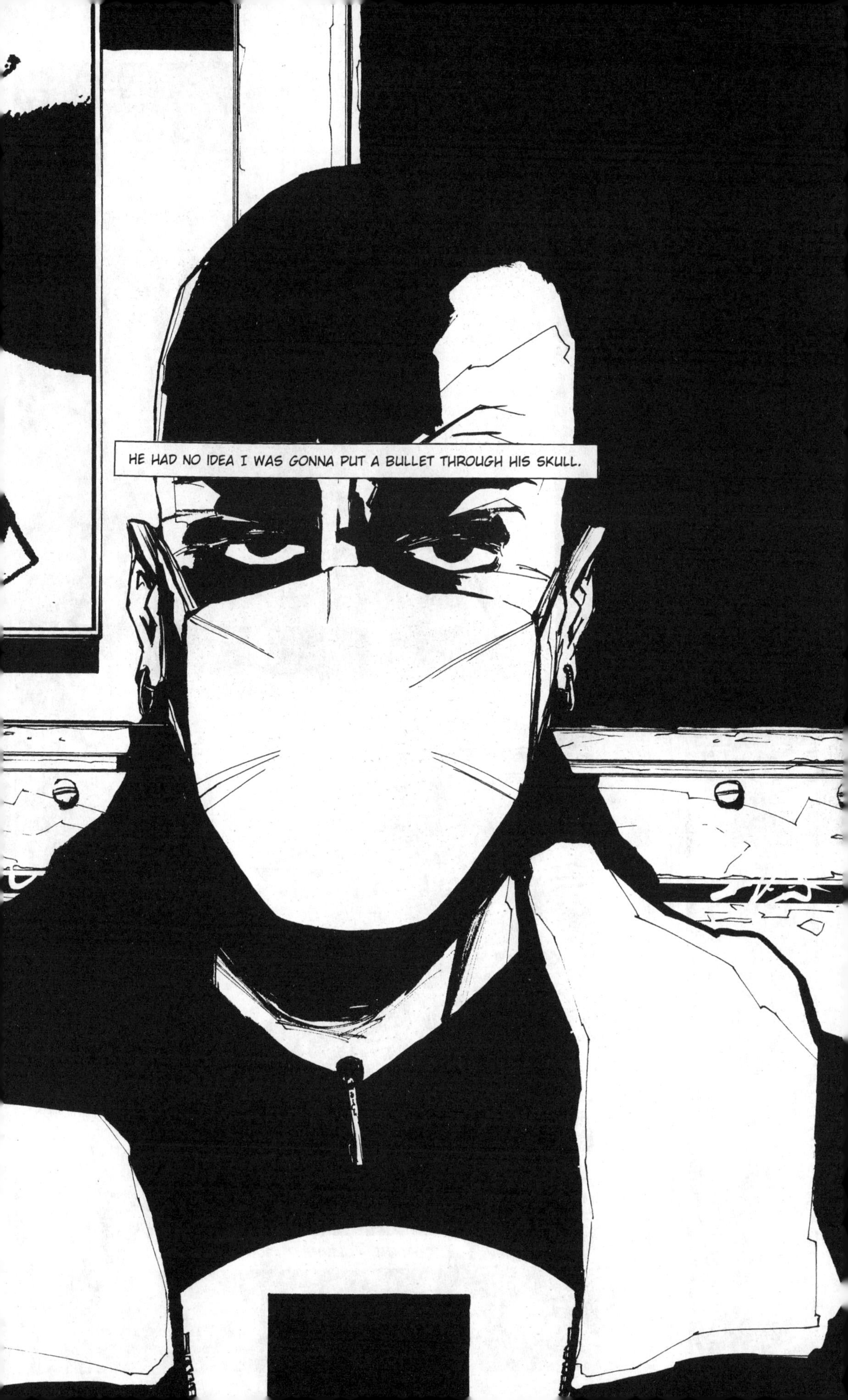
HE HAD NO IDEA I WAS GONNA PUT A BULLET THROUGH HIS SKULL.

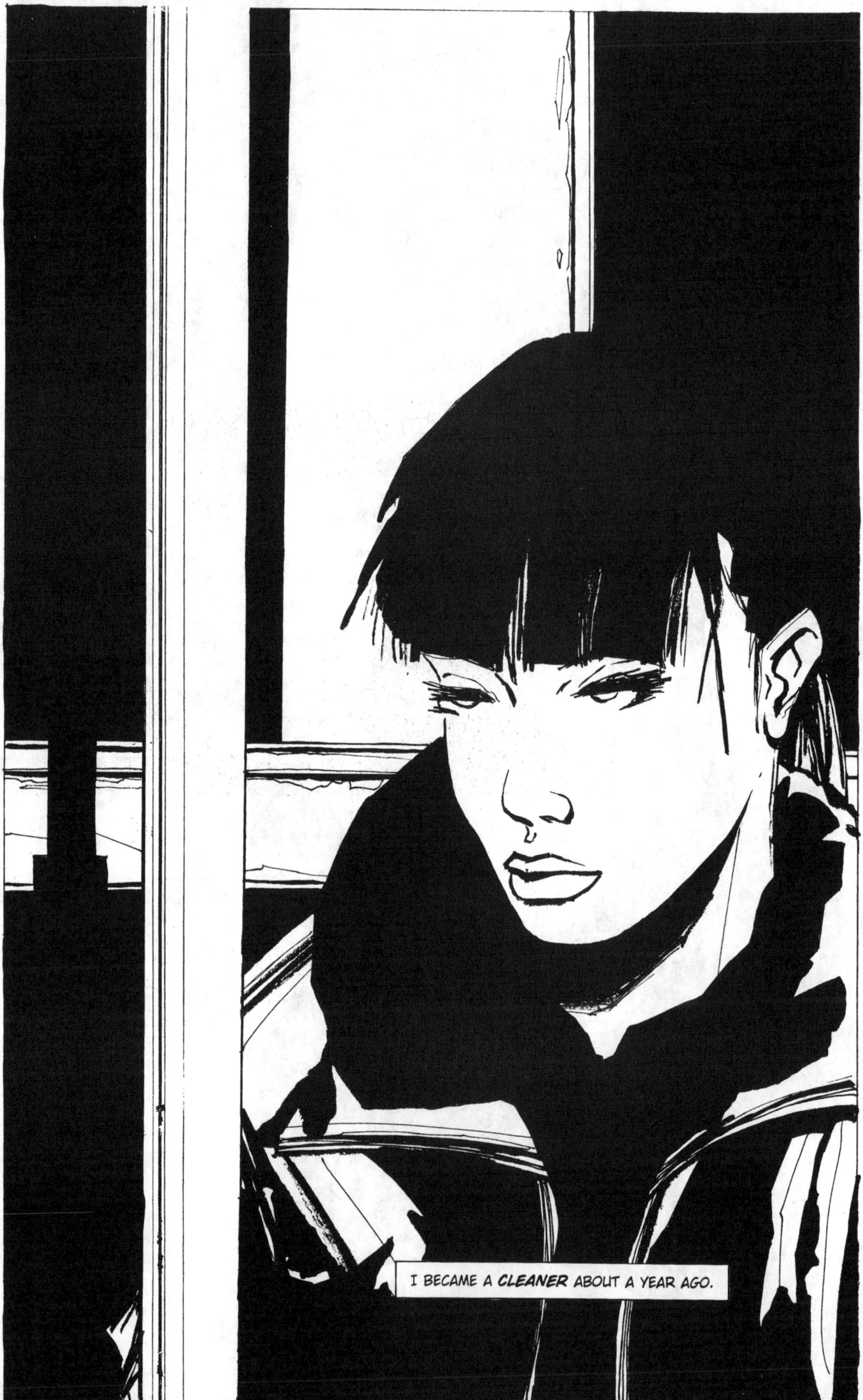
I BECAME A **CLEANER** ABOUT A YEAR AGO.

IT'S ALL ABOUT A GOOD SALARY, GREAT BENEFITS, AND THE *WARM FEELING* YOU GET AT THE END OF THE DAY, WHEN YOU GO HOME TO YOUR SWEET APARTMENT; KNOWING THAT BECAUSE YOU *SHOT* A 14-YEAR-OLD FOR *KEY-SCRATCHING* THE J TRAIN, THAT WOULD SOME HOW IMPROVE THE *QUALITY OF LIFE* IN OUR CITY.

I'VE HEARD *ALL* THE ARGUMENTS. PROPERTY VALUES ARE UP, THE CRIME RATE IS DOWN TO WHAT IT WAS *THIRTY YEARS AGO*, THERE'S PLENTY OF PARKING, AND YOU CAN WALK THROUGH *TIMES SQUARE* WITHOUT HAVING TO DODGE *HOOKERS* AND *JUNKIES* AND *MUGGERS*.

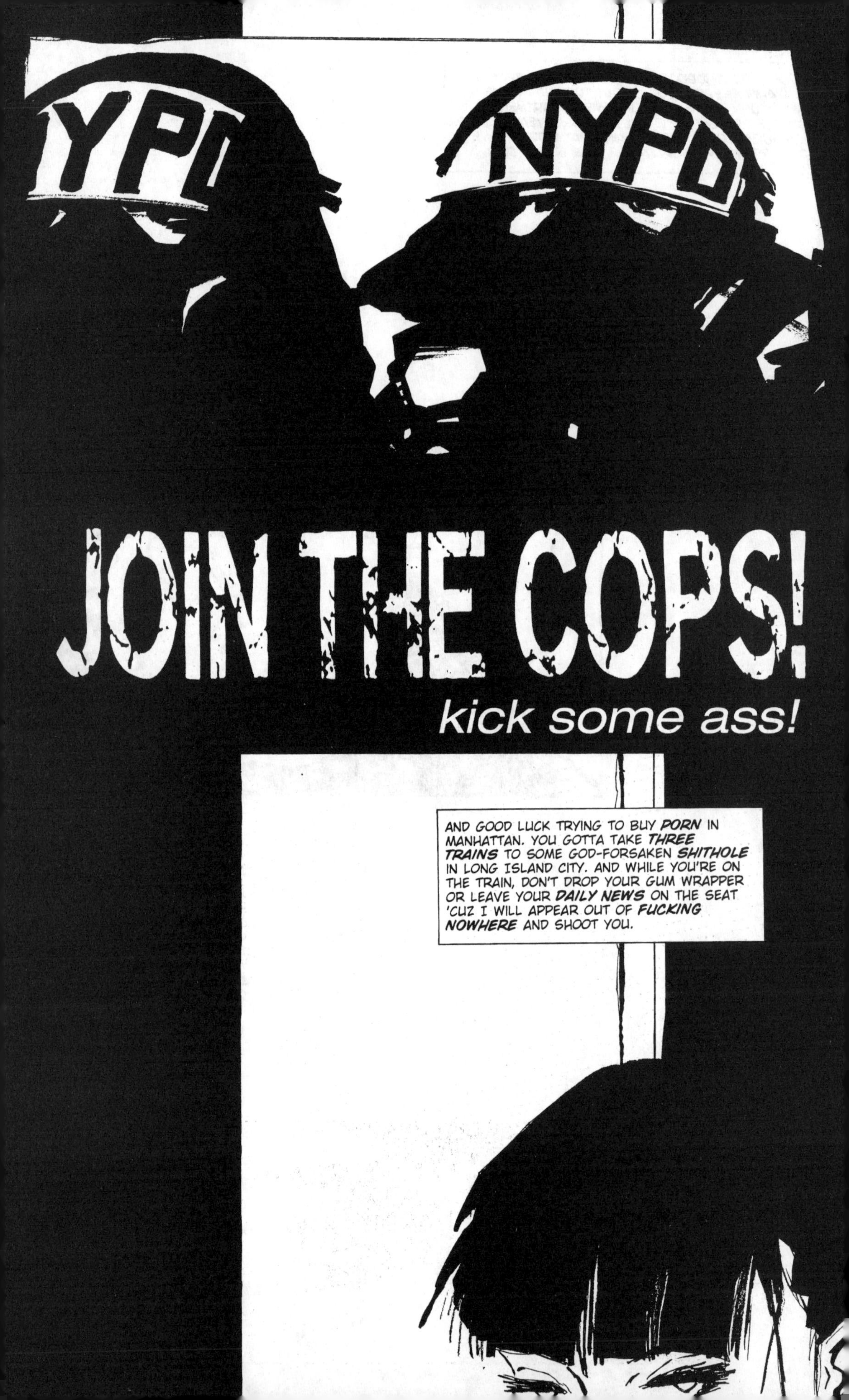

YPD
NYPD
JOIN THE COPS!
kick some ass!
AND GOOD LUCK TRYING TO BUY PORN IN MANHATTAN. YOU GOTTA TAKE THREE TRAINS TO SOME GOD-FORSAKEN SHITHOLE IN LONG ISLAND CITY. AND WHILE YOU'RE ON THE TRAIN, DON'T DROP YOUR GUM WRAPPER OR LEAVE YOUR DAILY NEWS ON THE SEAT 'CUZ I WILL APPEAR OUT OF FUCKING NOWHERE AND SHOOT YOU.

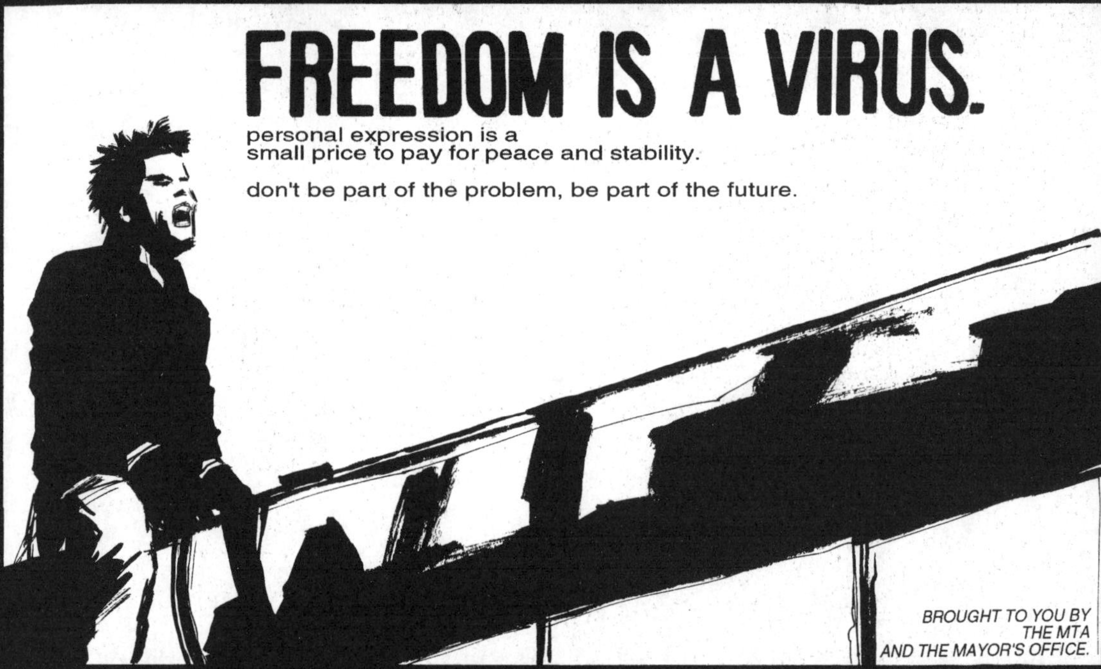
FREEDOM IS A VIRUS.
personal expression is a
small price to pay for peace and stability.
don't be part of the problem, be part of the future.
BROUGHT TO YOU BY
THE MTA
AND THE MAYOR'S OFFICE.

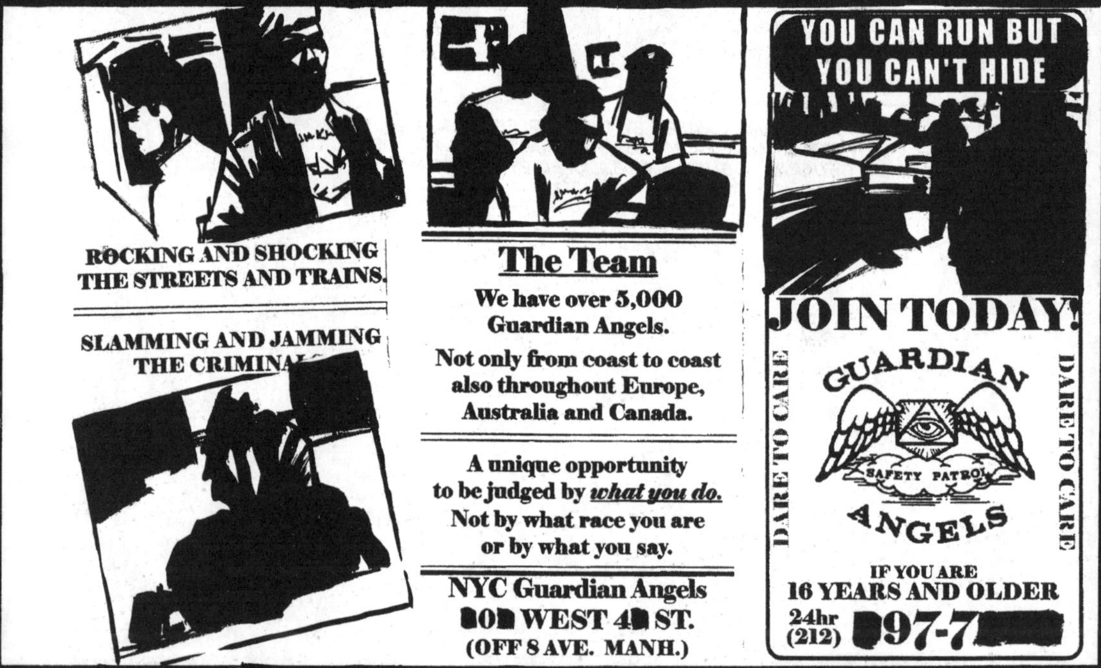
ROCKING AND SHOCKING
THE STREETS AND TRAINS.
SLAMMING AND JAMMING
THE CRIMINA
The Team
We have over 5,000
Guardian Angels.
Not only from coast to coast
also throughout Europe,
Australia and Canada.
A unique opportunity
to be judged by what you do.
Not by what race you are
or by what you say.
NYC Guardian Angels
[redacted] WEST 4[redacted] ST.
(OFF 8 AVE. MANH.)
YOU CAN RUN BUT
YOU CAN'T HIDE
JOIN TODAY!
DARE TO CARE
GUARDIAN
SAFETY PATROL
ANGELS
DARE TO CARE
IF YOU ARE
16 YEARS AND OLDER
24hr
(212) [redacted]97-7[redacted]

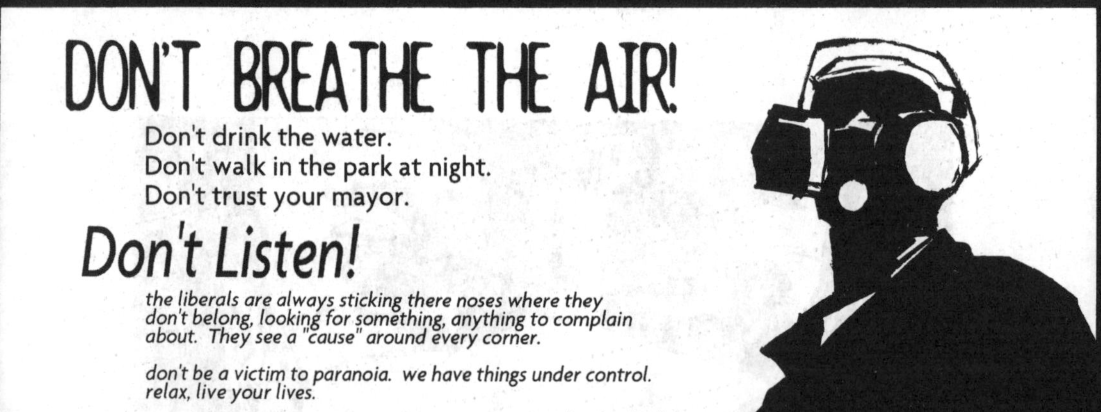
DON'T BREATHE THE AIR!
Don't drink the water.
Don't walk in the park at night.
Don't trust your mayor.
Don't Listen!
the liberals are always sticking there noses where they don't belong, looking for something, anything to complain about. They see a "cause" around every corner.
don't be a victim to paranoia. we have things under control. relax, live your lives.
the Mayor's Office

I'M FEARED BY MY FRIENDS AND FAMILY; *HATED* BY THE PEOPLE THAT MATTER THE MOST TO ME. MAYBE SOME RICH, OLD *WHITE WOMAN* FROM THE UPPER EAST SIDE LIKES ME BECAUSE WHEN SHE STEPS OUTSIDE, SHE ISN'T *FUCKIN' VISUALLY ASSAULTED* BY A NEWSPAPER BOX OR A HOTDOG VENDOR ON THE CORNER WHERE SHE DOESN'T THINK ONE SHOULD BE.

BUT THAT'S USELESS TO ME.

INSTEAD, WHAT HAPPENS EVERY NIGHT IS I GO HOME TO AN EMPTY APARTMENT WITH NO MESSAGES ON MY MACHINE, A FROZEN MICROWAVE DINNER, AND *300 CRAP CHANNELS* ON TV.

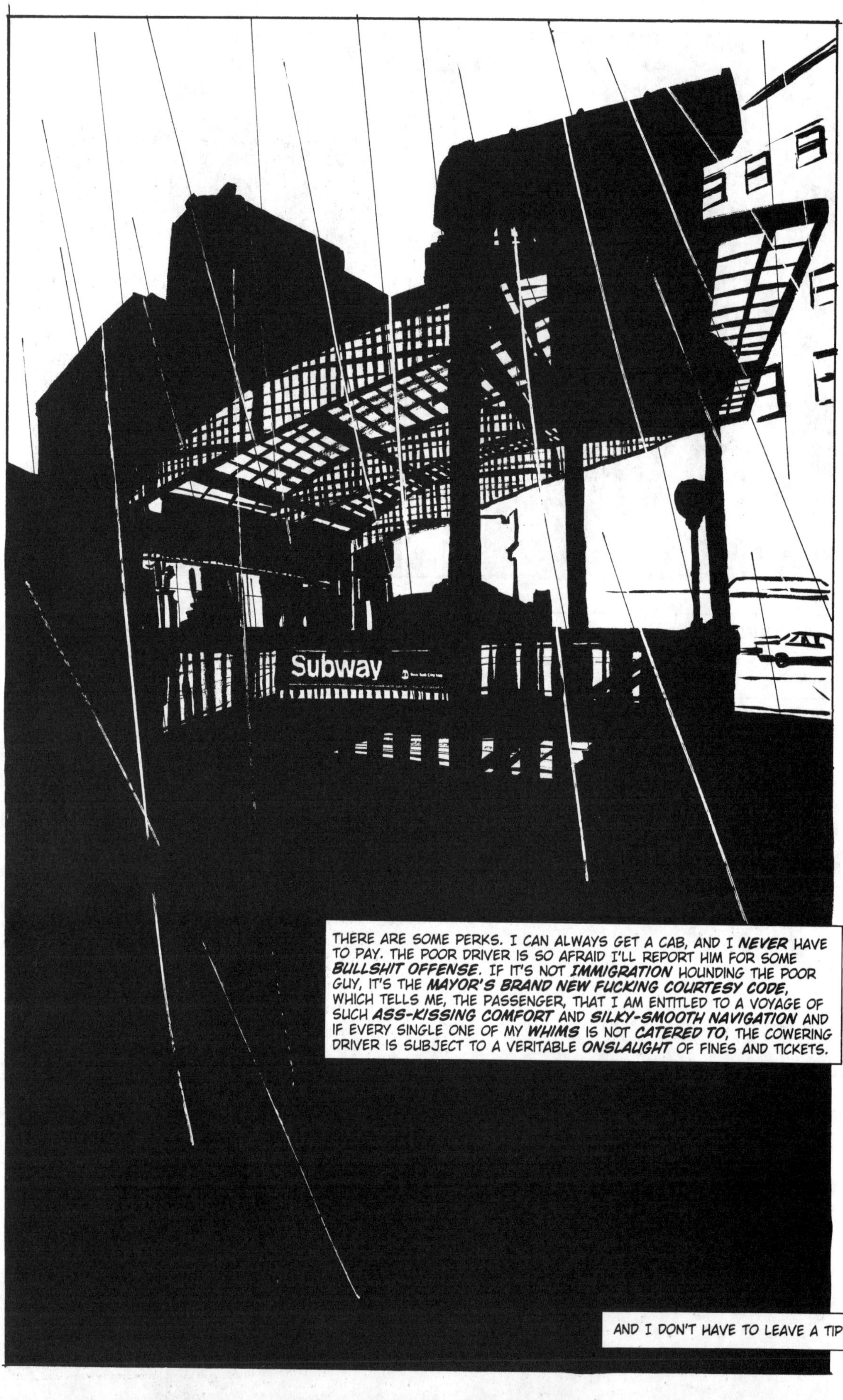
Subway
THERE ARE SOME PERKS. I CAN ALWAYS GET A CAB, AND I ***NEVER*** HAVE TO PAY. THE POOR DRIVER IS SO AFRAID I'LL REPORT HIM FOR SOME ***BULLSHIT OFFENSE***. IF IT'S NOT ***IMMIGRATION*** HOUNDING THE POOR GUY, IT'S THE ***MAYOR'S BRAND NEW FUCKING COURTESY CODE***, WHICH TELLS ME, THE PASSENGER, THAT I AM ENTITLED TO A VOYAGE OF SUCH ***ASS-KISSING COMFORT*** AND ***SILKY-SMOOTH NAVIGATION*** AND IF EVERY SINGLE ONE OF MY ***WHIMS*** IS NOT ***CATERED TO***, THE COWERING DRIVER IS SUBJECT TO A VERITABLE ***ONSLAUGHT*** OF FINES AND TICKETS.
AND I DON'T HAVE TO LEAVE A TIP.

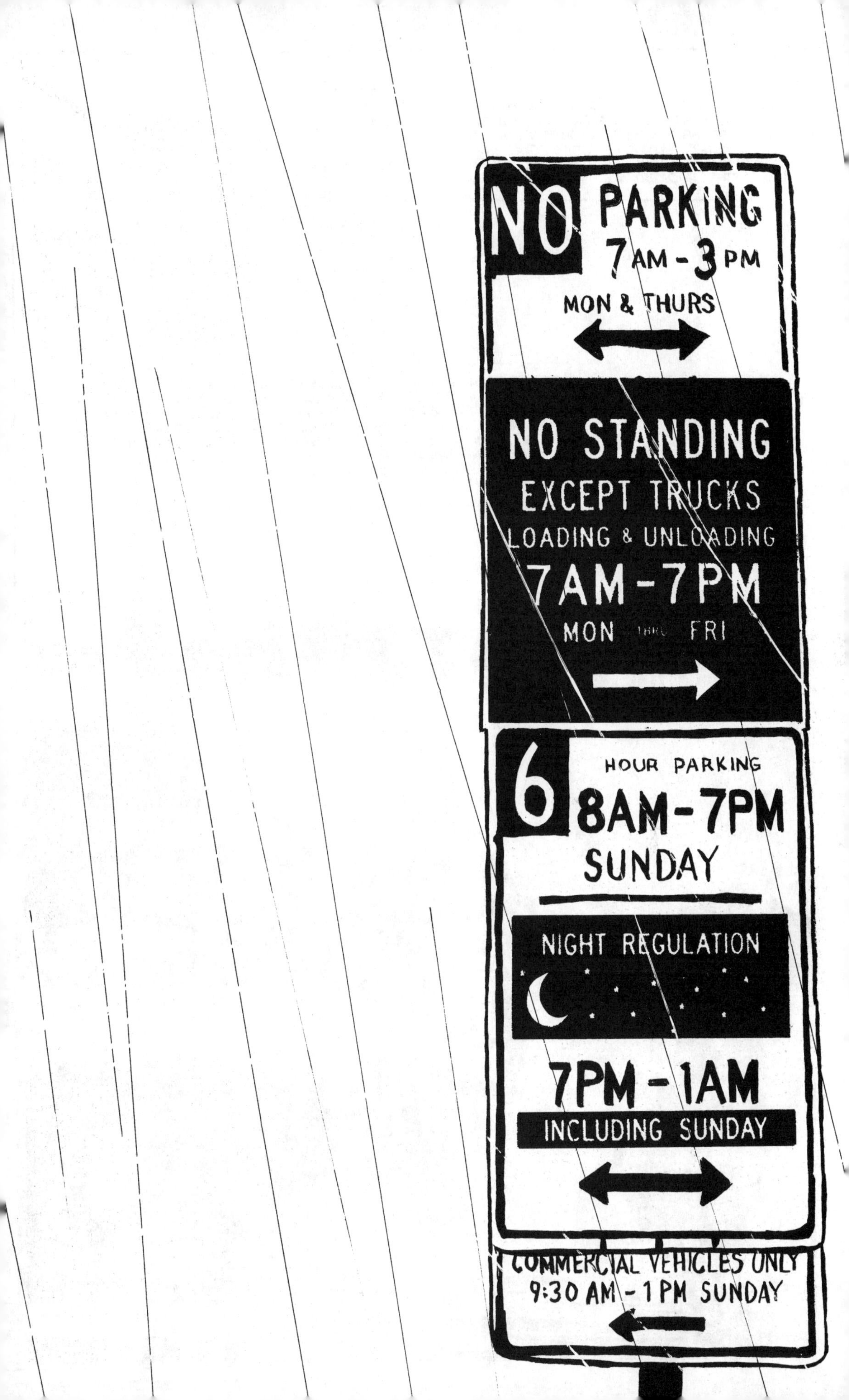
NO PARKING
7AM - 3PM
MON & THURS
NO STANDING
EXCEPT TRUCKS
LOADING & UNLOADING
7AM-7PM
MON THRU FRI
6 HOUR PARKING
8AM-7PM
SUNDAY
NIGHT REGULATION
7PM - 1AM
INCLUDING SUNDAY
COMMERCIAL VEHICLES ONLY
9:30 AM - 1 PM SUNDAY

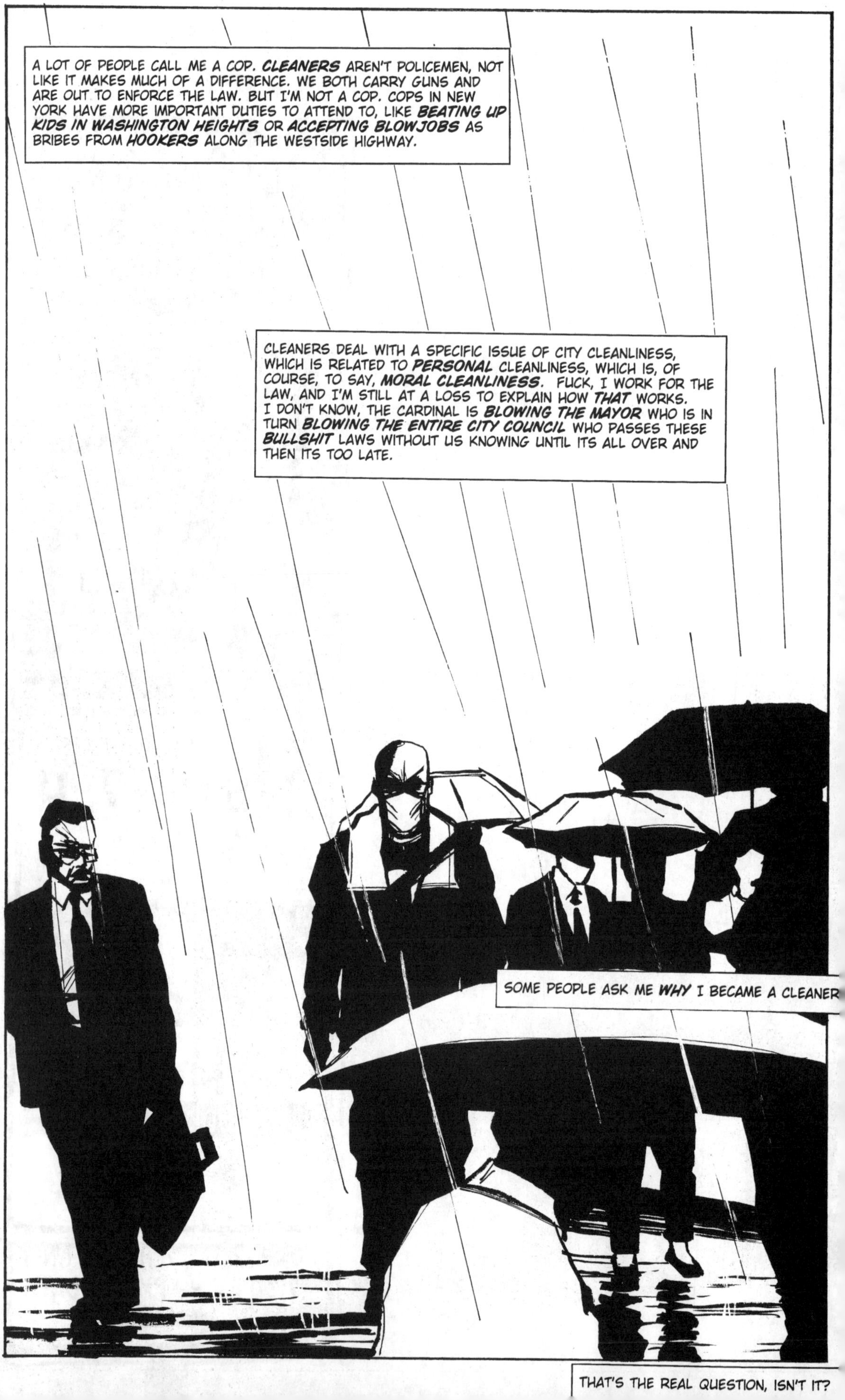
A LOT OF PEOPLE CALL ME A COP. CLEANERS AREN'T POLICEMEN, NOT LIKE IT MAKES MUCH OF A DIFFERENCE. WE BOTH CARRY GUNS AND ARE OUT TO ENFORCE THE LAW. BUT I'M NOT A COP. COPS IN NEW YORK HAVE MORE IMPORTANT DUTIES TO ATTEND TO, LIKE BEATING UP KIDS IN WASHINGTON HEIGHTS OR ACCEPTING BLOWJOBS AS BRIBES FROM HOOKERS ALONG THE WESTSIDE HIGHWAY.
CLEANERS DEAL WITH A SPECIFIC ISSUE OF CITY CLEANLINESS, WHICH IS RELATED TO PERSONAL CLEANLINESS, WHICH IS, OF COURSE, TO SAY, MORAL CLEANLINESS. FUCK, I WORK FOR THE LAW, AND I'M STILL AT A LOSS TO EXPLAIN HOW THAT WORKS. I DON'T KNOW, THE CARDINAL IS BLOWING THE MAYOR WHO IS IN TURN BLOWING THE ENTIRE CITY COUNCIL WHO PASSES THESE BULLSHIT LAWS WITHOUT US KNOWING UNTIL ITS ALL OVER AND THEN ITS TOO LATE.
SOME PEOPLE ASK ME WHY I BECAME A CLEANER
THAT'S THE REAL QUESTION, ISN'T IT?

THE MOST ***OBVIOUS*** ANSWER IS SOMETHING LIKE "MY DAD WAS A CLEANER", OR "I WANT TO MAKE THE STREETS CLEAN FOR OUR CHILDREN", OR EVEN SOMETHING LIKE "MY PARENTS WERE KILLED BY RANDOM LITTERING, SO I'VE DEDICATED MY LIFE TO CLEANLINESS". FUCK ***THAT*** NOISE. THAT SORT OF SHIT IS FOR ***STUPID PEOPLE*** WHO DON'T KNOW ANY BETTER.

I JOINED THE ***CLEANERS*** FOR THE SIMPLE REASON THAT I WAS ***BRAINWASHED***. I USED TO BE A REAL TV JUNKIE, PISSING AWAY MY LIFE WATCHING ***MUST SEE FUCKING TEDIUM***, AND THE ***SATURDAY MORNING PILE OF HORSESHIT***. SO WHEN CITY ELECTIONS STARTED BEING TELEVISED, I GOT HOOKED. MY BRAIN HAD BEEN ***NUMBED*** BY TALK SHOWS YEARS AGO, SO I WAS AN EASY TARGET. I LEARNED TO ***TRUST*** THE MAYOR, I ***BELIEVED IN HIM***, I VOTED FOR HIM.

AND WHEN HE FORMED THE CLEANERS, I JOINED.

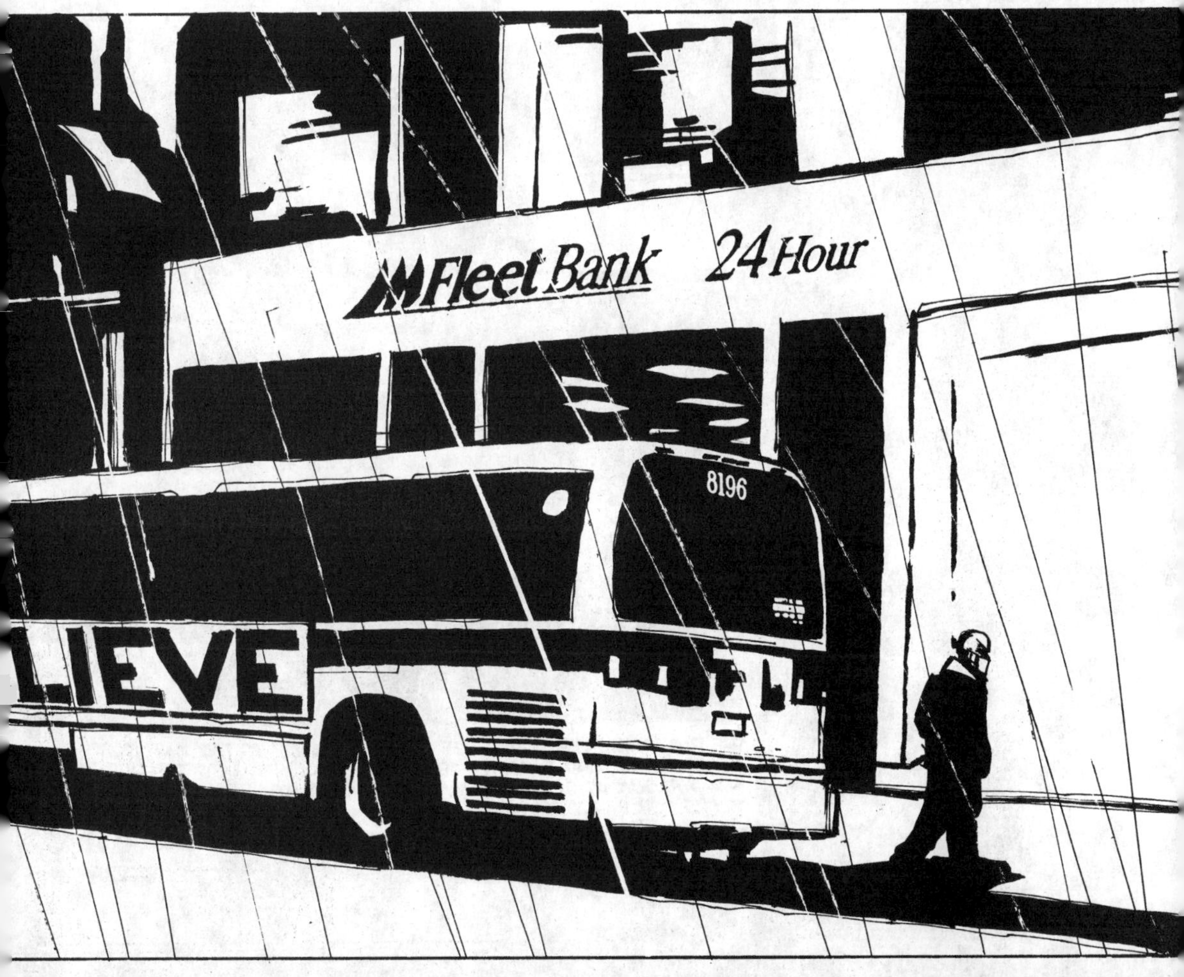
Fleet Bank 24 Hour
8196
LIEVE

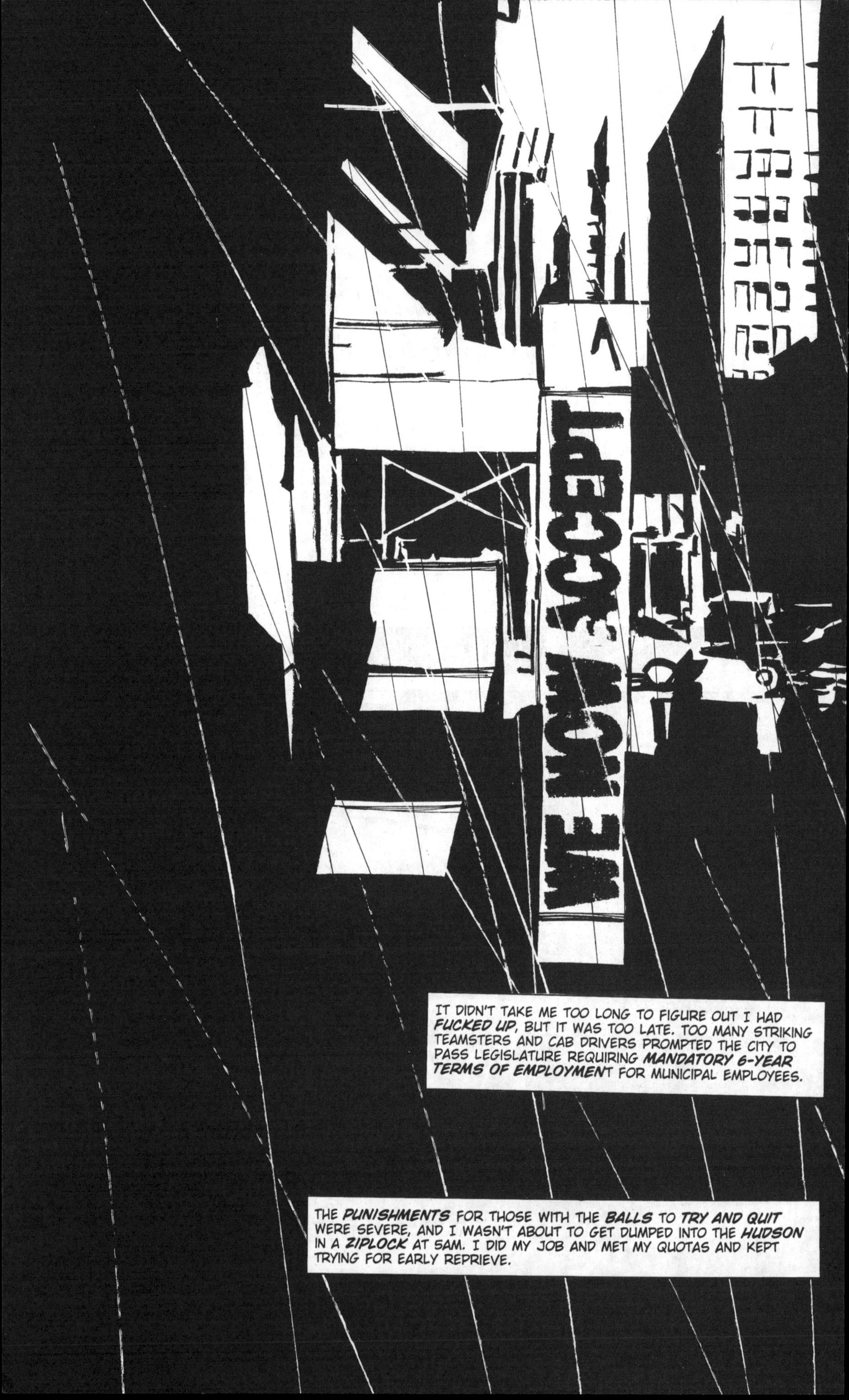
WE NOW ACCEPT
IT DIDN'T TAKE ME TOO LONG TO FIGURE OUT I HAD ***FUCKED UP***, BUT IT WAS TOO LATE. TOO MANY STRIKING TEAMSTERS AND CAB DRIVERS PROMPTED THE CITY TO PASS LEGISLATURE REQUIRING ***MANDATORY 6-YEAR TERMS OF EMPLOYMENT*** FOR MUNICIPAL EMPLOYEES.
THE ***PUNISHMENTS*** FOR THOSE WITH THE ***BALLS*** TO ***TRY AND QUIT*** WERE SEVERE, AND I WASN'T ABOUT TO GET DUMPED INTO THE ***HUDSON*** IN A ***ZIPLOCK*** AT 5AM. I DID MY JOB AND MET MY QUOTAS AND KEPT TRYING FOR EARLY REPRIEVE.

BACK TO THE ***BASTARD***, THE ONE PUTTING UP ***ILLEGAL POSTERS***, THE ONE LYING ON A ***SLAB*** IN THE CITY MORGUE WITH A ***BULLET HOLE*** IN HIS HEAD, THE ***FUCKING COCKSUCKER*** THAT FORCED ME TO MAKE MYSELF A ***MURDERER*** FOR THE ***HUNDREDTH TIME.***

I FEEL PRETTY ***SHITTY*** ABOUT KILLING HIM, BUT THAT'LL ONLY LAST A COUPLE DAYS. WHAT REALLY BOTHERS ME IS THAT I ***AGREED*** WITH WHAT HE WAS DOING.

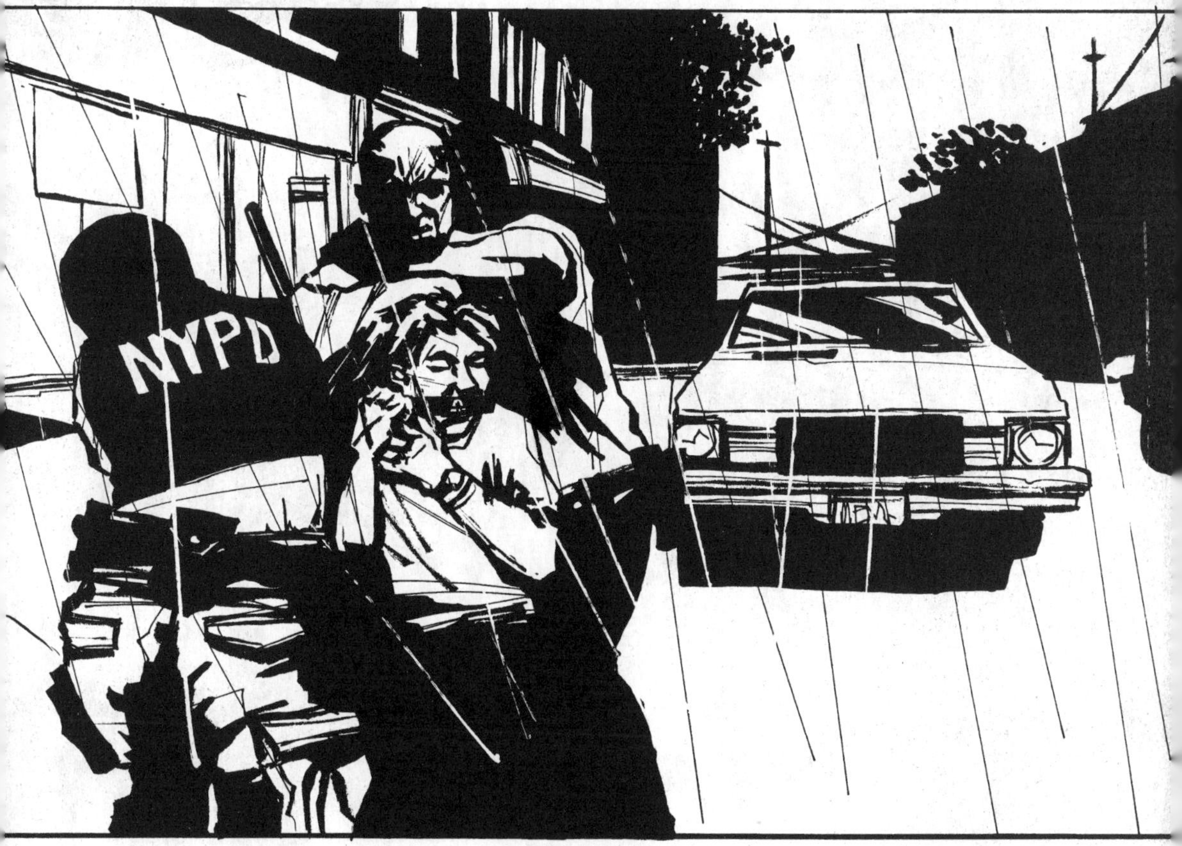
NYPD

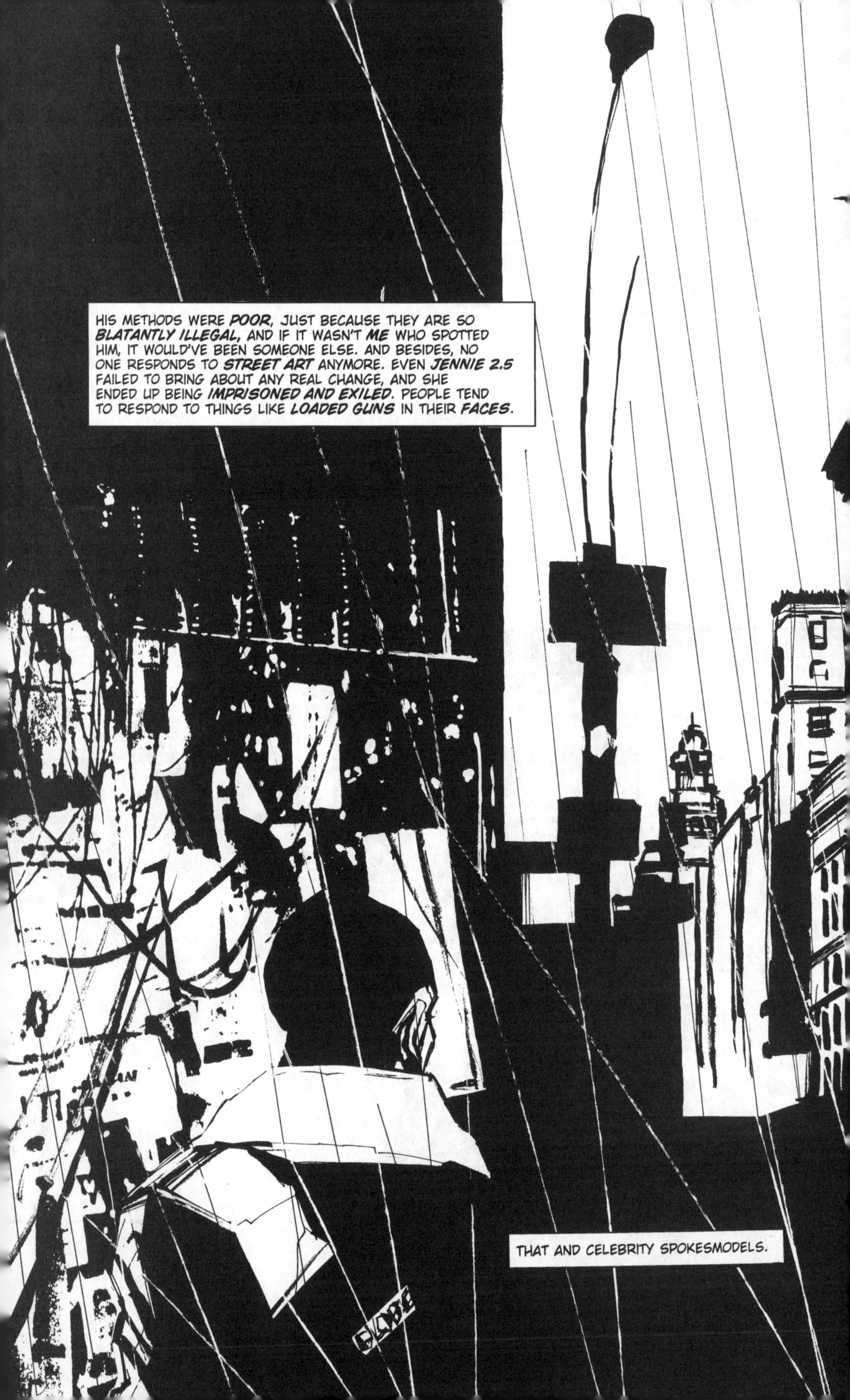
HIS METHODS WERE POOR, JUST BECAUSE THEY ARE SO BLATANTLY ILLEGAL, AND IF IT WASN'T ME WHO SPOTTED HIM, IT WOULD'VE BEEN SOMEONE ELSE. AND BESIDES, NO ONE RESPONDS TO STREET ART ANYMORE. EVEN JENNIE 2.5 FAILED TO BRING ABOUT ANY REAL CHANGE, AND SHE ENDED UP BEING IMPRISONED AND EXILED. PEOPLE TEND TO RESPOND TO THINGS LIKE LOADED GUNS IN THEIR FACES.
THAT AND CELEBRITY SPOKESMODELS.

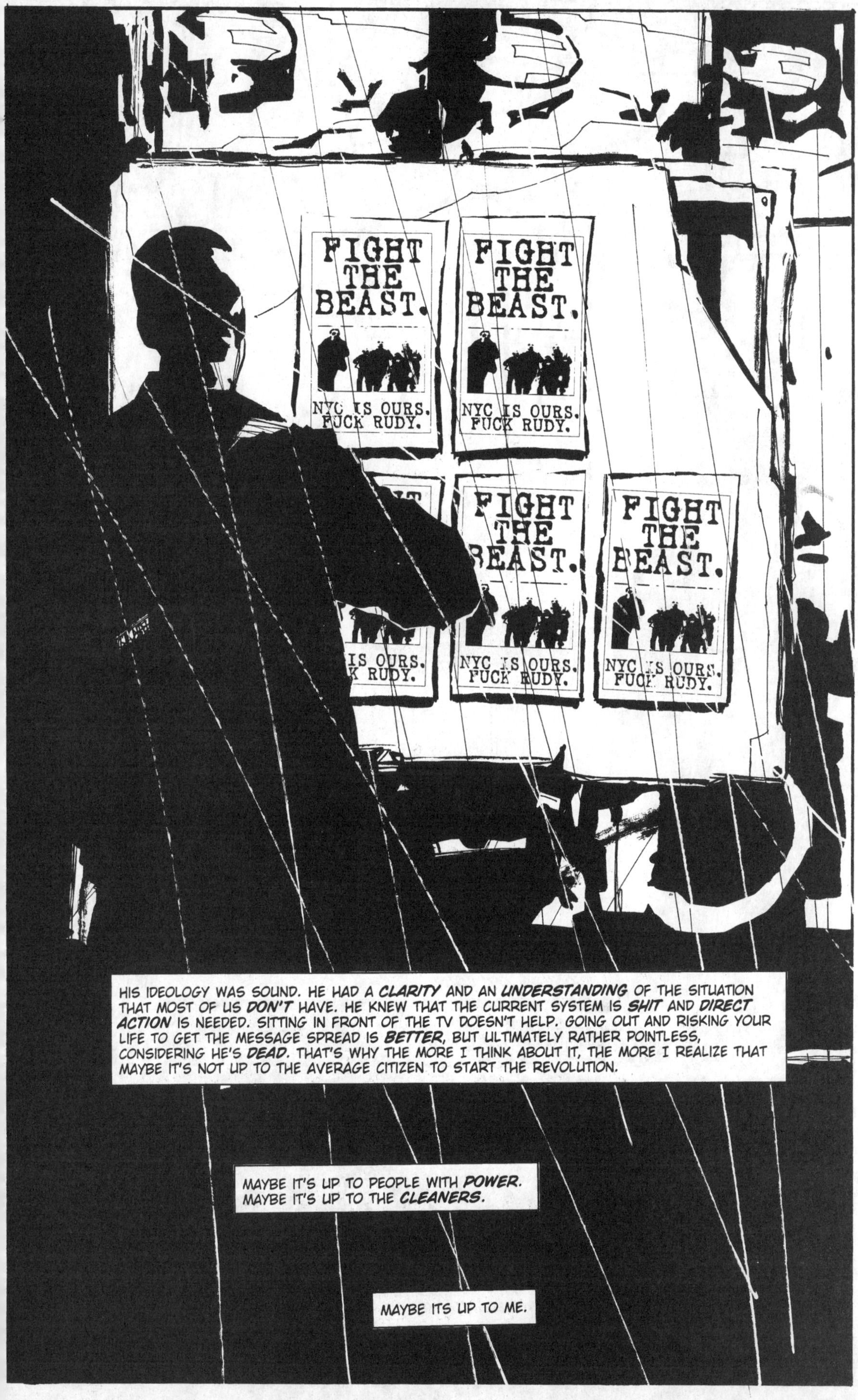
FIGHT THE BEAST.
NYC IS OURS. FUCK RUDY.
FIGHT THE BEAST.
NYC IS OURS. FUCK RUDY.
FIGHT THE BEAST.
NYC IS OURS. FUCK RUDY.
FIGHT THE BEAST.
NYC IS OURS. FUCK RUDY.
HIS IDEOLOGY WAS SOUND. HE HAD A *CLARITY* AND AN *UNDERSTANDING* OF THE SITUATION THAT MOST OF US *DON'T* HAVE. HE KNEW THAT THE CURRENT SYSTEM IS *SHIT* AND *DIRECT ACTION* IS NEEDED. SITTING IN FRONT OF THE TV DOESN'T HELP. GOING OUT AND RISKING YOUR LIFE TO GET THE MESSAGE SPREAD IS *BETTER*, BUT ULTIMATELY RATHER POINTLESS, CONSIDERING HE'S *DEAD*. THAT'S WHY THE MORE I THINK ABOUT IT, THE MORE I REALIZE THAT MAYBE IT'S NOT UP TO THE AVERAGE CITIZEN TO START THE REVOLUTION.
MAYBE IT'S UP TO PEOPLE WITH *POWER*. MAYBE IT'S UP TO THE *CLEANERS*.
MAYBE ITS UP TO ME.

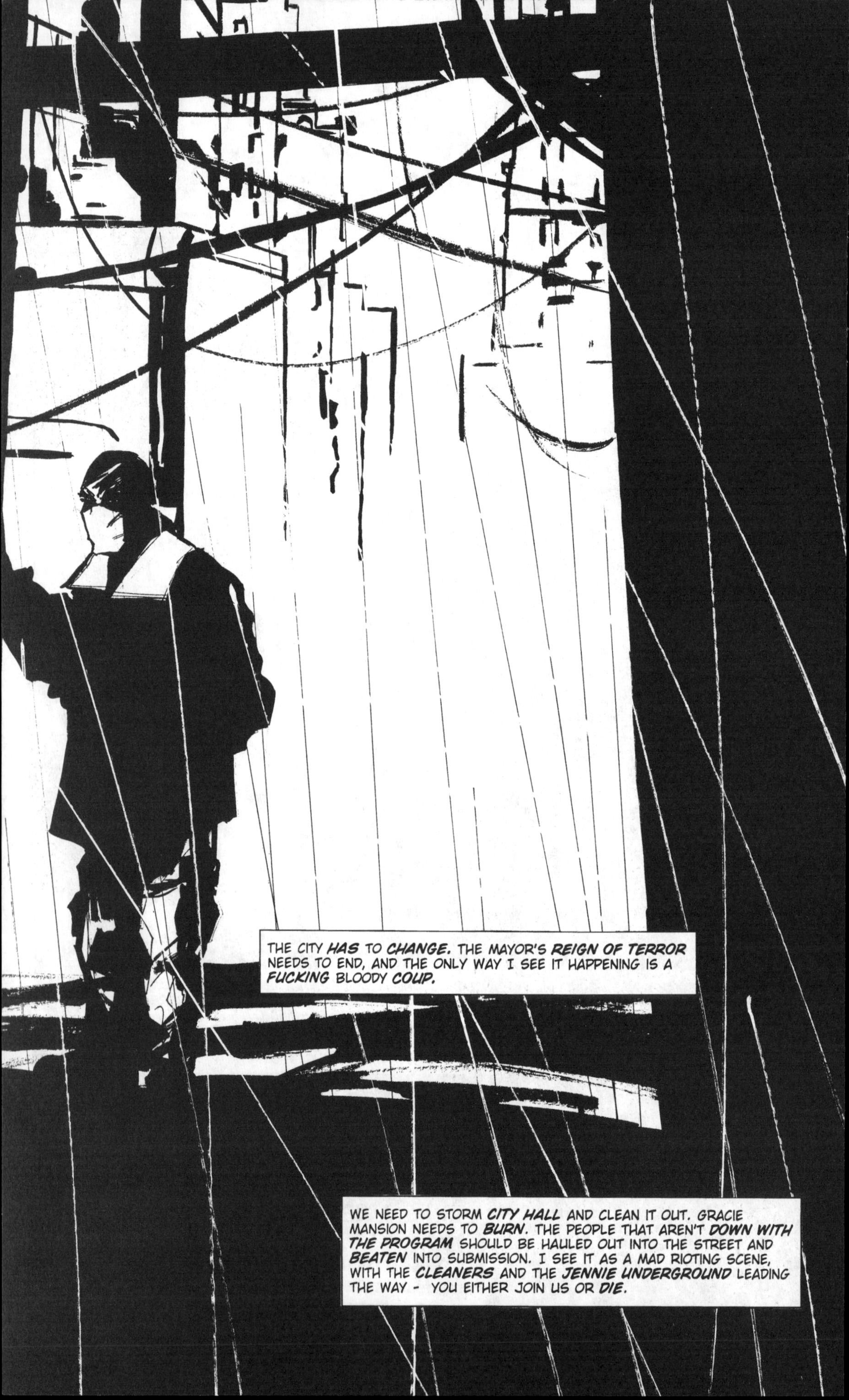
THE CITY HAS TO CHANGE. THE MAYOR'S REIGN OF TERROR NEEDS TO END, AND THE ONLY WAY I SEE IT HAPPENING IS A FUCKING BLOODY COUP.
WE NEED TO STORM CITY HALL AND CLEAN IT OUT. GRACIE MANSION NEEDS TO BURN. THE PEOPLE THAT AREN'T DOWN WITH THE PROGRAM SHOULD BE HAULED OUT INTO THE STREET AND BEATEN INTO SUBMISSION. I SEE IT AS A MAD RIOTING SCENE, WITH THE CLEANERS AND THE JENNIE UNDERGROUND LEADING THE WAY - YOU EITHER JOIN US OR DIE.

PUT THE *MOTHERFUCKING BOOT IN.*

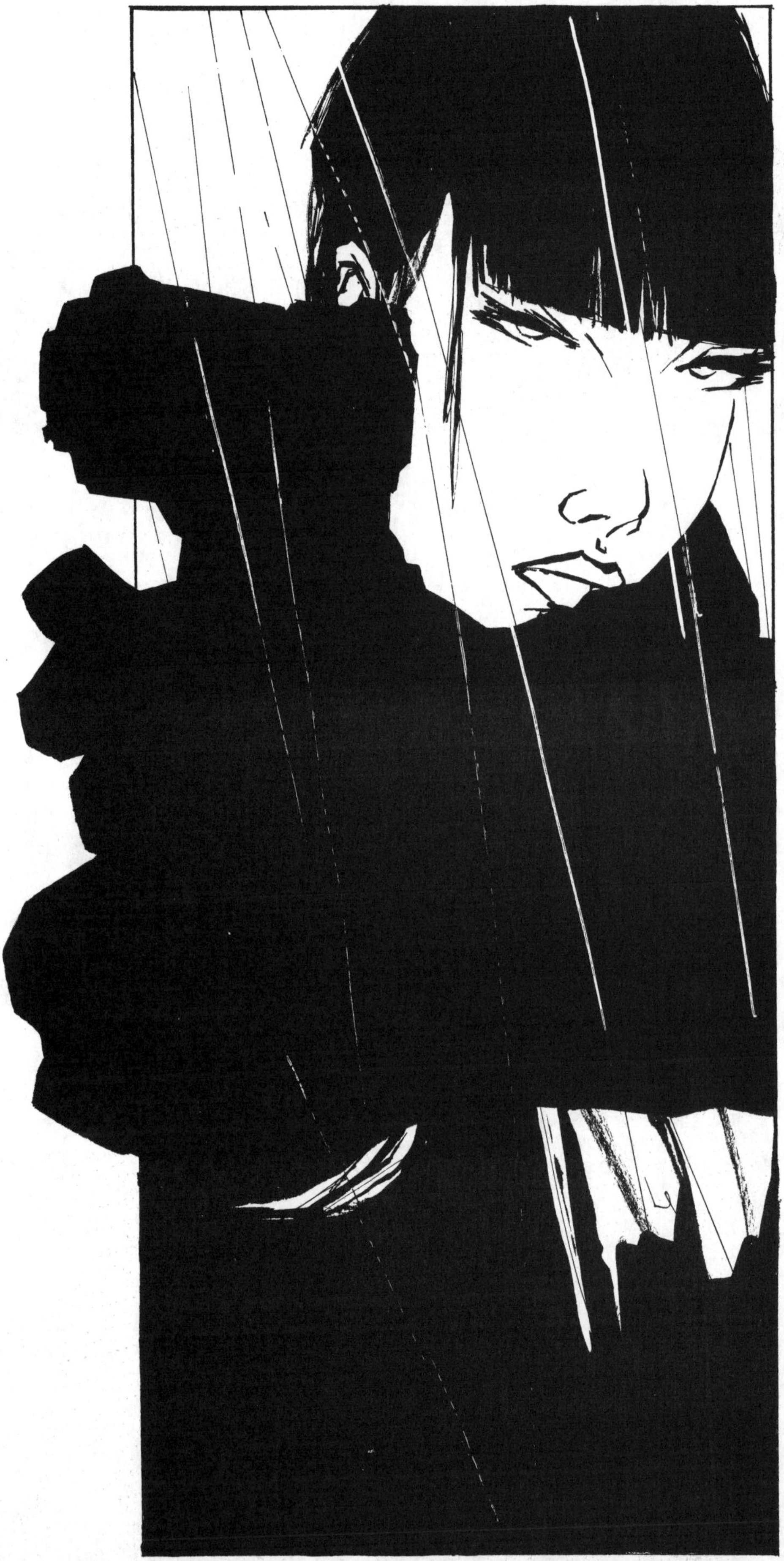

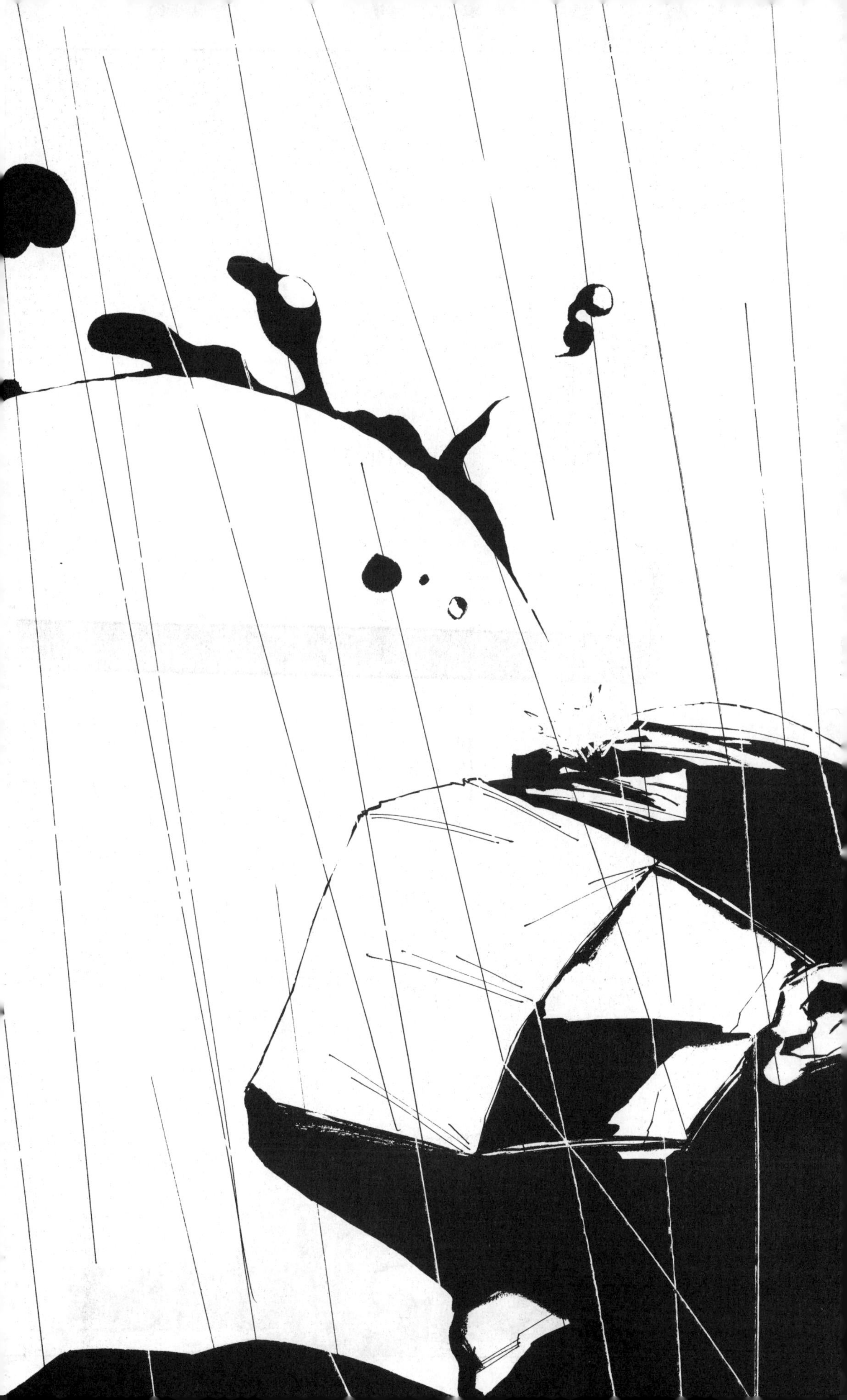

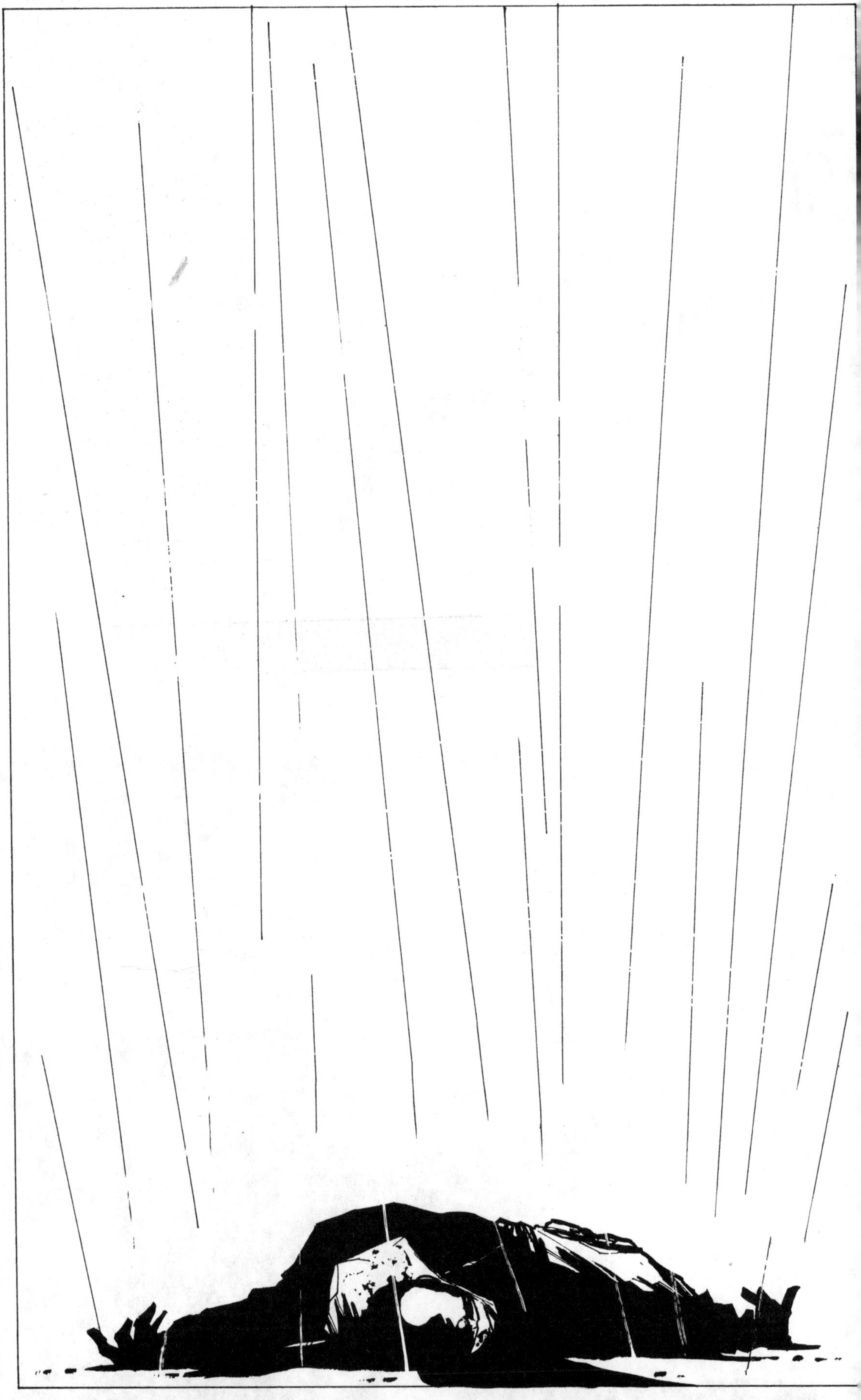

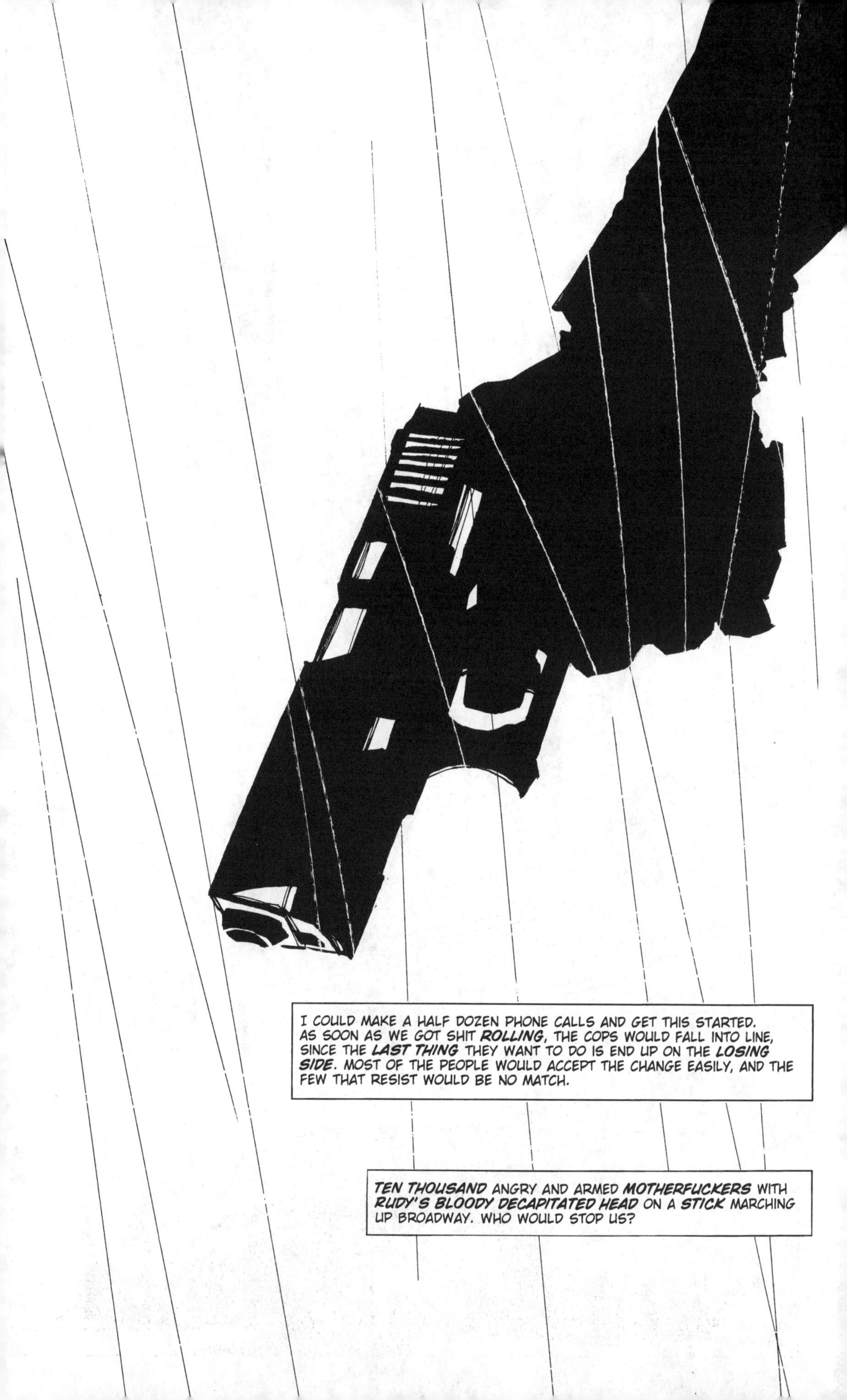
I COULD MAKE A HALF DOZEN PHONE CALLS AND GET THIS STARTED. AS SOON AS WE GOT SHIT ROLLING, THE COPS WOULD FALL INTO LINE, SINCE THE LAST THING THEY WANT TO DO IS END UP ON THE LOSING SIDE. MOST OF THE PEOPLE WOULD ACCEPT THE CHANGE EASILY, AND THE FEW THAT RESIST WOULD BE NO MATCH.
TEN THOUSAND ANGRY AND ARMED MOTHERFUCKERS WITH RUDY'S BLOODY DECAPITATED HEAD ON A STICK MARCHING UP BROADWAY. WHO WOULD STOP US?

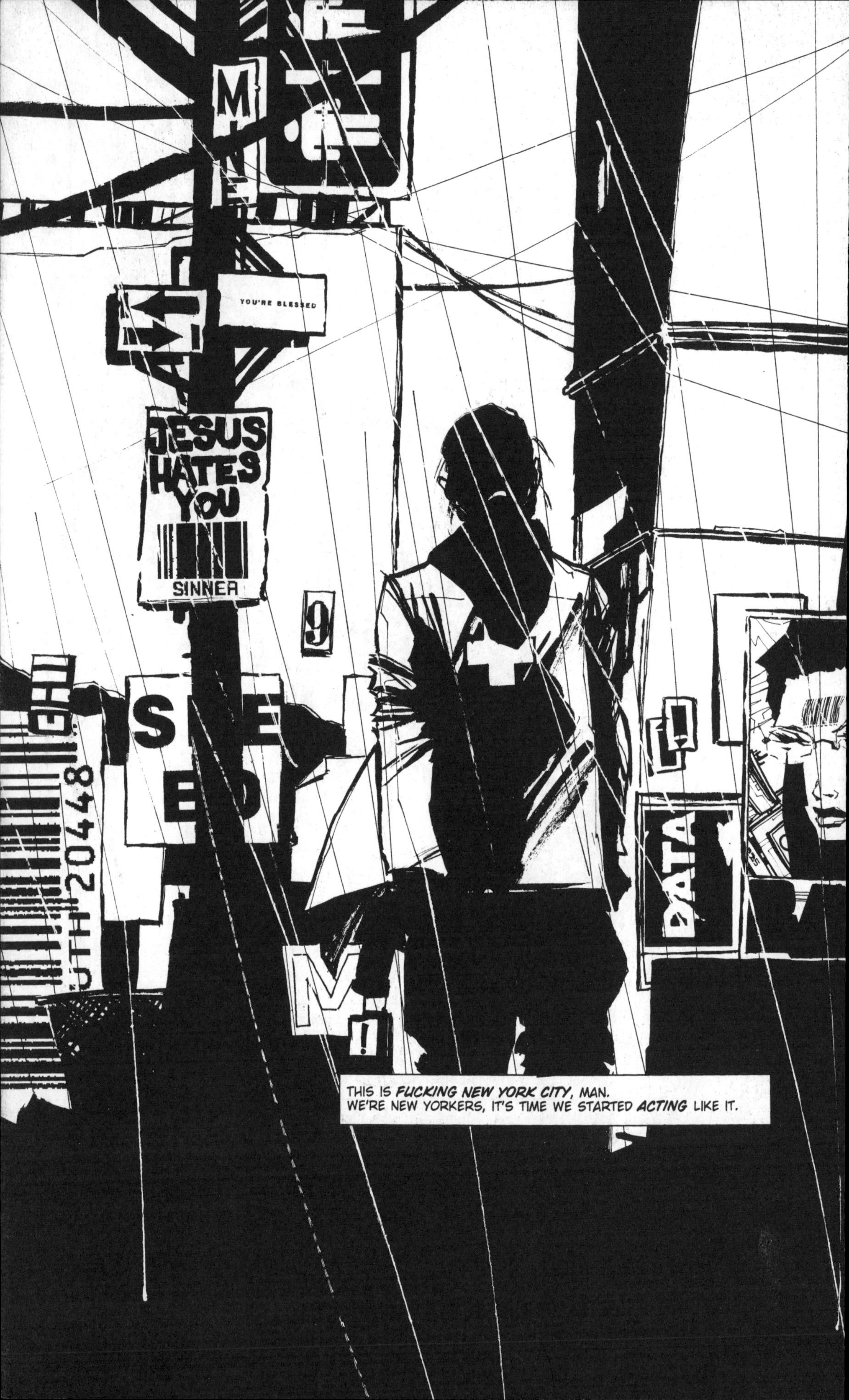
YOU'RE BLESSED
JESUS HATES YOU
SINNER
9
UTH 20448
DATA
THIS IS *FUCKING NEW YORK CITY*, MAN.
WE'RE NEW YORKERS, IT'S TIME WE STARTED *ACTING* LIKE IT.

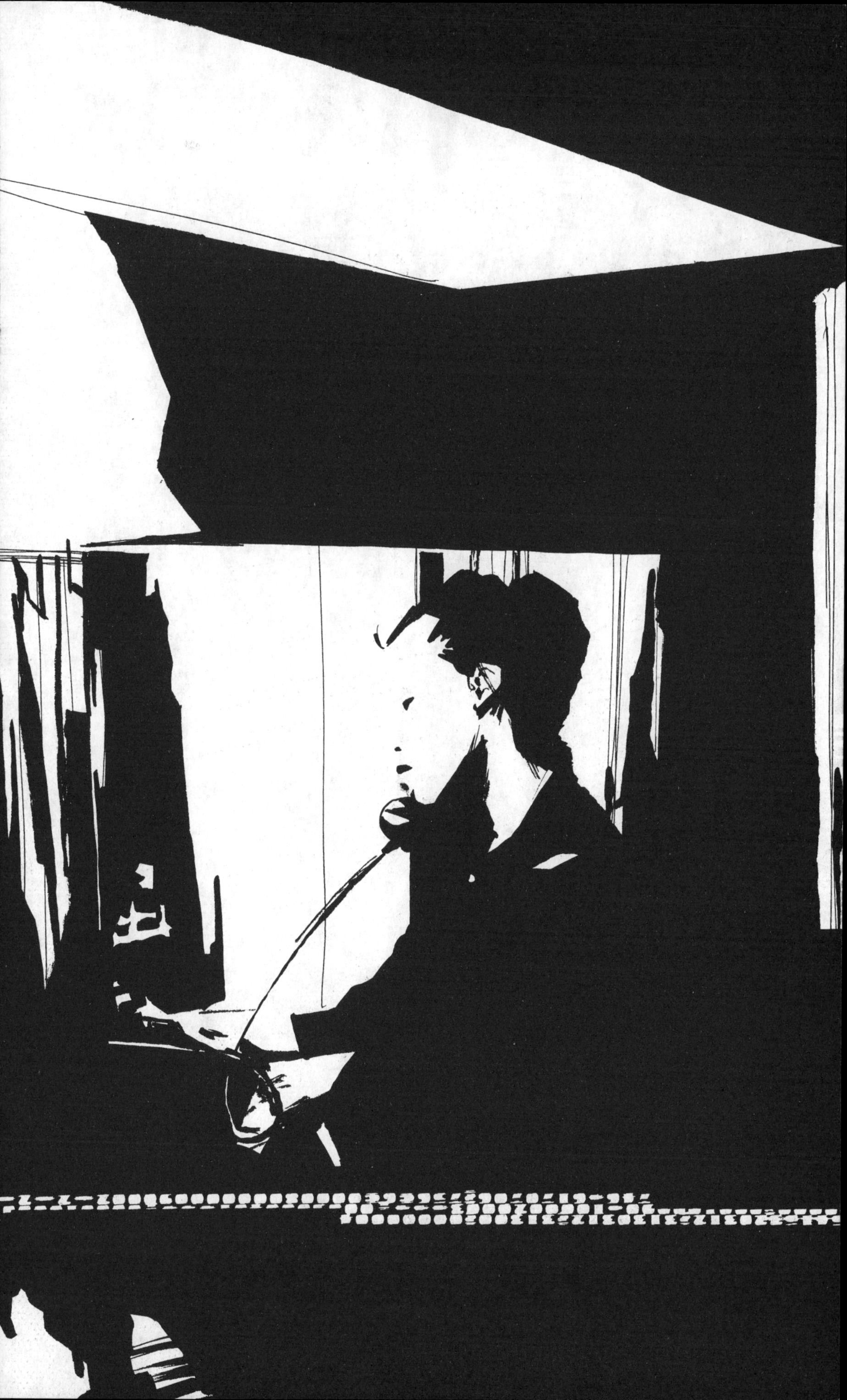

global   supermarket

"When one voice rules the nation
just because they're top of the pile
doesn't mean their vision is the clearest."

-Billy Bragg

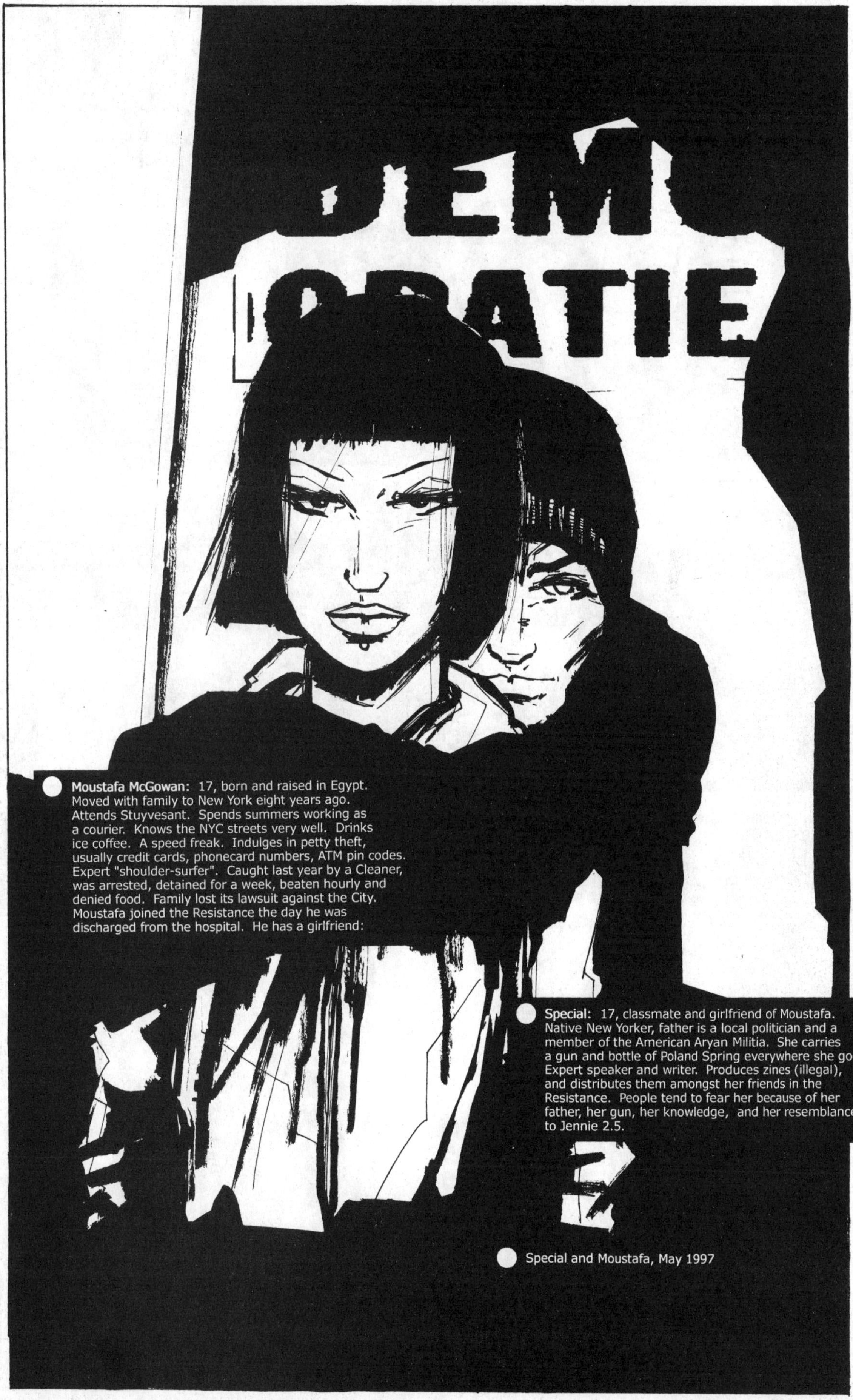
Moustafa McGowan: 17, born and raised in Egypt. Moved with family to New York eight years ago. Attends Stuyvesant. Spends summers working as a courier. Knows the NYC streets very well. Drinks ice coffee. A speed freak. Indulges in petty theft, usually credit cards, phonecard numbers, ATM pin codes. Expert "shoulder-surfer". Caught last year by a Cleaner, was arrested, detained for a week, beaten hourly and denied food. Family lost its lawsuit against the City. Moustafa joined the Resistance the day he was discharged from the hospital. He has a girlfriend:
Special: 17, classmate and girlfriend of Moustafa. Native New Yorker, father is a local politician and a member of the American Aryan Militia. She carries a gun and bottle of Poland Spring everywhere she goes. Expert speaker and writer. Produces zines (illegal), and distributes them amongst her friends in the Resistance. People tend to fear her because of her father, her gun, her knowledge, and her resemblance to Jennie 2.5.
Special and Moustafa, May 1997

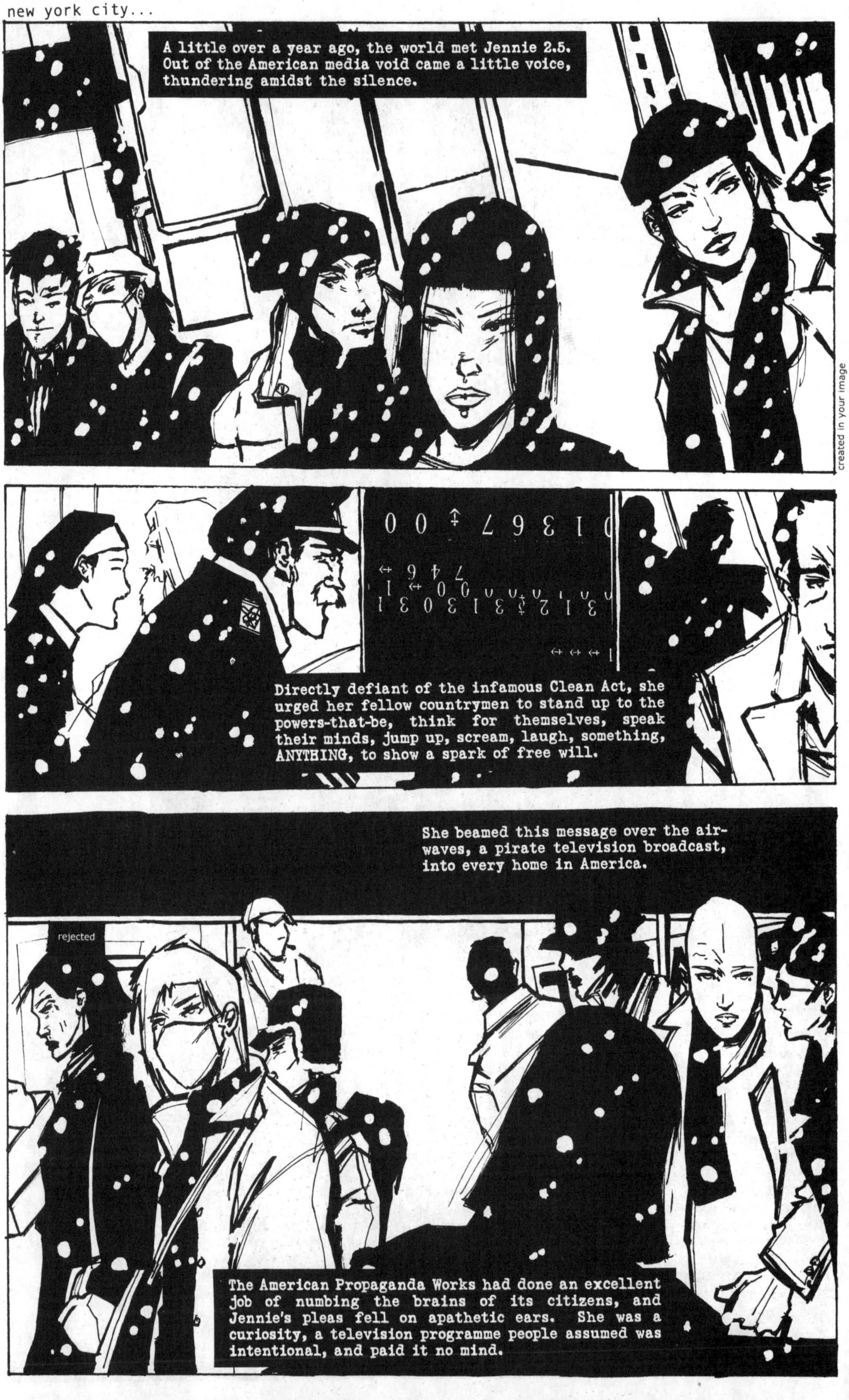
new york city...
A little over a year ago, the world met Jennie 2.5. Out of the American media void came a little voice, thundering amidst the silence.
created in your image
Directly defiant of the infamous Clean Act, she urged her fellow countrymen to stand up to the powers-that-be, think for themselves, speak their minds, jump up, scream, laugh, something, ANYTHING, to show a spark of free will.
She beamed this message over the air-waves, a pirate television broadcast, into every home in America.
rejected
The American Propaganda Works had done an excellent job of numbing the brains of its citizens, and Jennie's pleas fell on apathetic ears. She was a curiosity, a television programme people assumed was intentional, and paid it no mind.

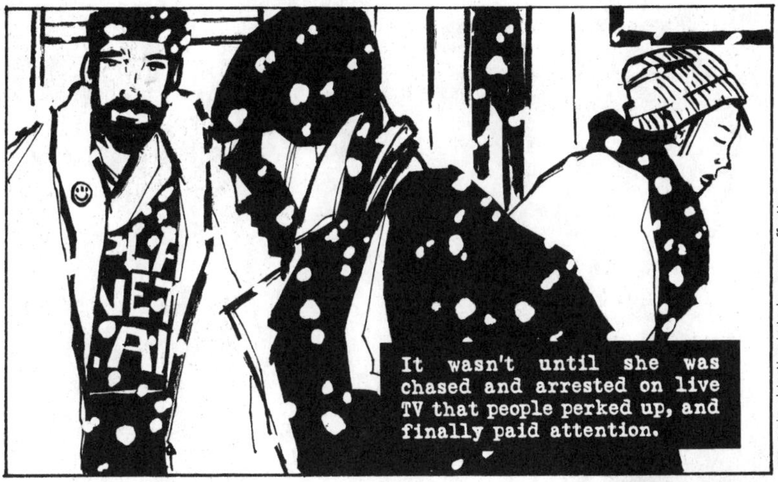
It wasn't until she was chased and arrested on live TV that people perked up, and finally paid attention.

my main objective is to be more effective

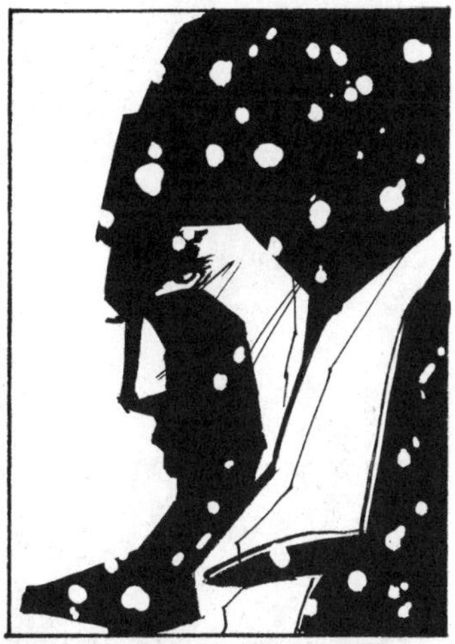

Her trial was televised, as an example to the people of what happens if you defy the established order. She was imprisoned for a short time, then exiled. Within America, and the rest of the world, the myth of Jennie 2.5 is well known, and many imitators have sprung up in her absence. None have come close to achieving what she has.

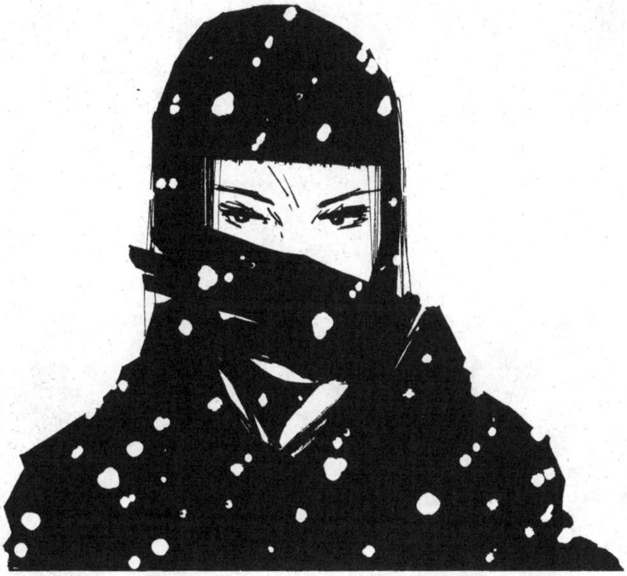

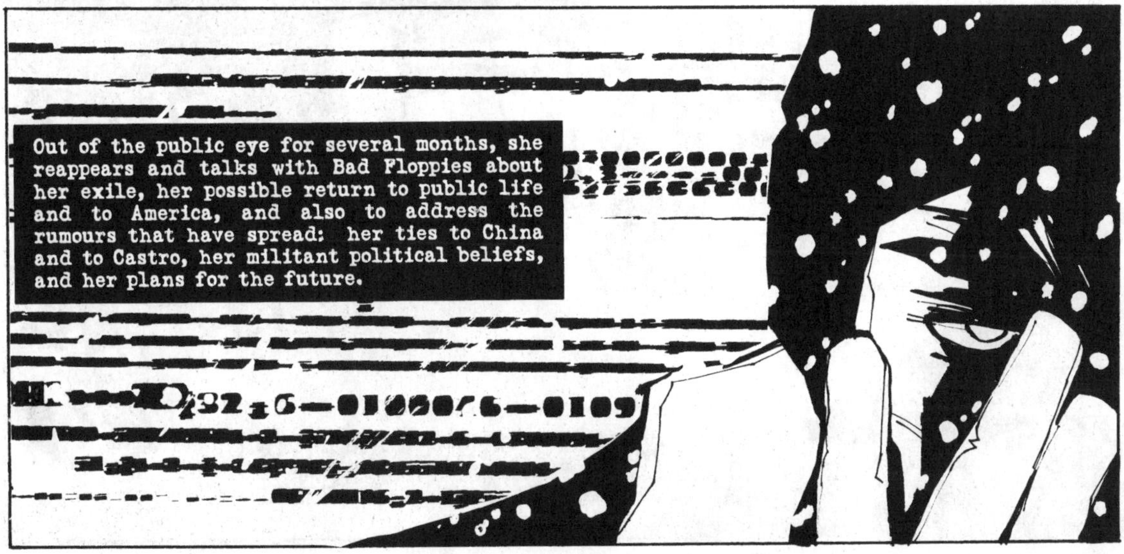
Out of the public eye for several months, she reappears and talks with Bad Floppies about her exile, her possible return to public life and to America, and also to address the rumours that have spread: her ties to China and to Castro, her militant political beliefs, and her plans for the future.

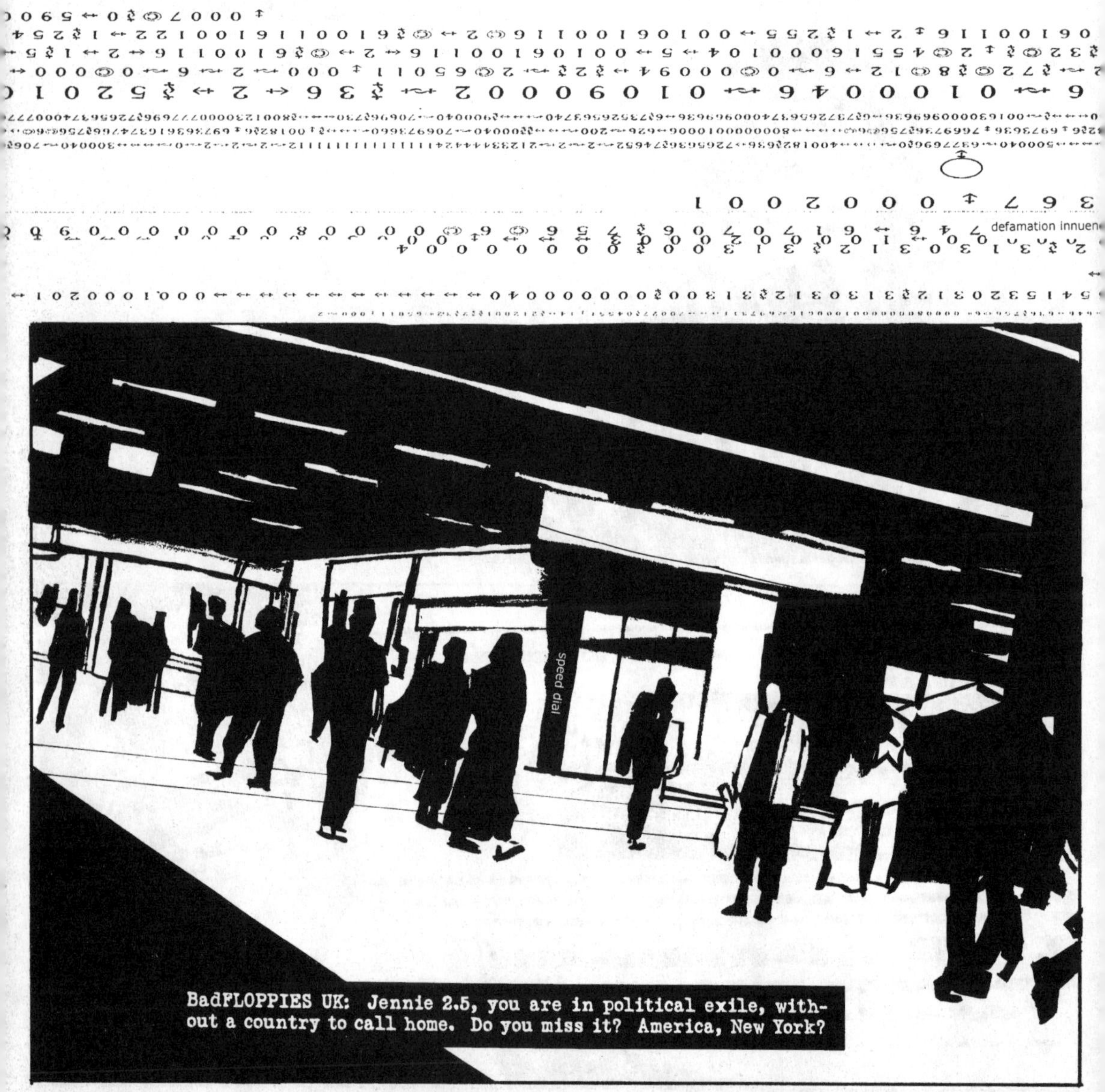
defamation innuen
speed dial
BadFLOPPIES UK: Jennie 2.5, you are in political exile, without a country to call home. Do you miss it? America, New York?

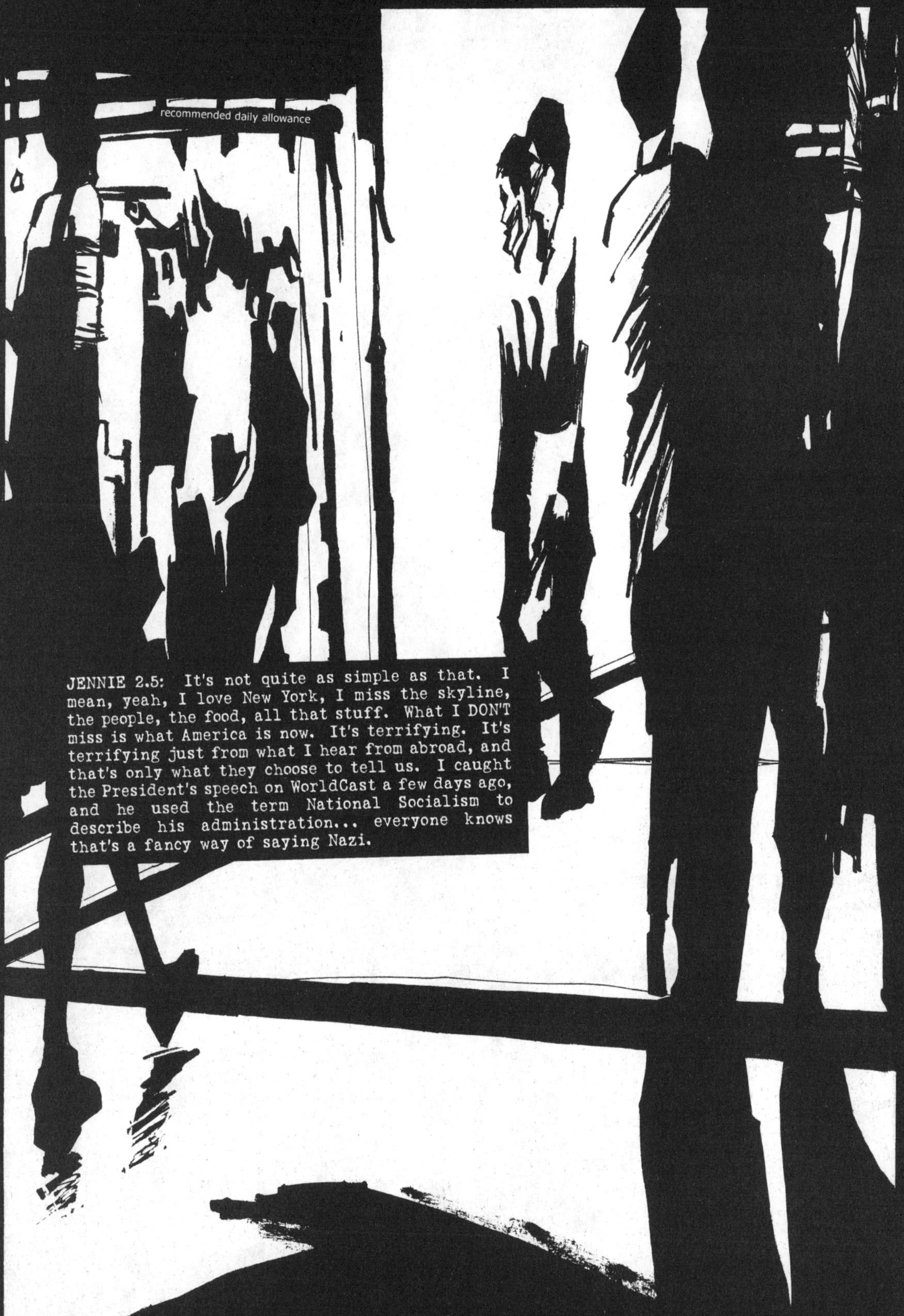
JENNIE 2.5: It's not quite as simple as that. I mean, yeah, I love New York, I miss the skyline, the people, the food, all that stuff. What I DON'T miss is what America is now. It's terrifying. It's terrifying just from what I hear from abroad, and that's only what they choose to tell us. I caught the President's speech on WorldCast a few days ago, and he used the term National Socialism to describe his administration... everyone knows that's a fancy way of saying Nazi.

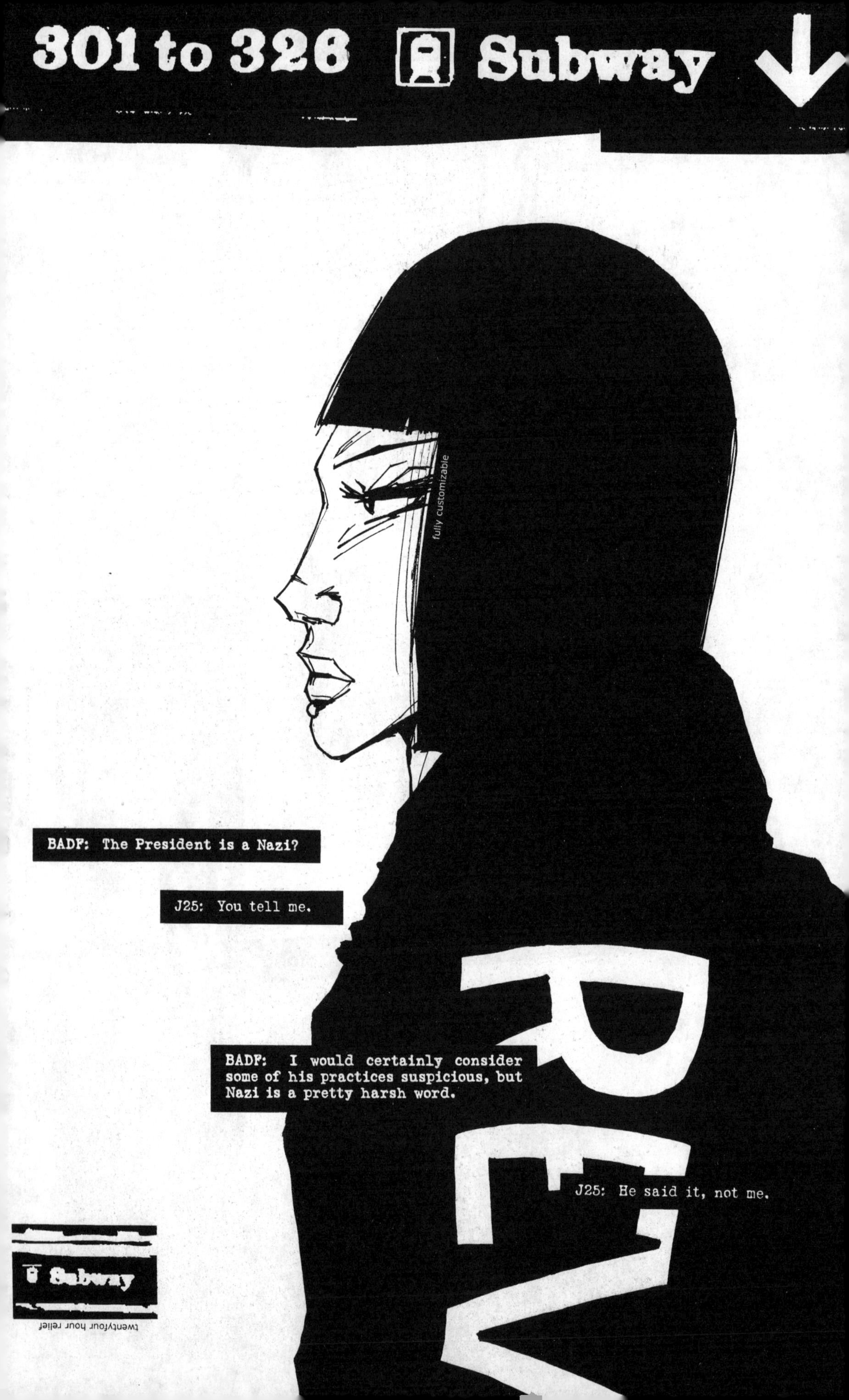
301 to 326 Subway
fully customizable
BADF: The President is a Nazi?
J25: You tell me.
BADF: I would certainly consider some of his practices suspicious, but Nazi is a pretty harsh word.
J25: He said it, not me.
REV
Subway
twentyfour hour relief

BADF: True. You've made your intentions to break your exile and return to America public knowledge. And it seems these intentions to spread the word will guarantee American authorities to be waiting for you when you arrive. Why are you taking this risk, and aren't you worried about your safety?

J25: Yes, and no. I don't expect to be immediately arrested. I do expect to be trailed and bugged. They exiled me instead of imprisoning me for a reason. I probably should have been killed. I think its because I am well known, and I have the ability to generate interest in whatever, and they like that. I think they want me to work for them.

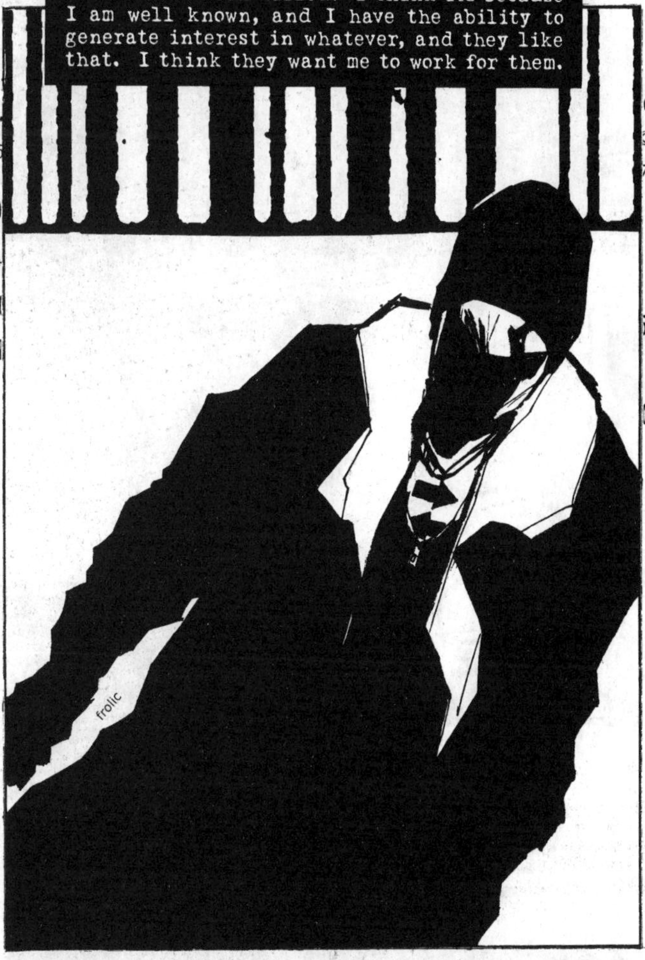
frolic

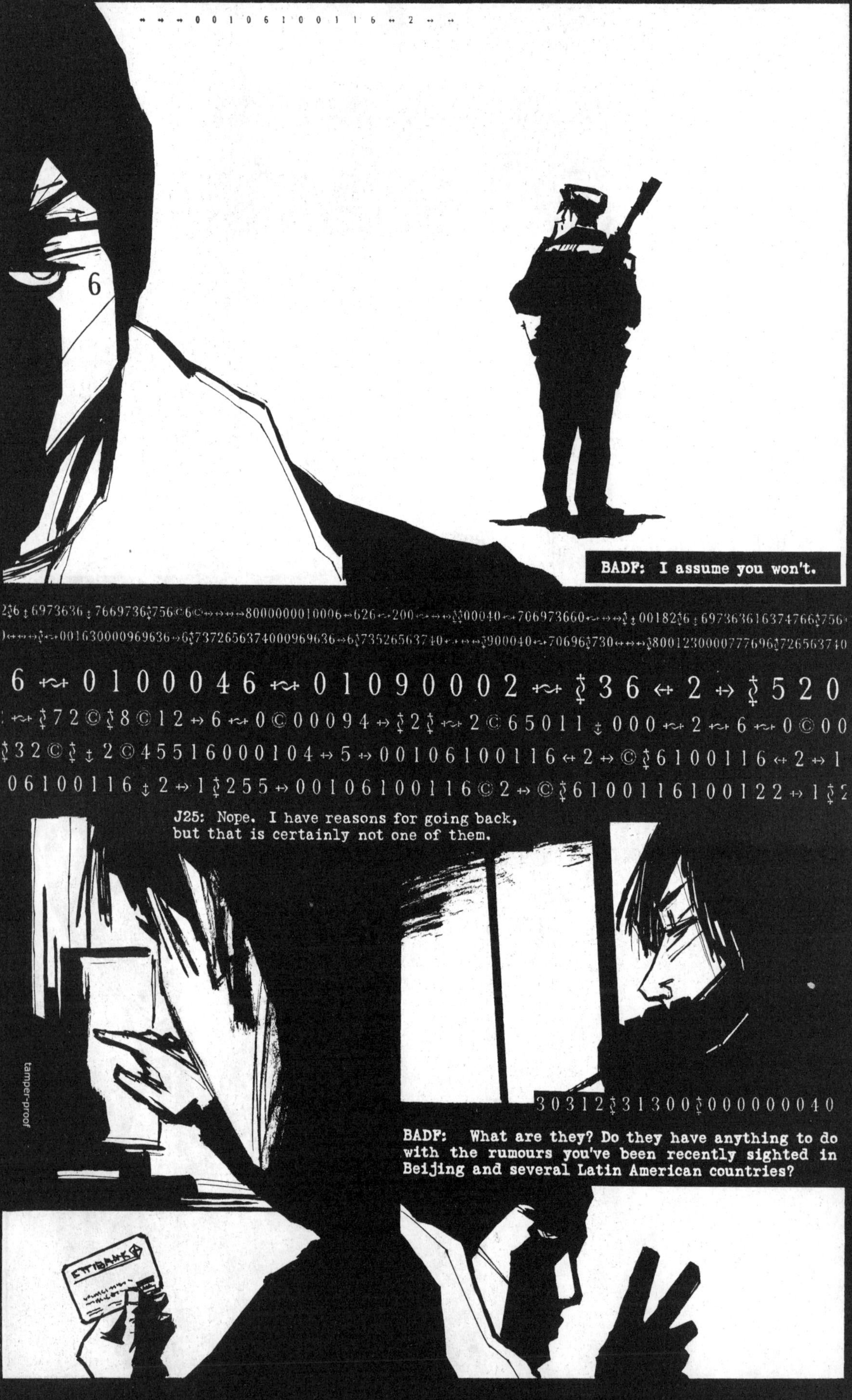
BADF: I assume you won't.
J25: Nope. I have reasons for going back, but that is certainly not one of them.
BADF: What are they? Do they have anything to do with the rumours you've been recently sighted in Beijing and several Latin American countries?
never better
tamper-proof

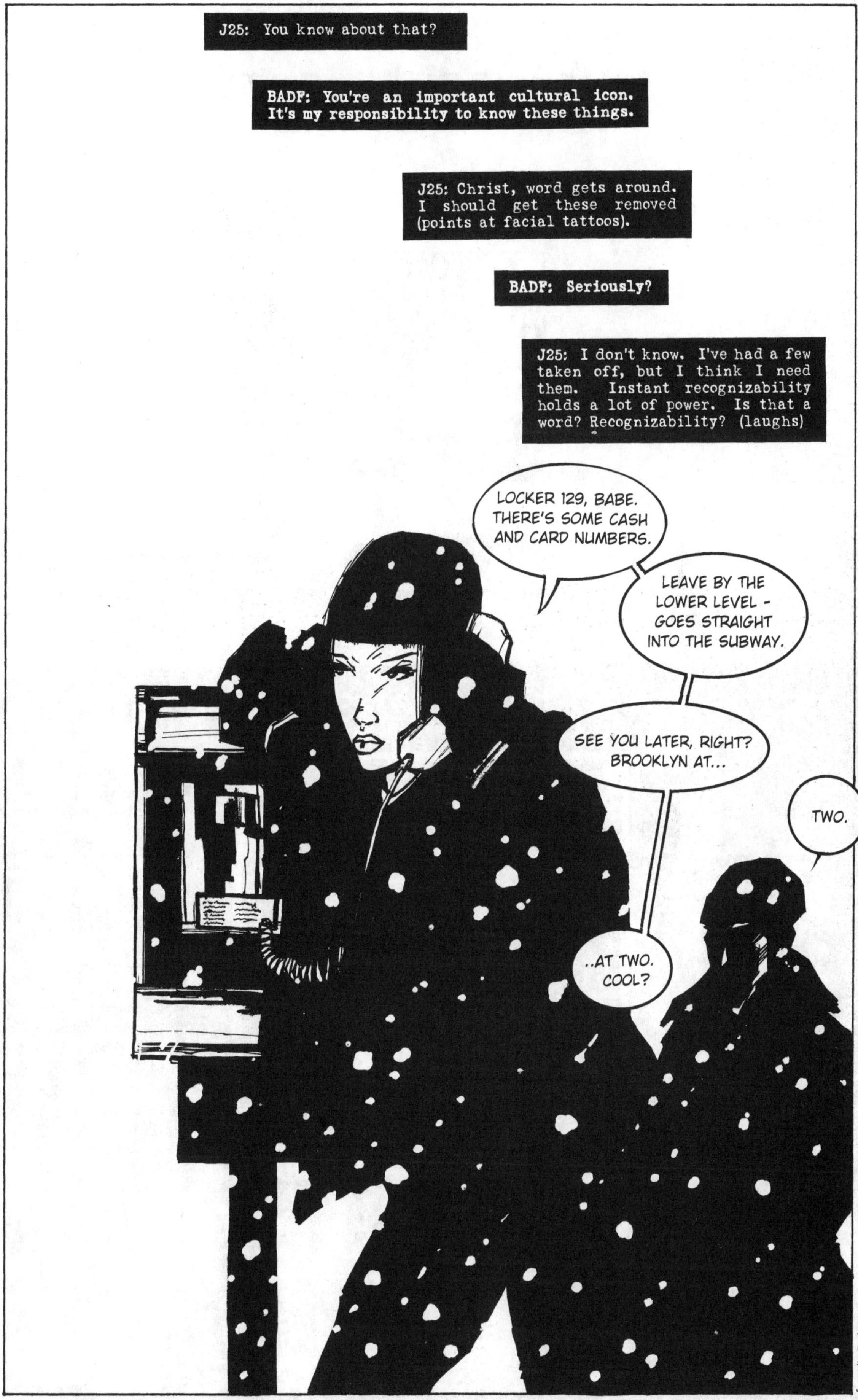
J25: You know about that?
BADF: You're an important cultural icon. It's my responsibility to know these things.
J25: Christ, word gets around. I should get these removed (points at facial tattoos).
BADF: Seriously?
J25: I don't know. I've had a few taken off, but I think I need them. Instant recognizability holds a lot of power. Is that a word? Recognizability? (laughs)
LOCKER 129, BABE. THERE'S SOME CASH AND CARD NUMBERS.
LEAVE BY THE LOWER LEVEL - GOES STRAIGHT INTO THE SUBWAY.
SEE YOU LATER, RIGHT? BROOKLYN AT...
TWO.
..AT TWO. COOL?

your worst enemy.

your ultimate salvation.

MADONNA
AND
CHILD

who do you love?

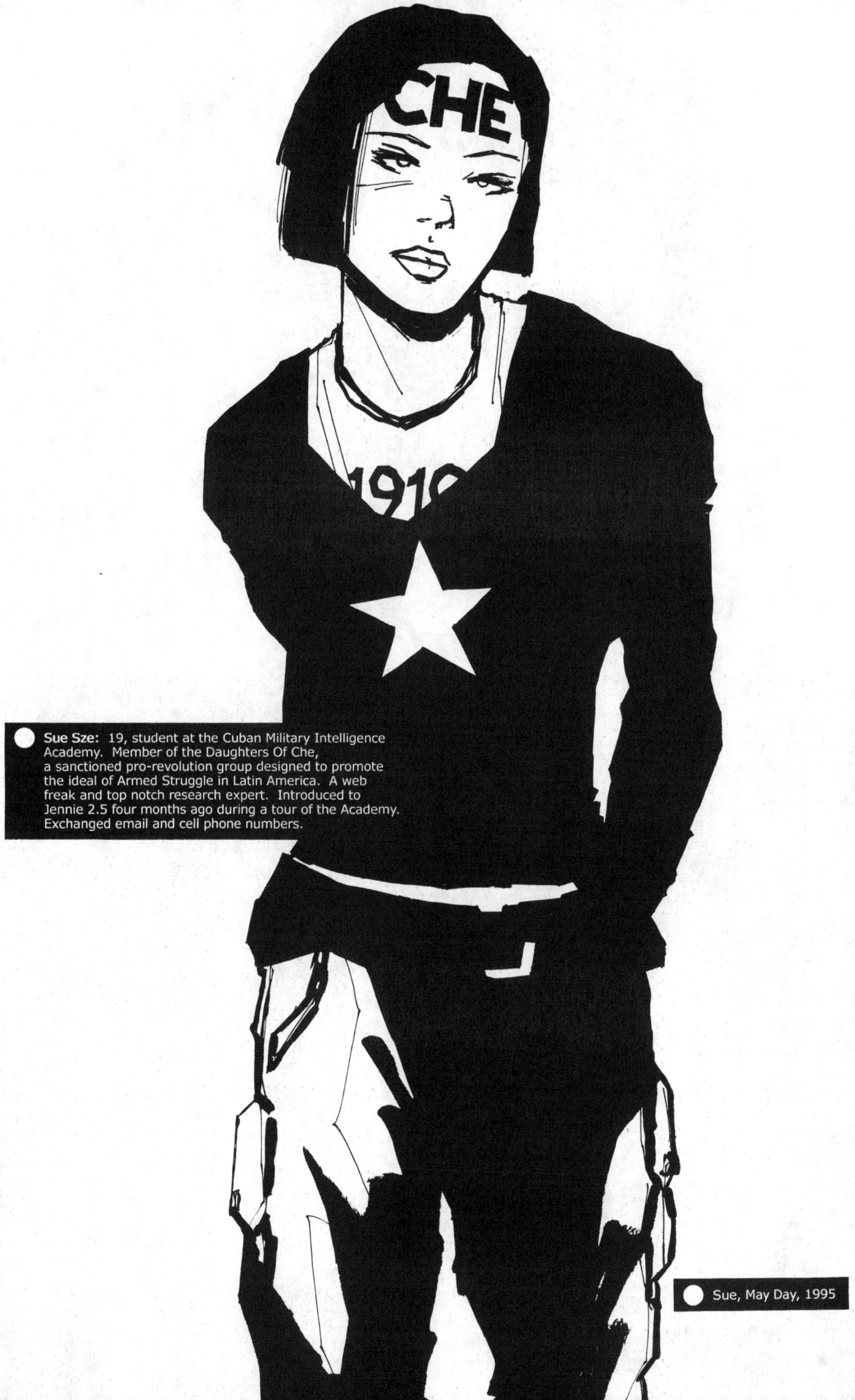
CHE
Sue Sze: 19, student at the Cuban Military Intelligence Academy. Member of the Daughters Of Che, a sanctioned pro-revolution group designed to promote the ideal of Armed Struggle in Latin America. A web freak and top notch research expert. Introduced to Jennie 2.5 four months ago during a tour of the Academy. Exchanged email and cell phone numbers.
Sue, May Day, 1995

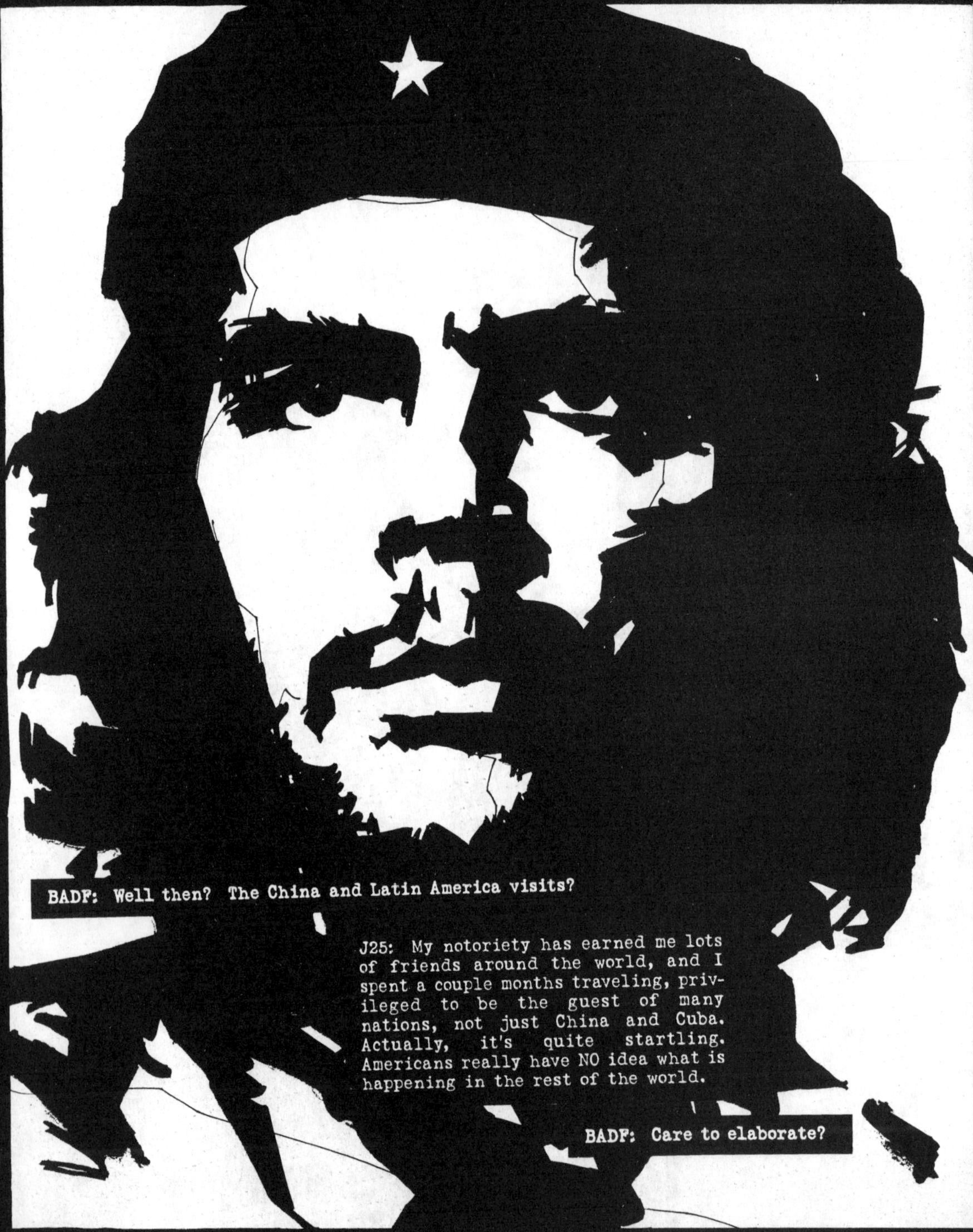

BADF: Well then? The China and Latin America visits?

J25: My notoriety has earned me lots of friends around the world, and I spent a couple months traveling, privileged to be the guest of many nations, not just China and Cuba. Actually, it's quite startling. Americans really have NO idea what is happening in the rest of the world.

BADF: Care to elaborate?

havana...

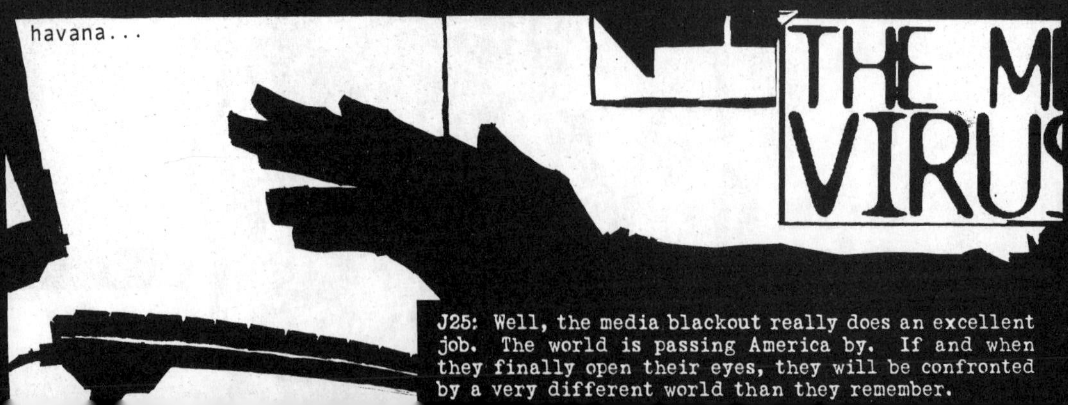
THE M
VIRU

J25: Well, the media blackout really does an excellent job. The world is passing America by. If and when they finally open their eyes, they will be confronted by a very different world than they remember.

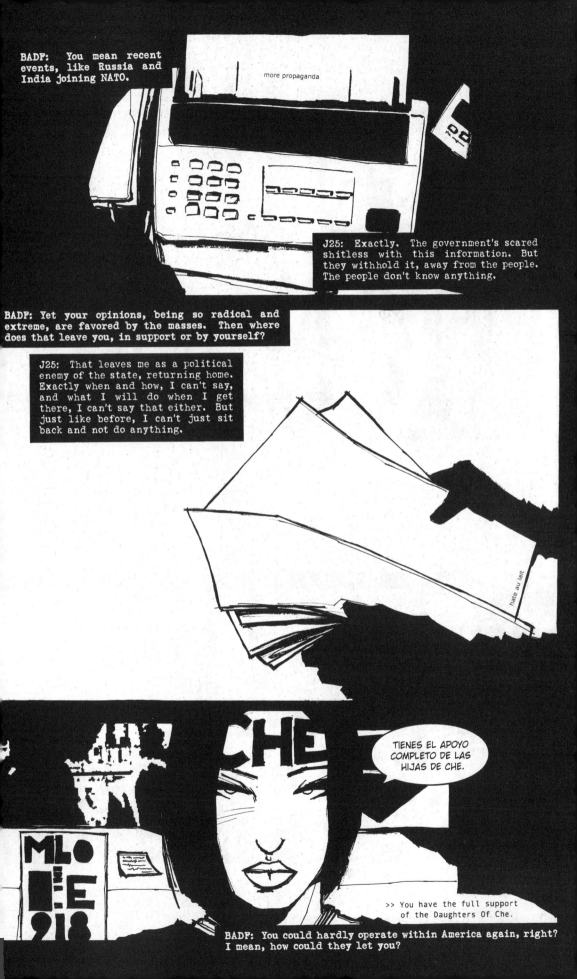

BADF: You mean recent events, like Russia and India joining NATO.

more propaganda

J25: Exactly. The government's scared shitless with this information. But they withhold it, away from the people. The people don't know anything.

BADF: Yet your opinions, being so radical and extreme, are favored by the masses. Then where does that leave you, in support or by yourself?

J25: That leaves me as a political enemy of the state, returning home. Exactly when and how, I can't say, and what I will do when I get there, I can't say that either. But just like before, I can't just sit back and not do anything.

hate au lait

TIENES EL APOYO COMPLETO DE LAS HIJAS DE CHE.

>> You have the full support of the Daughters Of Che.

BADF: You could hardly operate within America again, right? I mean, how could they let you?

"...imperialism at its worst."

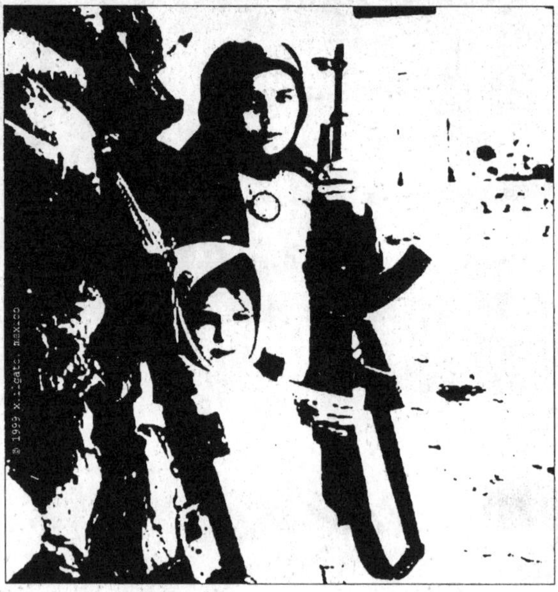

two sisters, aged 7 and 16, pose with weapons recently supplied by the L.A.C.A.S.

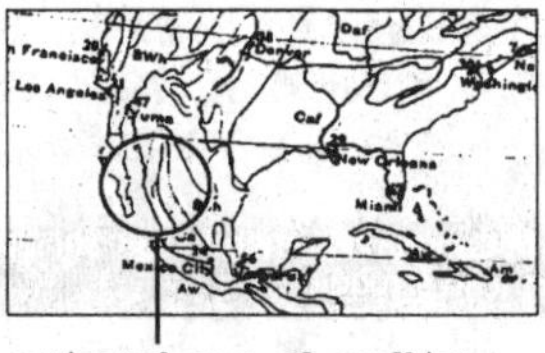

estimated area of conflict. US warplanes prevent aerial reconnaissance.

this poorly digitized photo, recently sent out via email from our news correspondent in Mexico shows a peasant population preparing themselves for a war with America they will, in all likelihood, lose. and with their defeat will come death, starvation, slave labor, and conscription into the mighty American war machine. this is Imperialism at its worst.

who watches who? who watches you?

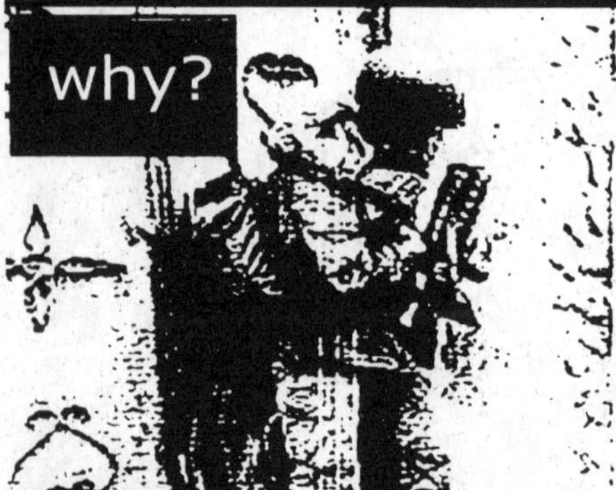
why?

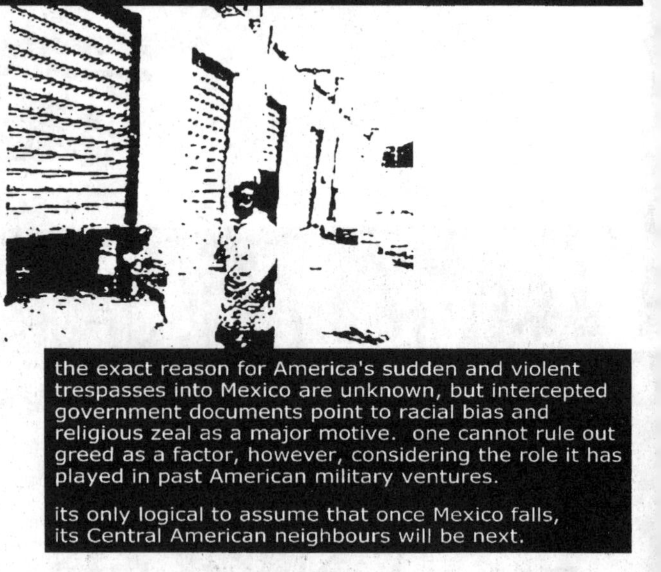

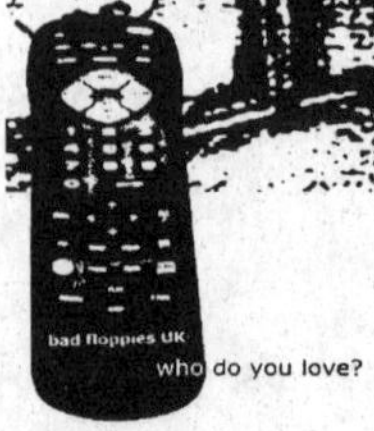
bad floppies UK
who do you love?

the exact reason for America's sudden and violent trespasses into Mexico are unknown, but intercepted government documents point to racial bias and religious zeal as a major motive. one cannot rule out greed as a factor, however, considering the role it has played in past American military ventures.

its only logical to assume that once Mexico falls, its Central American neighbours will be next.

Heavy: 28, student at Vancouver Film School. Originally from Seattle, he smuggles information and supplies across the border to friends and family on a regular basis. Formed a Resistance chapter in Canada two months ago to support the anti-American struggle.

Tadpole and Heavy, 1992

Tadpole: 22, student at Emily Carr. Longtime friend of Heavy, helps out with his information trafficking and maintains a website and database for the Resistance internationally. Bought a copy of the Anarchist Cookbook a year ago and runs a small bomb factory from her basement.

J25: They couldn't. I epitomize The One Who Fought Them and Won, more or less. I am Hope, and the last thing America wants its people feeling is hope. They would kill me before that happened, for sure. I want to see my home, see my friends, and get a feel for the political climate. After that, we shall see.

vancouver...

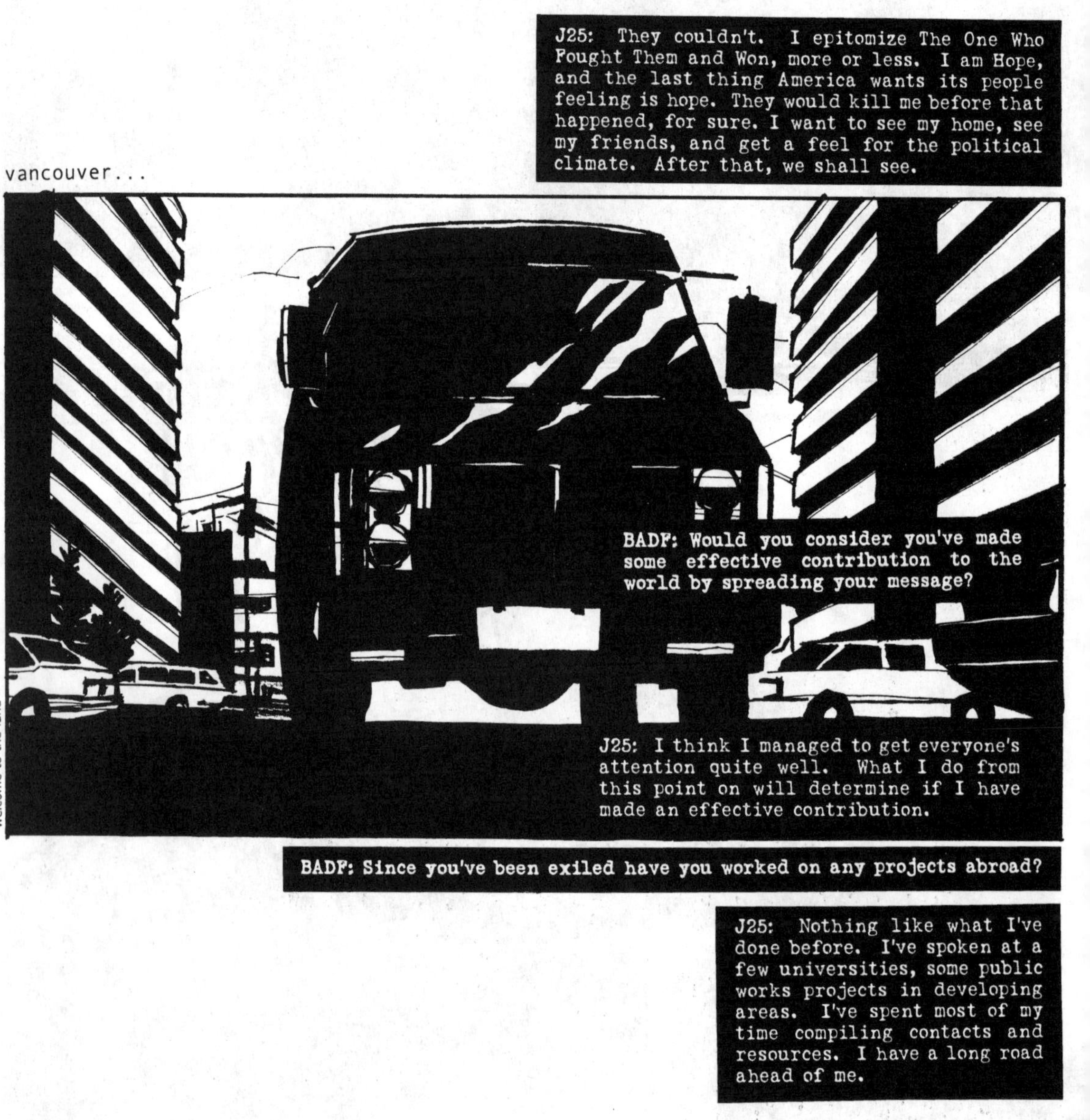

BADF: Would you consider you've made some effective contribution to the world by spreading your message?

J25: I think I managed to get everyone's attention quite well. What I do from this point on will determine if I have made an effective contribution.

BADF: Since you've been exiled have you worked on any projects abroad?

J25: Nothing like what I've done before. I've spoken at a few universities, some public works projects in developing areas. I've spent most of my time compiling contacts and resources. I have a long road ahead of me.

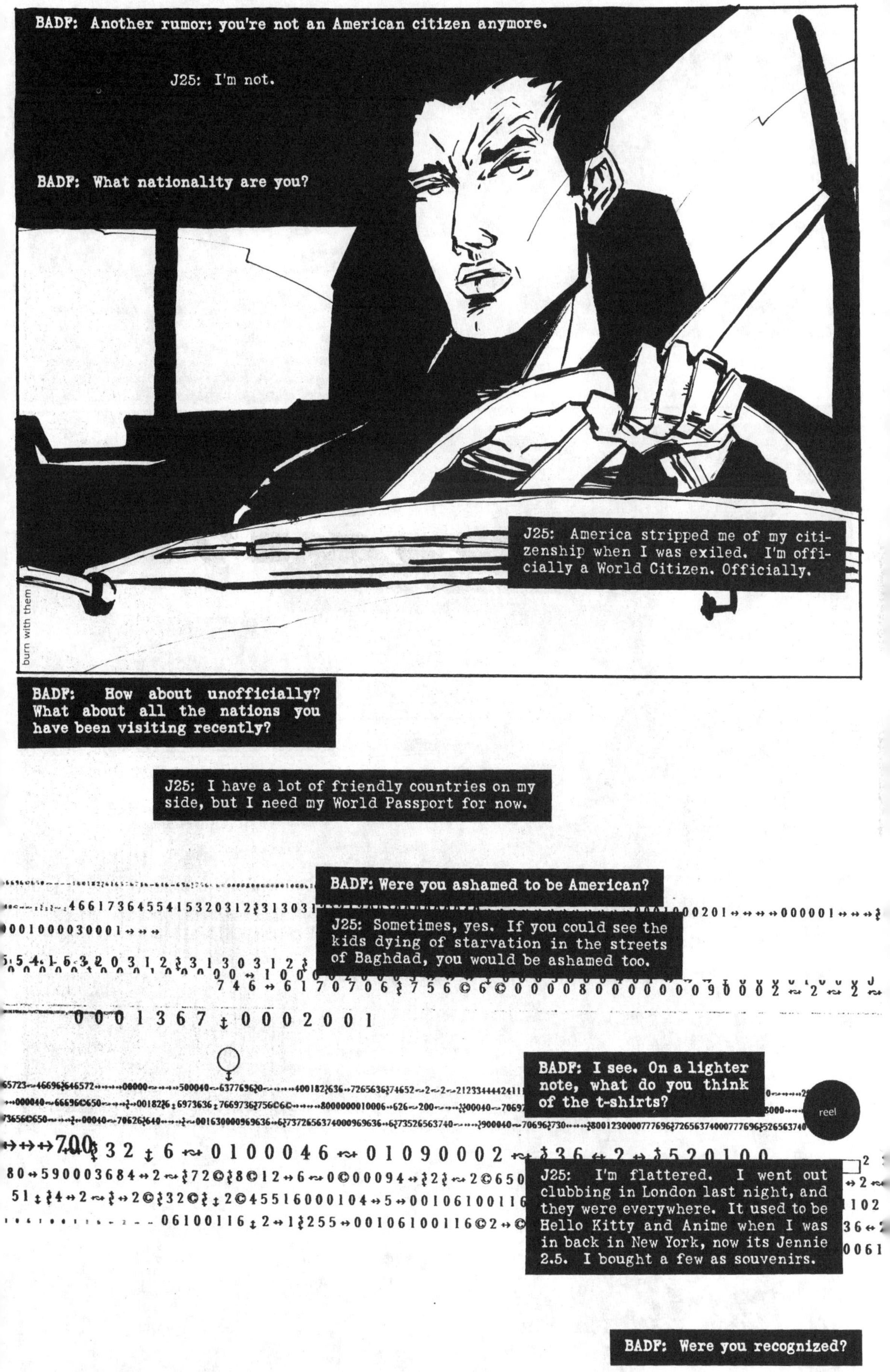
BADF: Another rumor: you're not an American citizen anymore.
J25: I'm not.
BADF: What nationality are you?
J25: America stripped me of my citizenship when I was exiled. I'm officially a World Citizen. Officially.
burn with them

BADF: How about unofficially? What about all the nations you have been visiting recently?

J25: I have a lot of friendly countries on my side, but I need my World Passport for now.

BADF: Were you ashamed to be American?

J25: Sometimes, yes. If you could see the kids dying of starvation in the streets of Baghdad, you would be ashamed too.

BADF: I see. On a lighter note, what do you think of the t-shirts?

reel

J25: I'm flattered. I went out clubbing in London last night, and they were everywhere. It used to be Hello Kitty and Anime when I was in back in New York, now its Jennie 2.5. I bought a few as souvenirs.

BADF: Were you recognized?

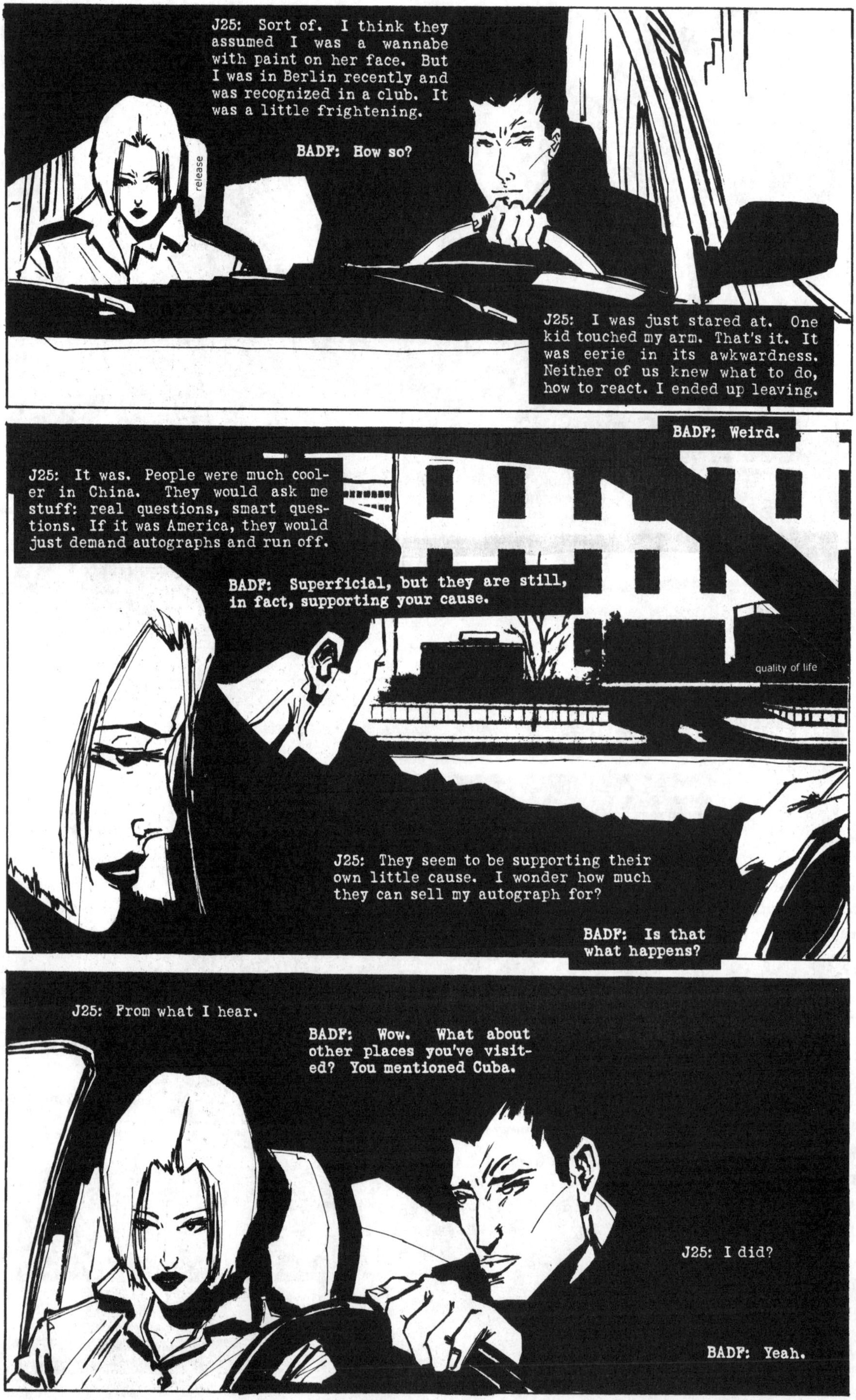
J25: Sort of. I think they assumed I was a wannabe with paint on her face. But I was in Berlin recently and was recognized in a club. It was a little frightening.
BADF: How so?
release
J25: I was just stared at. One kid touched my arm. That's it. It was eerie in its awkwardness. Neither of us knew what to do, how to react. I ended up leaving.
BADF: Weird.
J25: It was. People were much cooler in China. They would ask me stuff: real questions, smart questions. If it was America, they would just demand autographs and run off.
BADF: Superficial, but they are still, in fact, supporting your cause.
quality of life
J25: They seem to be supporting their own little cause. I wonder how much they can sell my autograph for?
BADF: Is that what happens?
J25: From what I hear.
BADF: Wow. What about other places you've visited? You mentioned Cuba.
J25: I did?
BADF: Yeah.

J25: Oh. Well, Cuba was a cool place. I have a lot of respect for Castro and his administration. I mean, they stood up to America, said 'fuck you', and got away with it. Even with the Soviets backing them, it's still pretty hardcore. And they WON.

BADF: You're compared to Che a lot.

J25: I heard that a couple times. I don't agree. He is a revolutionary god. Committed, tough, self-sacrificing. He changed the world. I wish I could be that way.

BADF: In many ways you are.

J25: No I'm not. I could be, maybe. I want to be.

BADF: Is that what you have planned? Armed struggle? A revolution?

J25: America would certainly benefit from a revolution. A lot of similarities can be drawn from its current state to Batista's Cuba in 1958. In that case, a dozen determined men with virtually no resources overthrew the government, thumbed their noses at the world, and are still in power 40 years later. If they did it, someone could do it with America.

BADF: Someone like you?

J25: Someone like me.

BADF: Specifically you?

J25: I can't answer that.

BADF: Are you a Communist?

J25: I've been called that. I've been called a Socialist, a Leninist-Marxist, an Anarchist. Call me all of those if you want. I am what you see before you.

BADF: You wrote an article for the Review recently, in which praised Maoist theory.

J25: Mao probably had the clearest vision of them all. He was a genius. It's no wonder China is as powerful as it is.

BADF: What about Tibet? And its blatant human rights violations?

J25: American exaggerations. I mean, those things exist. What China did to Tibet is unspeakable, I offer no excuses for them. But its not always as simple as we make it out to be. One common Western trait to assume your views are correct and everyone else's is wrong.

Who are we, as Westerners, to say that China can't stomp all over Tibet if they want to? It's their business. We aren't the police of the world, despite what America says or does. We don't have to like it, but forcing our opinions on everyone is wrong.

BADF: Point taken. But it's a chilling stance to take. It's not a popular stance.

J25: I know its not. But it's the CORRECT opinion.

ONE OF THE STEWARDESSES. SHE'S BLOND, ABOUT 35-40. SHE'LL HAND YOU A PASSPORT AND VISA. MEET US OUT FRONT. WE CAN TALK ABOUT THE BORDER THEN.

BADF: Good luck convincing people of that.

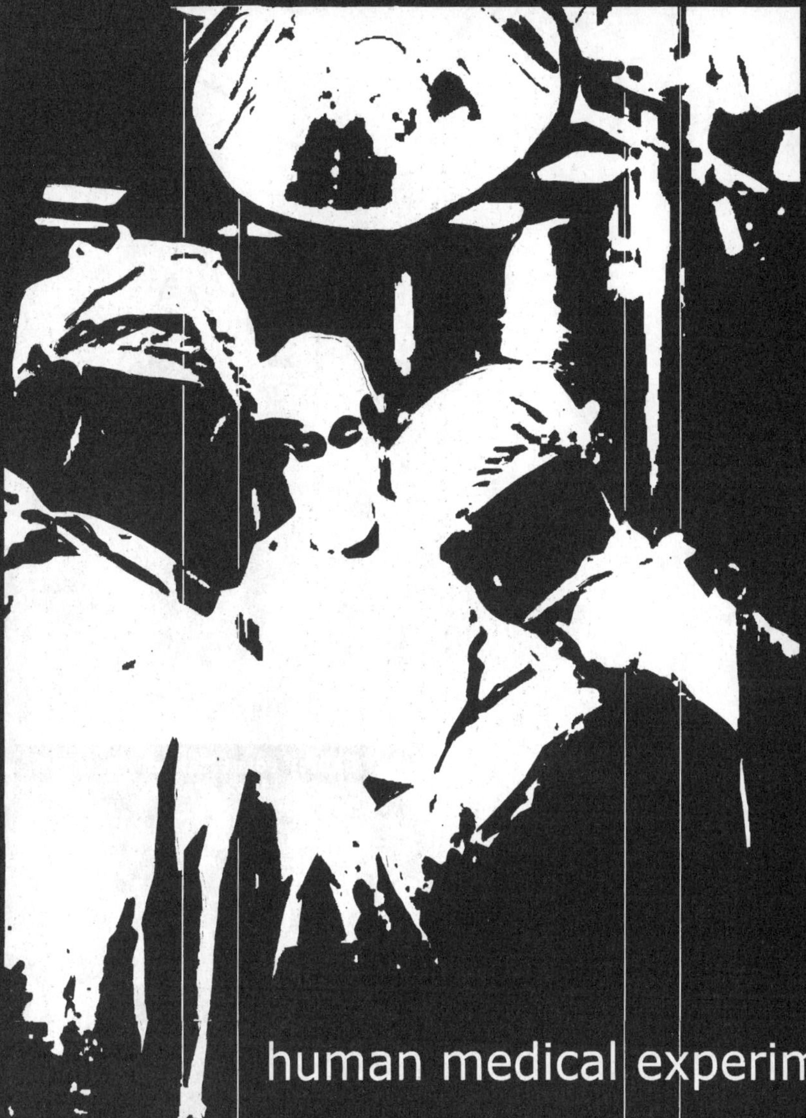

human medical experimentation--

it's like a bad dream.

but it happened. the japanese. the nazis.

a horrible by-product of conflict. prisoners of war put to use.

countries looking for an advantage. any advantage.

but that was a long time ago. we are more civilized now.

Nevada. 1998.
a small government-funded research complex.

a paranoid America. millennial dread. world opinion not in their favor.

they turn to history for answers.

--it never went away.

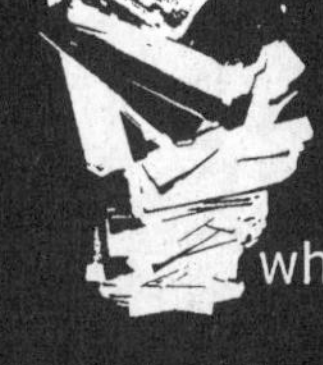
bad floppies

who do you love?

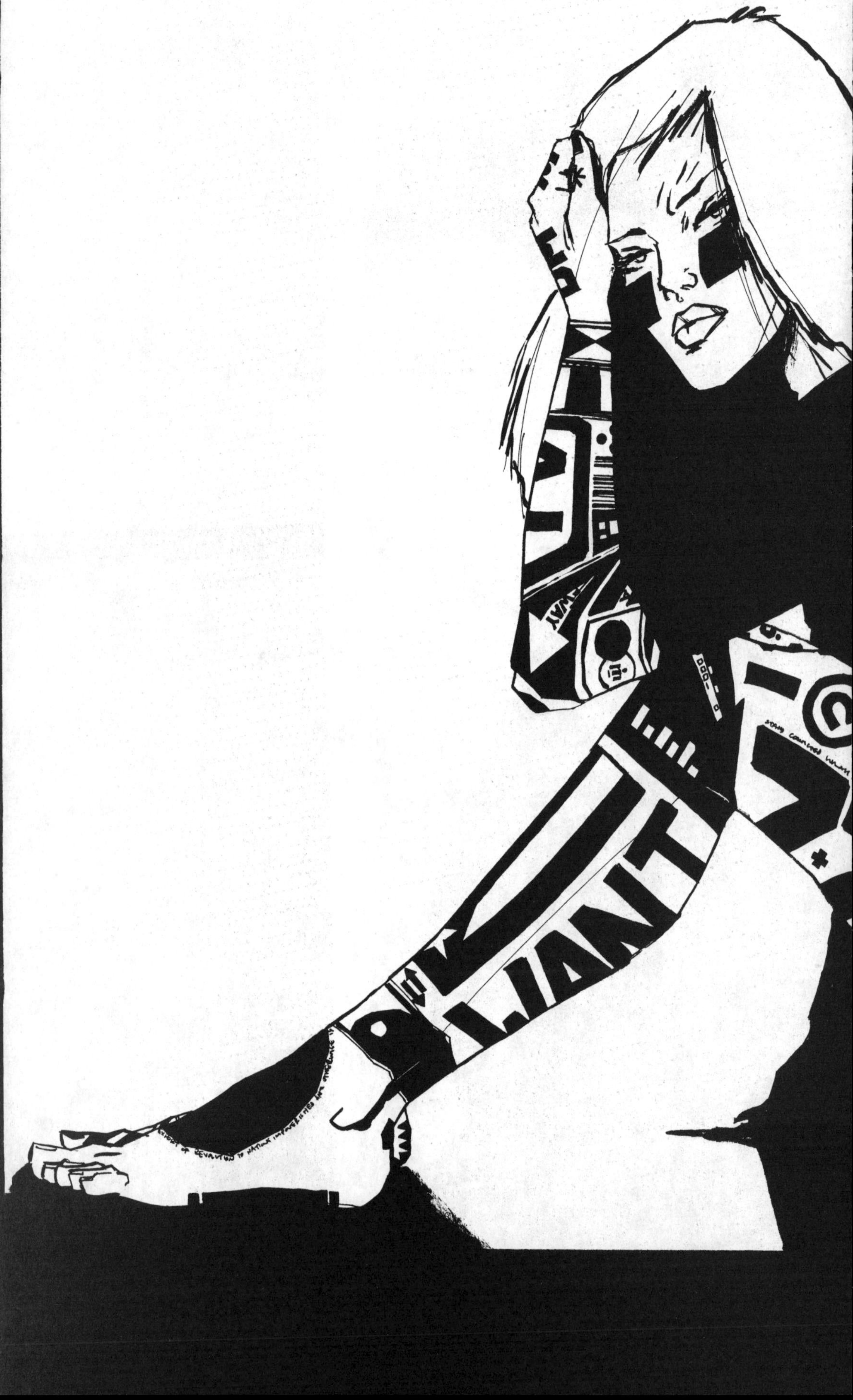
WANT

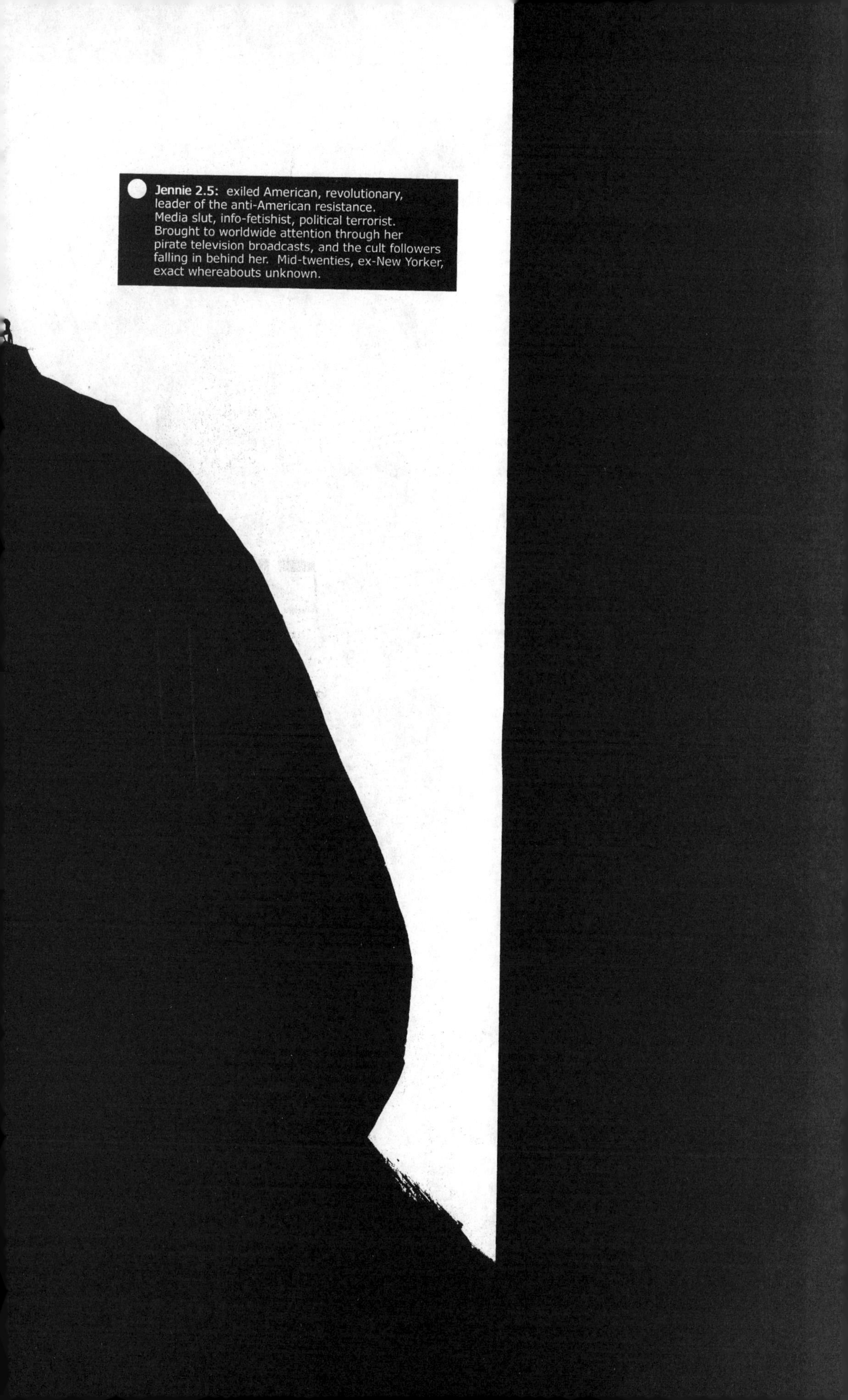
Jennie 2.5: exiled American, revolutionary, leader of the anti-American resistance. Media slut, info-fetishist, political terrorist. Brought to worldwide attention through her pirate television broadcasts, and the cult followers falling in behind her. Mid-twenties, ex-New Yorker, exact whereabouts unknown.

J25: Well, I plan to be in America by the time this interview hits the stands. I still have the problem of getting past customs, and getting the needed cards and IDs to get by once I am there. I have some people on that as we speak.

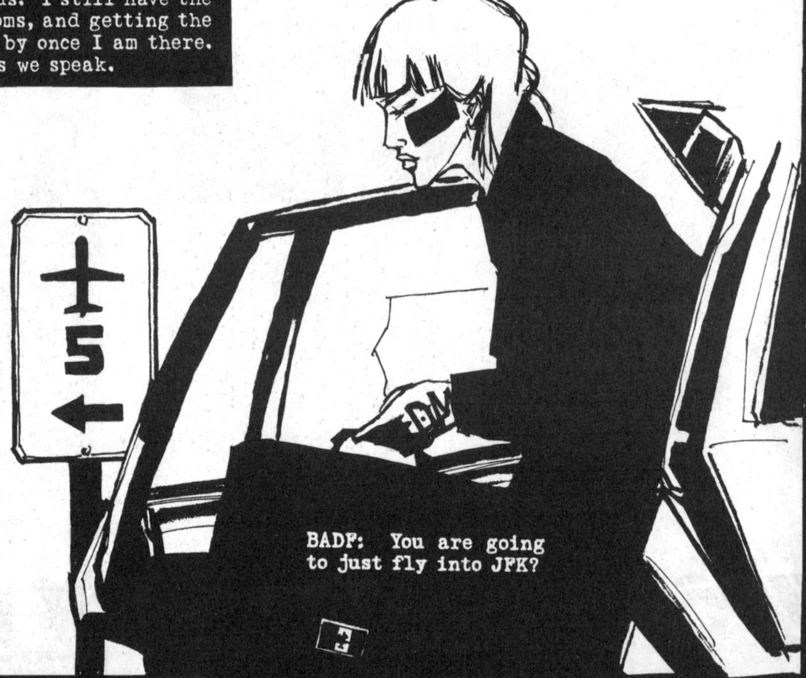
5

BADF: You are going to just fly into JFK?

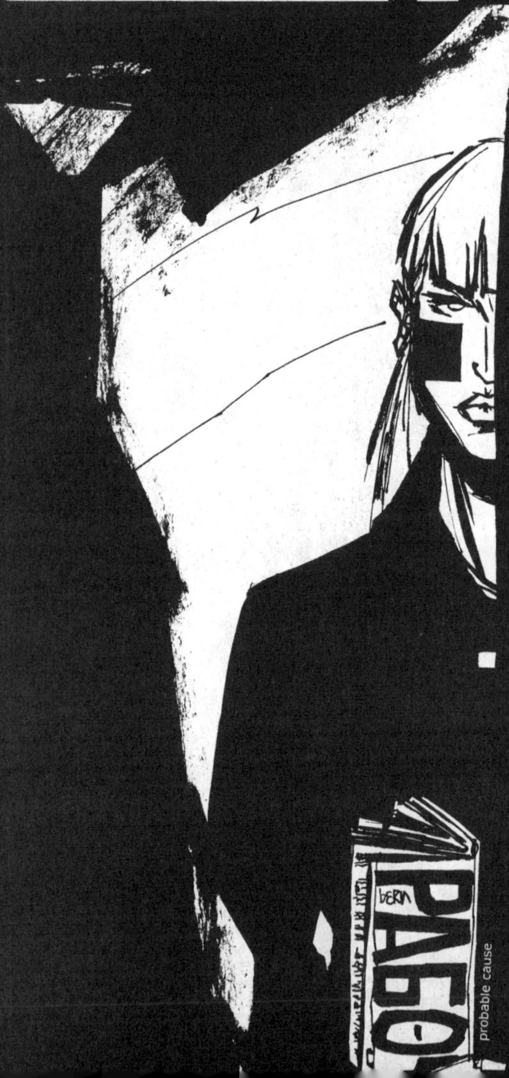
РАБО

J25: I didn't say that. I mean, it may be that simple, or not. There are groups in Canada and Mexico that would be happy to help me out, but the border guards in America are pretty severe, so maybe I will have to think a little unconventionally. Any ideas?

BADF: Umm...

J25: I'm kidding. I'm not worried. I'll make it in. Getting out may be a different story.

BADF: Good luck with that. Do you consider yourself to be a role model?

J25: You mean like for kids?

BADF: Whomever.

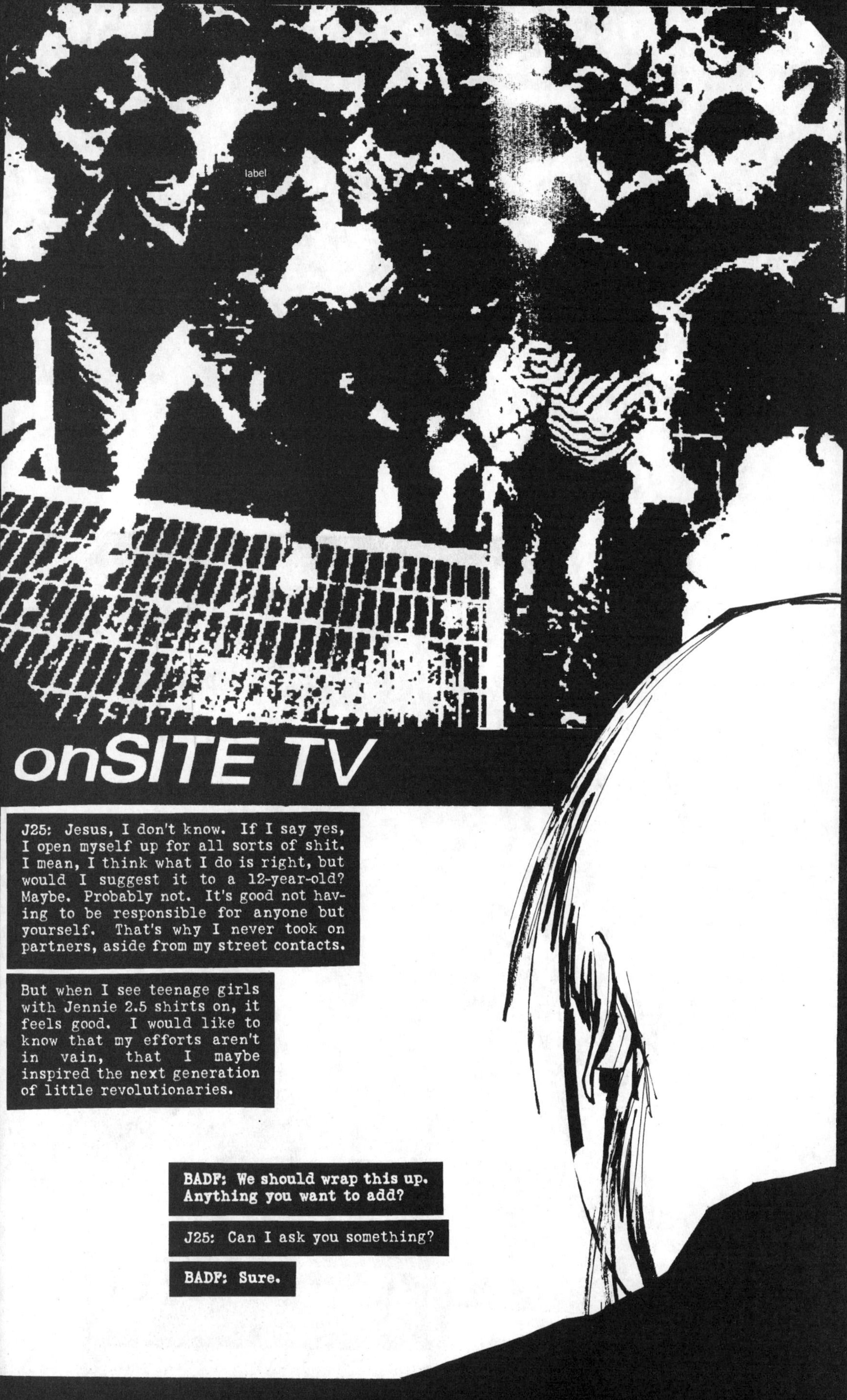

onSITE TV
J25: Jesus, I don't know. If I say yes, I open myself up for all sorts of shit. I mean, I think what I do is right, but would I suggest it to a 12-year-old? Maybe. Probably not. It's good not having to be responsible for anyone but yourself. That's why I never took on partners, aside from my street contacts.
But when I see teenage girls with Jennie 2.5 shirts on, it feels good. I would like to know that my efforts aren't in vain, that I maybe inspired the next generation of little revolutionaries.
BADF: We should wrap this up. Anything you want to add?
J25: Can I ask you something?
BADF: Sure.

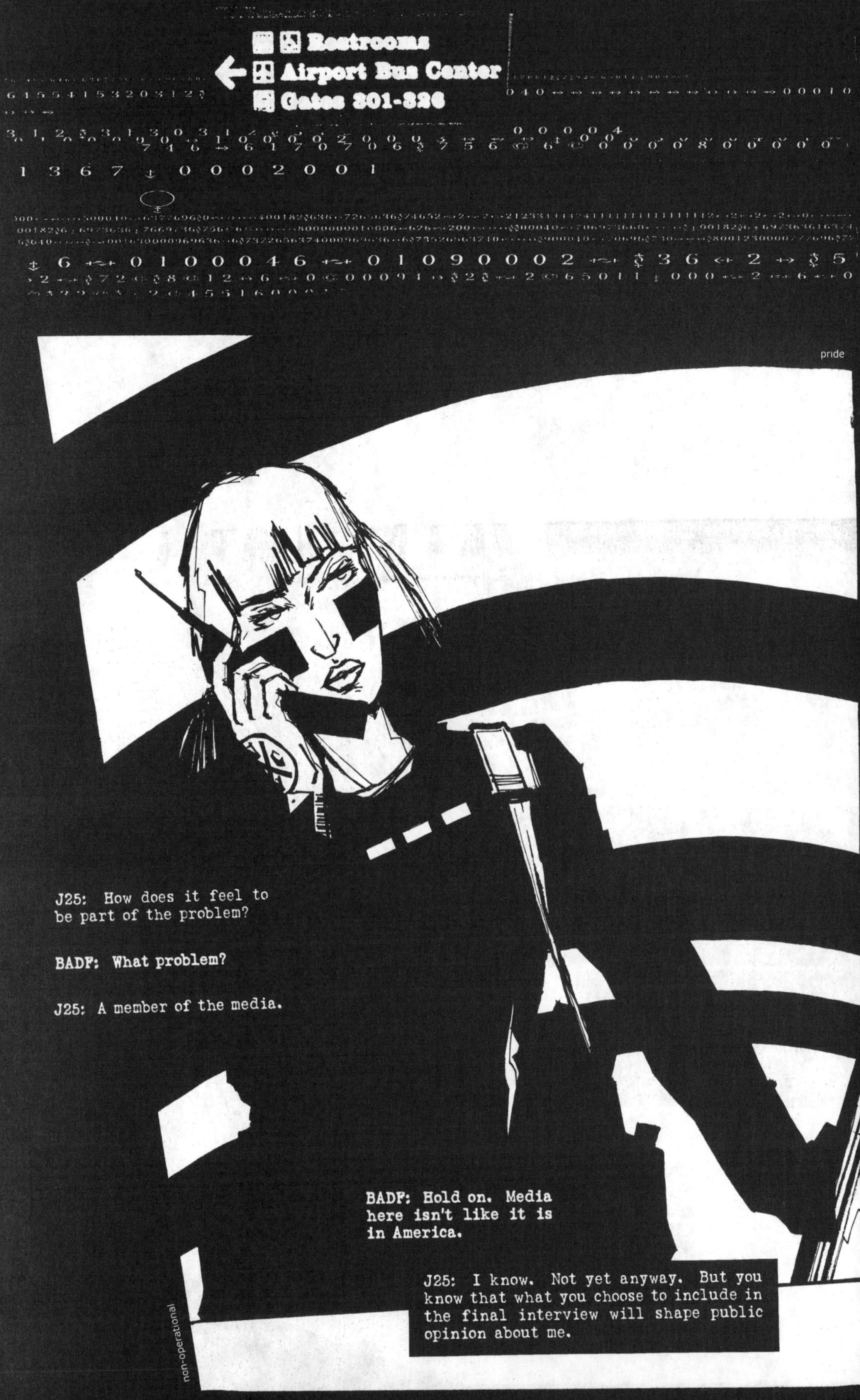
Restrooms
Airport Bus Center
Gates 301-326
1 3 6 7 0 0 0 2 0 0 1
J25: How does it feel to be part of the problem?
BADF: What problem?
J25: A member of the media.
BADF: Hold on. Media here isn't like it is in America.
J25: I know. Not yet anyway. But you know that what you choose to include in the final interview will shape public opinion about me.

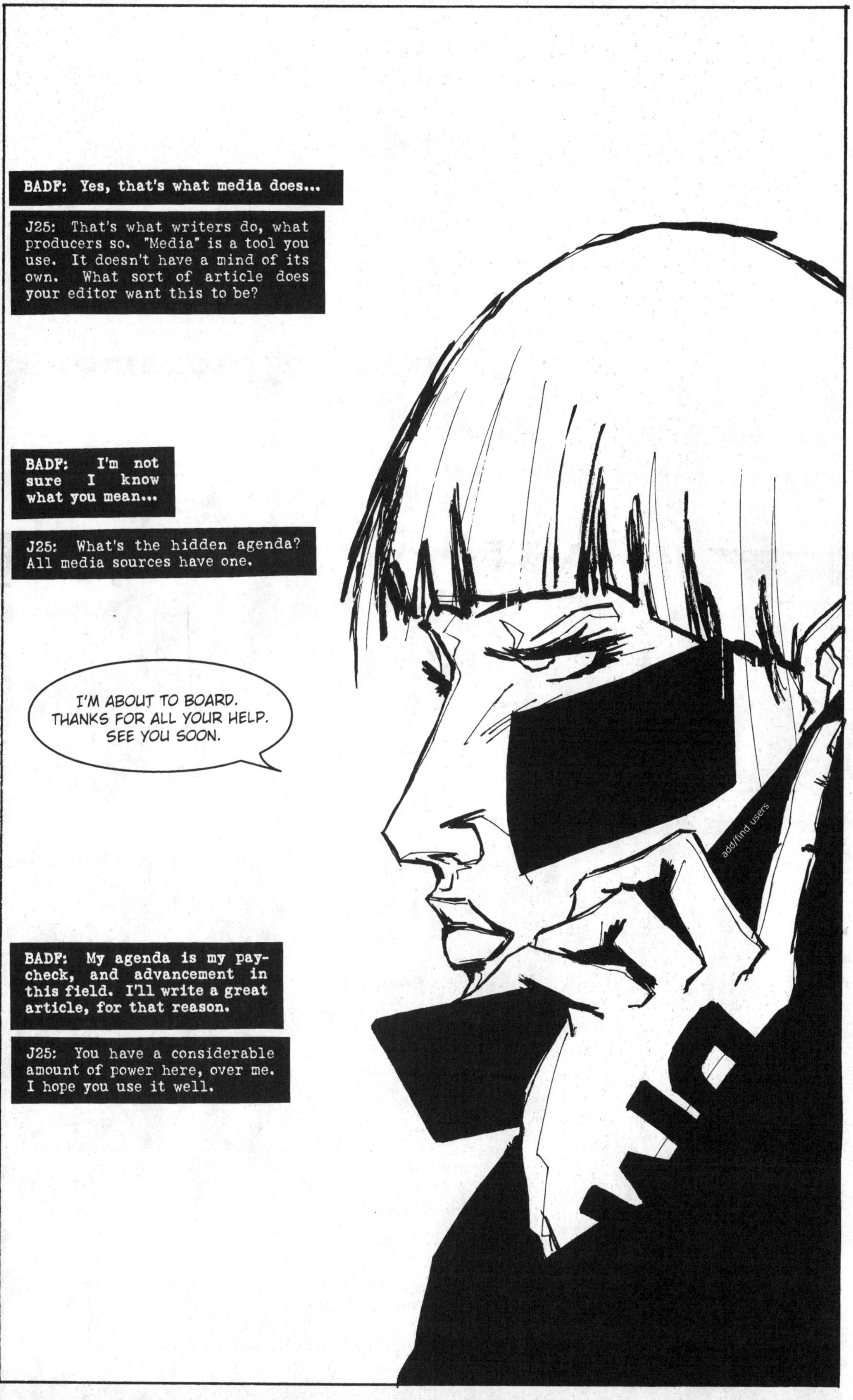
BADF: Yes, that's what media does...
J25: That's what writers do, what producers so. "Media" is a tool you use. It doesn't have a mind of its own. What sort of article does your editor want this to be?
BADF: I'm not sure I know what you mean...
J25: What's the hidden agenda? All media sources have one.
I'M ABOUT TO BOARD. THANKS FOR ALL YOUR HELP. SEE YOU SOON.
add/find users
BADF: My agenda is my paycheck, and advancement in this field. I'll write a great article, for that reason.
J25: You have a considerable amount of power here, over me. I hope you use it well.

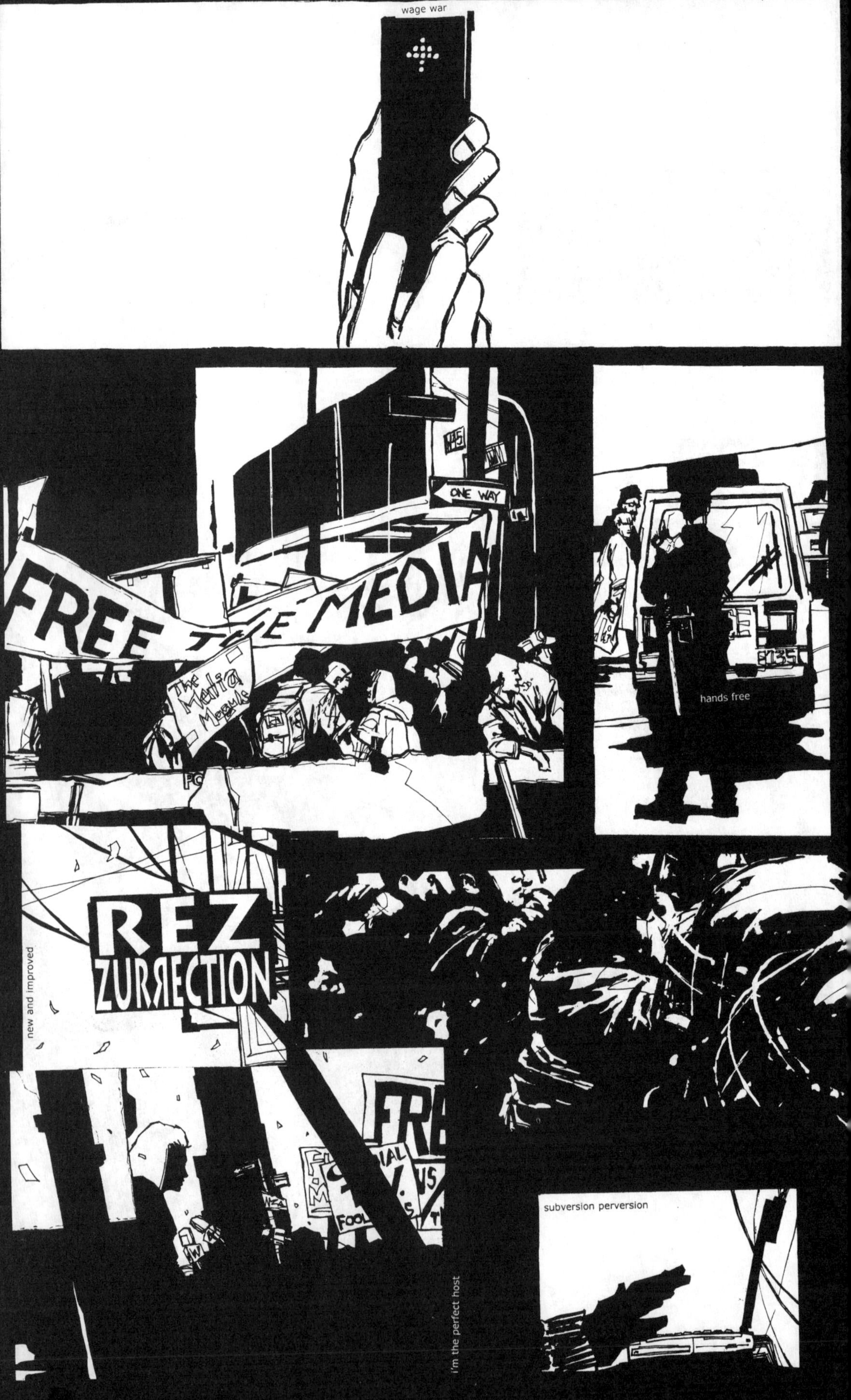
wage war
ONE WAY
FREE THE MEDIA
The Media Moguls
hands free
new and improved
REZ
ZURRECTION
i'm the perfect host
subversion perversion

After the interview, she took a short tour of our offices and left. Her cell phone had rung several times during our discussion, and she excused herself each time to answer it. She checked her email before she left. She turned down our offers for dinner.

She carries herself with a sort of pride, a determination, and a little bit of ego. I was left wondering what its like to wander the globe without a place to call home, being pulled in several directions by countries and corporations that all want her for themselves.

She is very much aware of her importance and her role in world events, whatever may happen.

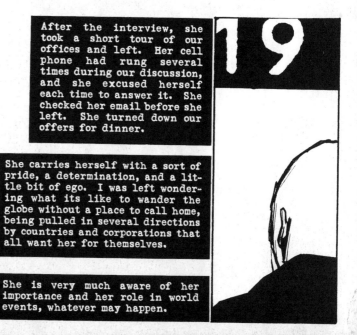

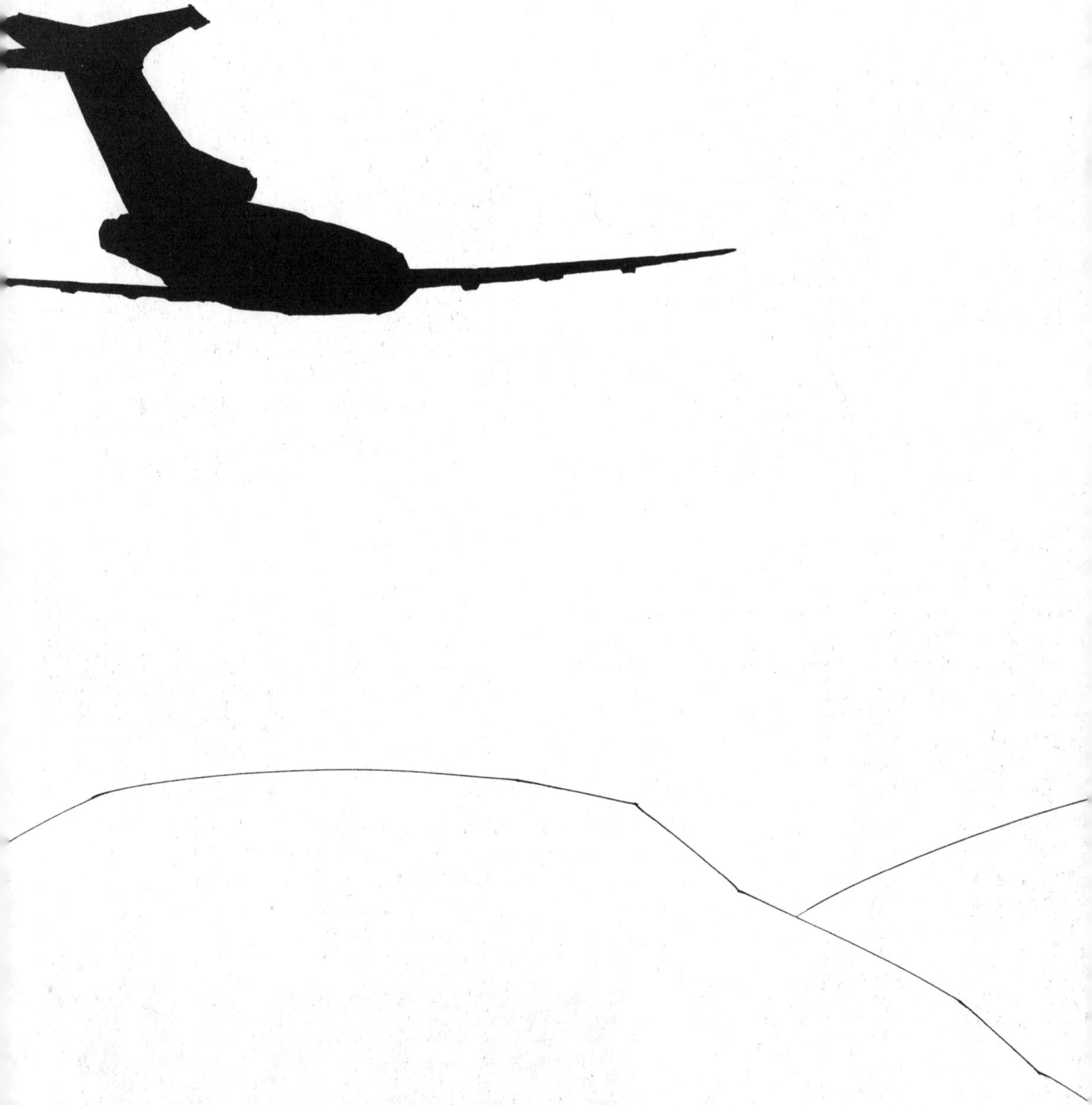

I am left with a feeling of excited unpredictability. Whatever she does, wherever, whenever, its gonna be fucking huge. I can't wait.

DRTY DATA

"I'LL BE GENTLE"

>.as global citizens entering the third millenium, free and un*restrict*ed communication with each other is essential and inevitable. state borders will cease to exist, race will become a non-issue, and social--

standing and caste status will be obliterated. digital existence is the next step in human development. the cerulean hue of active-matrix samsung laptop flatscreens will reflect in the eyes of our children who sit in libraries jacked into a T3, fingers tapping notes to penpals half a planet away at several hundred kilobytes a second.

the collective keystrokes of a world's population will define who we are, as a species of animals at

mental lightspeed.

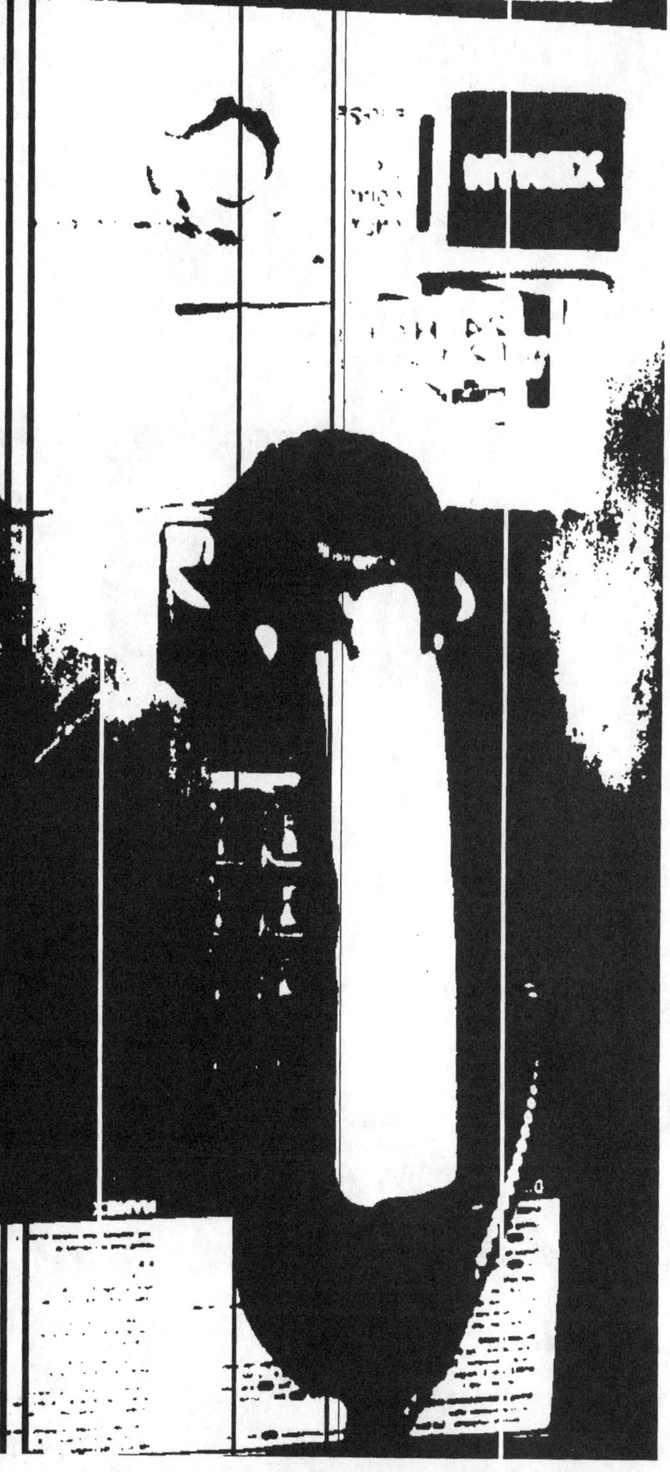

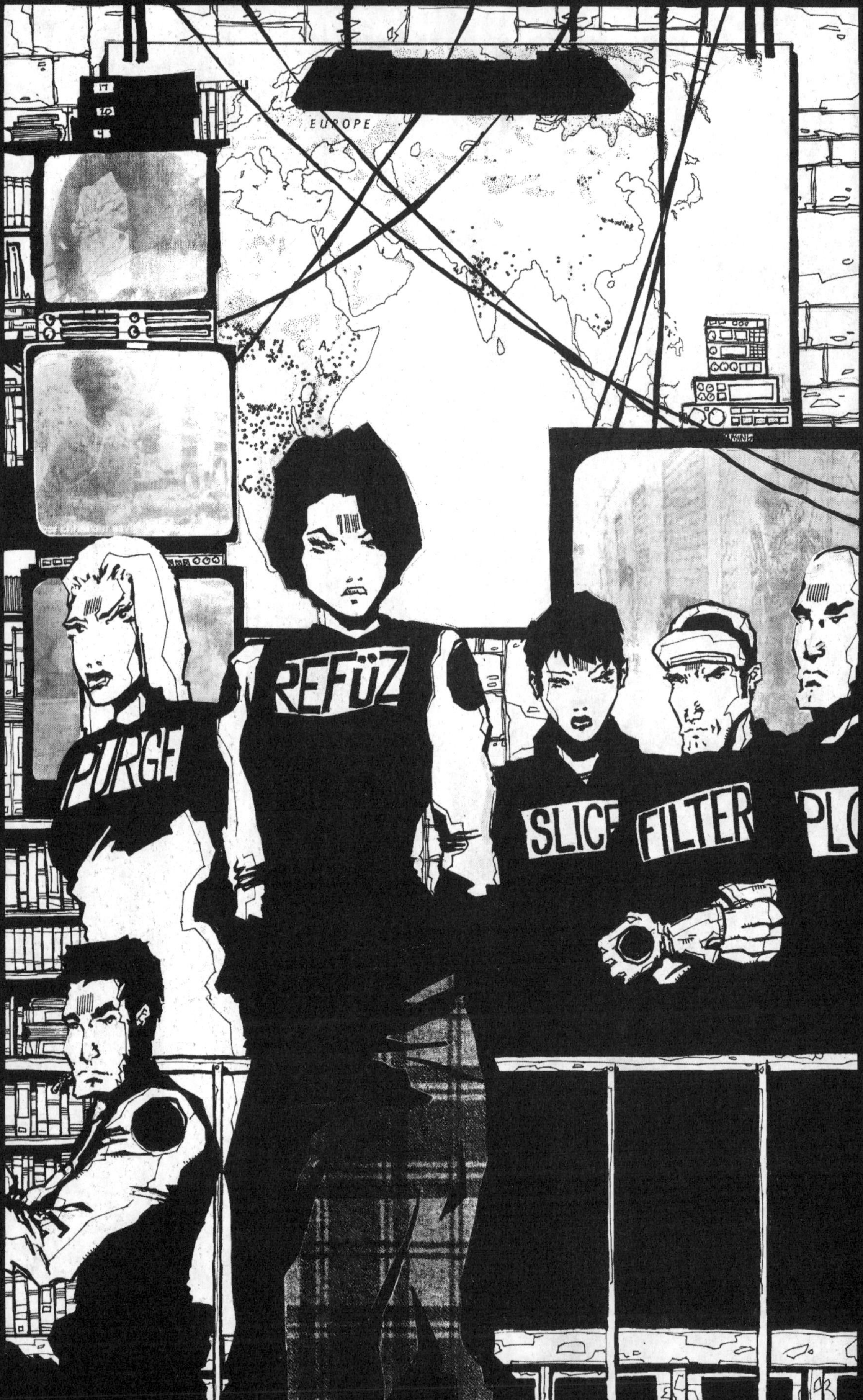
EUROPE
REFÜZ
PURGE
SLICE
FILTER
PLO

FROM THE JOURNAL OF JENNIE 2.5

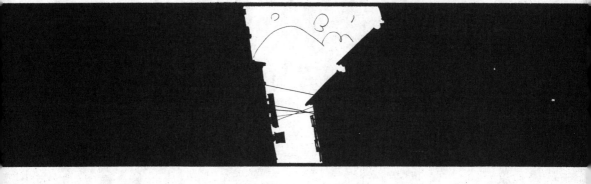

I'VE BEEN BACK IN THE CITY TWO WEEKS NOW.

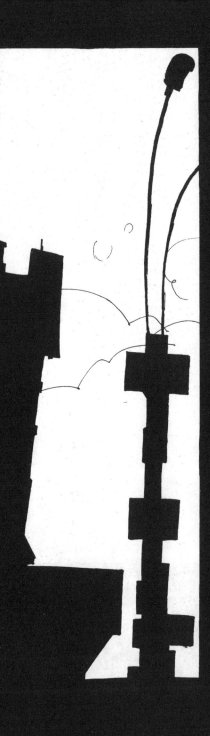

TWO WEEKS IN A FORGOTTEN WAREHOUSE SPACE
IN BROOKLYN, STARING OUT THE WINDOWS OVER
DUMBO, LOOKING AT MANHATTAN, THINKING, WISHING.

TWO WEEKS OF FAXES COMING IN ALMOST HOURLY,
THE PAPER ROLLING OUT ONTO THE FLOOR IN GREAT PILES.

TWO WEEKS OF THE PHONE RINGING,
AND ME NOT ANSWERING IT.

I'M TERRIBLY AFRAID OF THE CITY,
WHEN ONCE I USED TO LOVE IT LIKE A MOTHER .
IT USED TO REPRESENT LIFE AND HOPE AND LOVE
FOR ME, ART AND RISK AND EUPHORIA.

EVEN AT ITS WORST IT STILL COMFORTED ME,
ESPECIALLY ON THOSE LONG NIGHTS WHEN I USED
TO SLEEP ON THE STREET. I WAS NEVER EVER AFRAID
OF IT, NOT LIKE I AM NOW.

FUCK, I'M TERRIFIED TO EVEN LEAVE THE BUILDING.
WHAT THE HELL IS WRONG WITH ME?

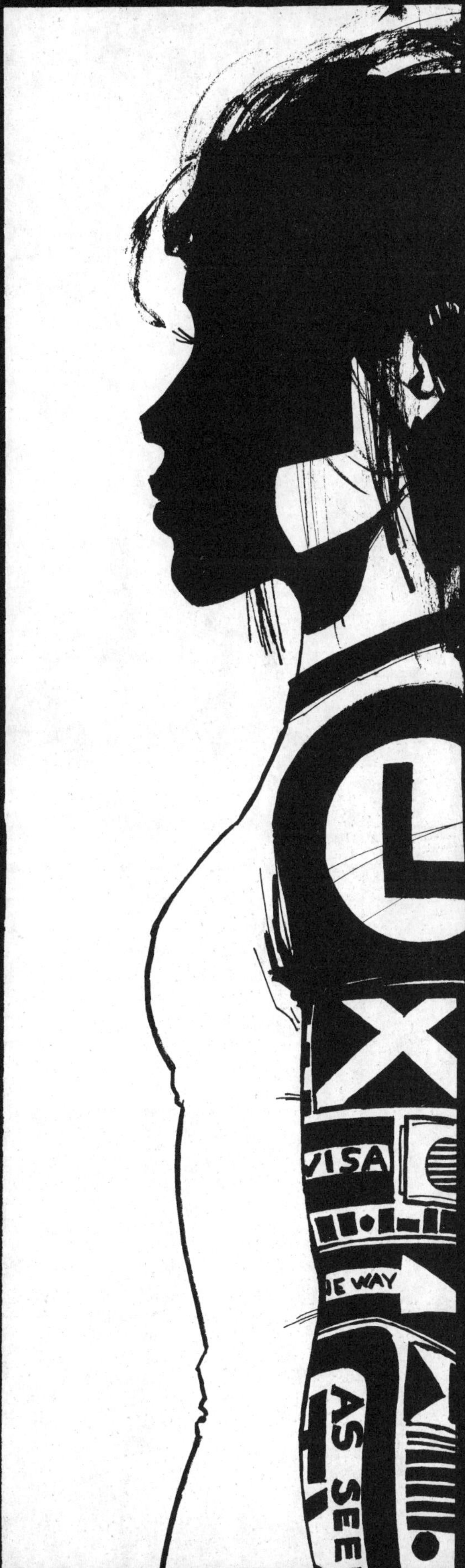
VISA
AS SEE

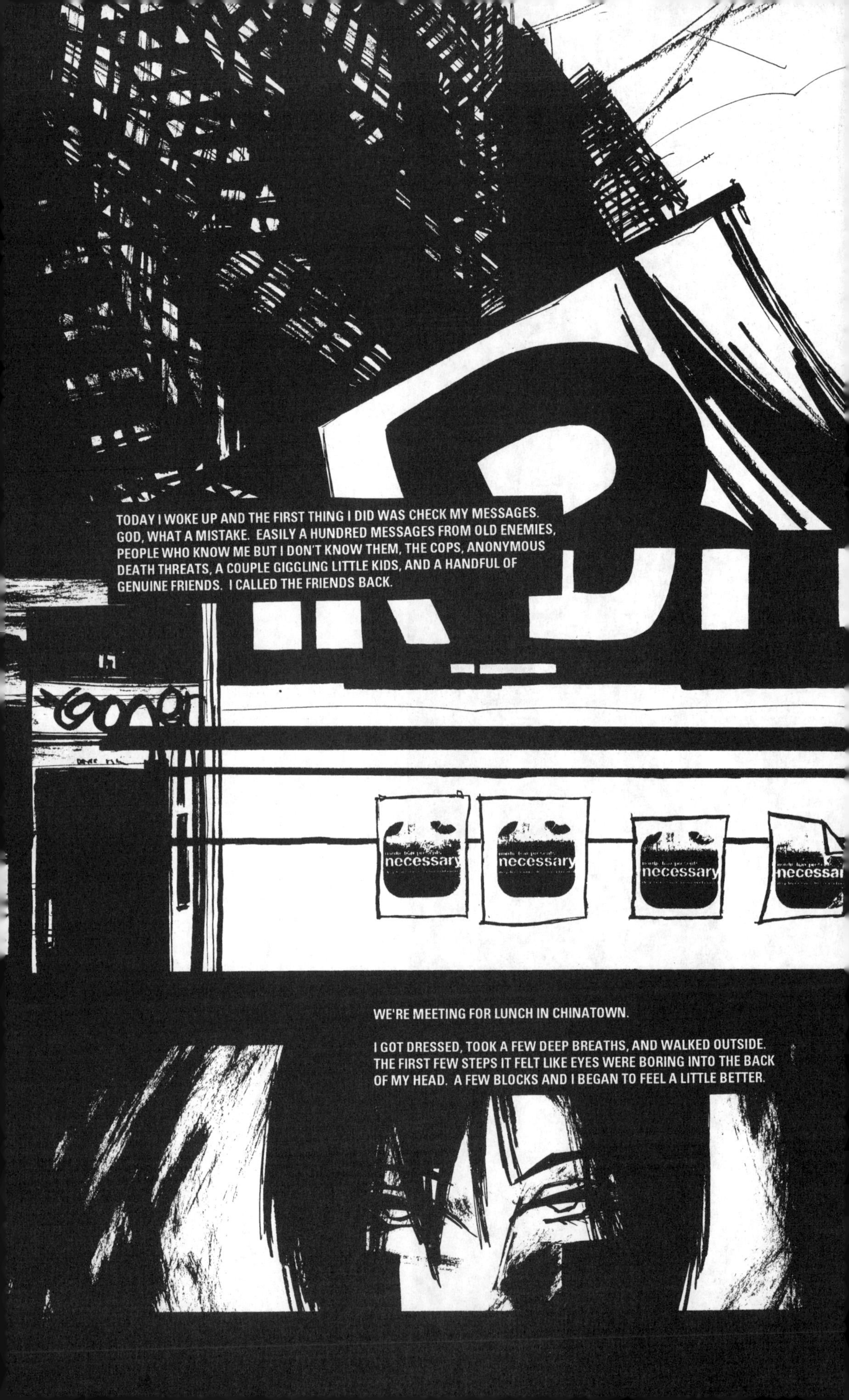
TODAY I WOKE UP AND THE FIRST THING I DID WAS CHECK MY MESSAGES. GOD, WHAT A MISTAKE. EASILY A HUNDRED MESSAGES FROM OLD ENEMIES, PEOPLE WHO KNOW ME BUT I DON'T KNOW THEM, THE COPS, ANONYMOUS DEATH THREATS, A COUPLE GIGGLING LITTLE KIDS, AND A HANDFUL OF GENUINE FRIENDS. I CALLED THE FRIENDS BACK.
necessary
necessary
necessary
necessar
WE'RE MEETING FOR LUNCH IN CHINATOWN.
I GOT DRESSED, TOOK A FEW DEEP BREATHS, AND WALKED OUTSIDE. THE FIRST FEW STEPS IT FELT LIKE EYES WERE BORING INTO THE BACK OF MY HEAD. A FEW BLOCKS AND I BEGAN TO FEEL A LITTLE BETTER.

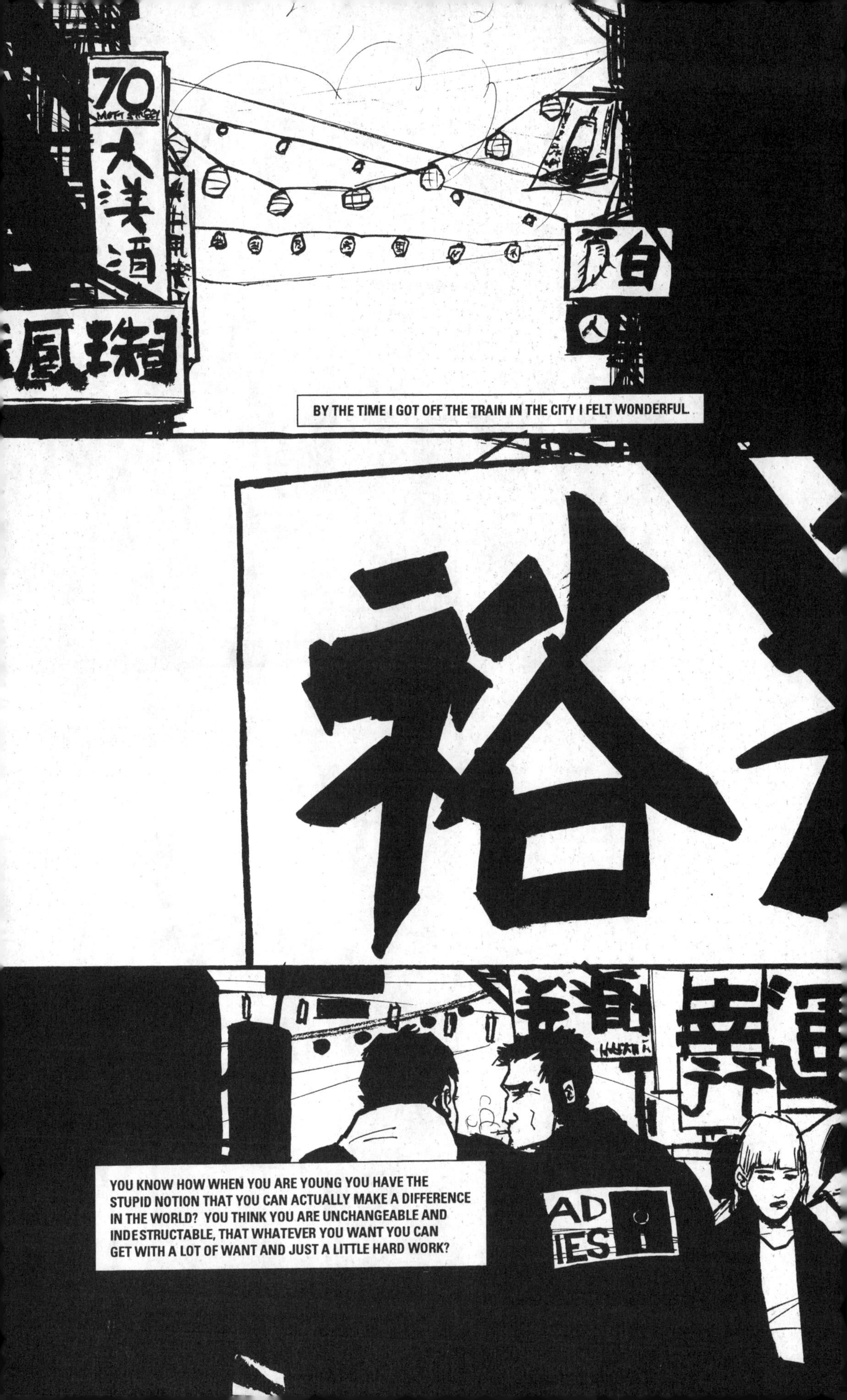
70
BY THE TIME I GOT OFF THE TRAIN IN THE CITY I FELT WONDERFUL.
YOU KNOW HOW WHEN YOU ARE YOUNG YOU HAVE THE STUPID NOTION THAT YOU CAN ACTUALLY MAKE A DIFFERENCE IN THE WORLD? YOU THINK YOU ARE UNCHANGEABLE AND INDESTRUCTABLE, THAT WHATEVER YOU WANT YOU CAN GET WITH A LOT OF WANT AND JUST A LITTLE HARD WORK?

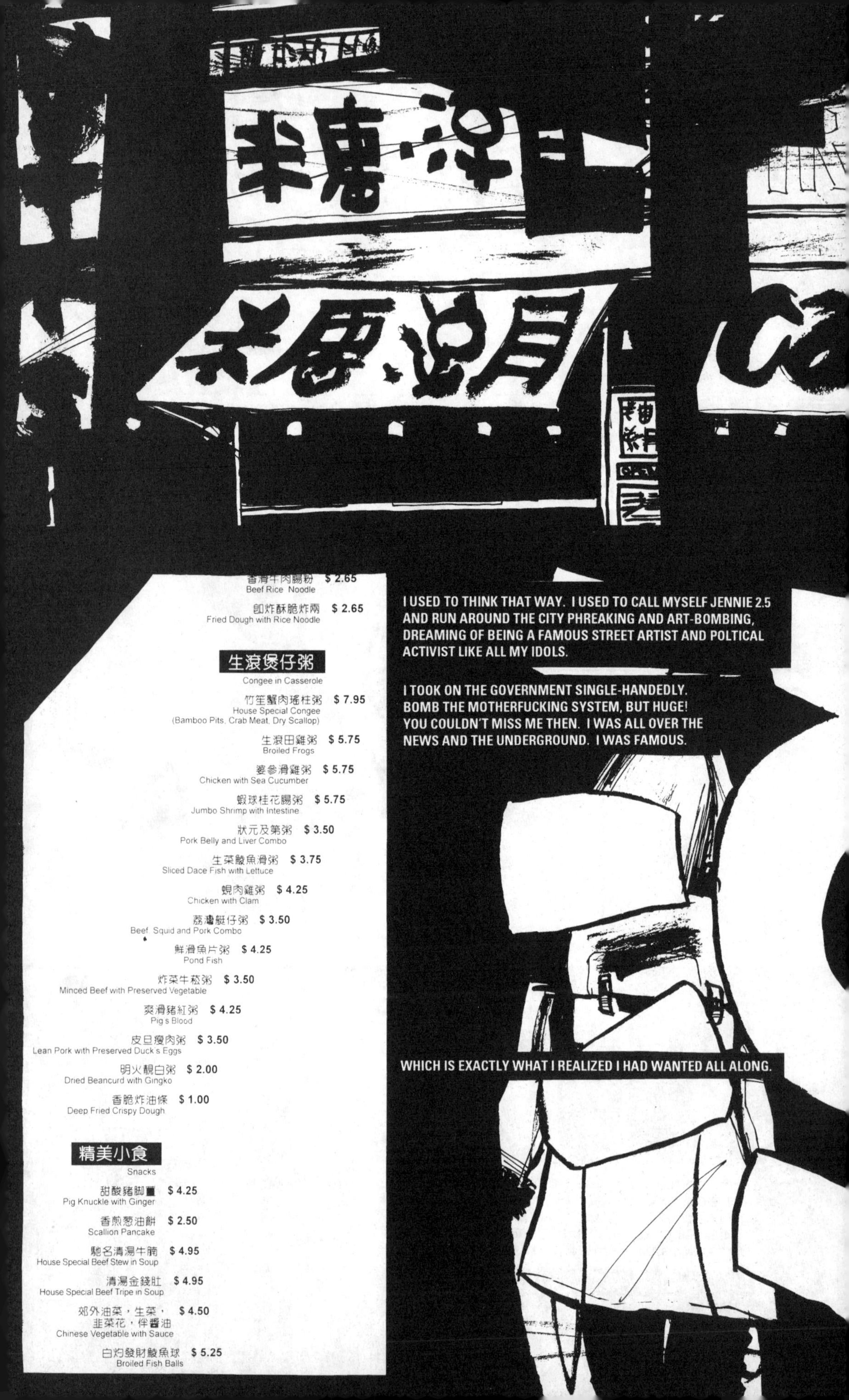

香滑牛肉腸粉 $ 2.65
Beef Rice Noodle
即炸酥脆炸兩 $ 2.65
Fried Dough with Rice Noodle
生滾煲仔粥
Congee in Casserole
竹笙蟹肉瑤柱粥 $ 7.95
House Special Congee
(Bamboo Pits, Crab Meat, Dry Scallop)
生滾田雞粥 $ 5.75
Broiled Frogs
婆参滑雞粥 $ 5.75
Chicken with Sea Cucumber
蝦球桂花腸粥 $ 5.75
Jumbo Shrimp with Intestine
狀元及第粥 $ 3.50
Pork Belly and Liver Combo
生菜鯪魚滑粥 $ 3.75
Sliced Dace Fish with Lettuce
蜆肉雞粥 $ 4.25
Chicken with Clam
艇仔粥 $ 3.50
Beef, Squid and Pork Combo
鮮滑魚片粥 $ 4.25
Pond Fish
炸菜牛菘粥 $ 3.50
Minced Beef with Preserved Vegetable
爽滑豬紅粥 $ 4.25
Pig's Blood
皮旦瘦肉粥 $ 3.50
Lean Pork with Preserved Duck's Eggs
明火靚白粥 $ 2.00
Dried Beancurd with Gingko
香脆炸油條 $ 1.00
Deep Fried Crispy Dough
精美小食
Snacks
甜酸豬腳薑 $ 4.25
Pig Knuckle with Ginger
香煎葱油餅 $ 2.50
Scallion Pancake
馳名清湯牛腩 $ 4.95
House Special Beef Stew in Soup
清湯金錢肚 $ 4.95
House Special Beef Tripe in Soup
郊外油菜，生菜，韭菜花，伴醤油 $ 4.50
Chinese Vegetable with Sauce
白灼發財鯪魚球 $ 5.25
Broiled Fish Balls
I USED TO THINK THAT WAY. I USED TO CALL MYSELF JENNIE 2.5 AND RUN AROUND THE CITY PHREAKING AND ART-BOMBING, DREAMING OF BEING A FAMOUS STREET ARTIST AND POLTICAL ACTIVIST LIKE ALL MY IDOLS.
I TOOK ON THE GOVERNMENT SINGLE-HANDEDLY. BOMB THE MOTHERFUCKING SYSTEM, BUT HUGE! YOU COULDN'T MISS ME THEN. I WAS ALL OVER THE NEWS AND THE UNDERGROUND. I WAS FAMOUS.
WHICH IS EXACTLY WHAT I REALIZED I HAD WANTED ALL ALONG.

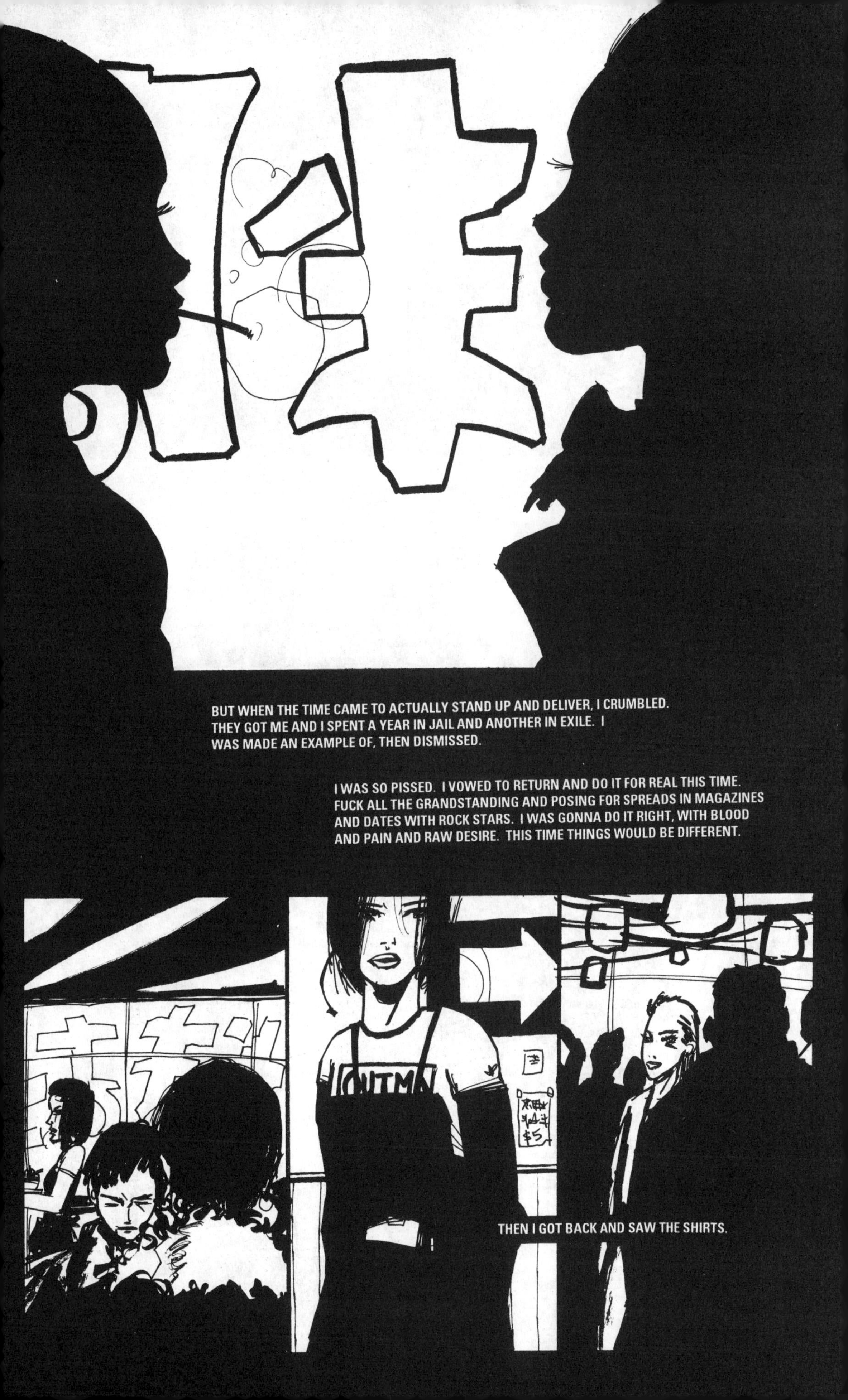
BUT WHEN THE TIME CAME TO ACTUALLY STAND UP AND DELIVER, I CRUMBLED. THEY GOT ME AND I SPENT A YEAR IN JAIL AND ANOTHER IN EXILE. I WAS MADE AN EXAMPLE OF, THEN DISMISSED.
I WAS SO PISSED. I VOWED TO RETURN AND DO IT FOR REAL THIS TIME. FUCK ALL THE GRANDSTANDING AND POSING FOR SPREADS IN MAGAZINES AND DATES WITH ROCK STARS. I WAS GONNA DO IT RIGHT, WITH BLOOD AND PAIN AND RAW DESIRE. THIS TIME THINGS WOULD BE DIFFERENT.
THEN I GOT BACK AND SAW THE SHIRTS.

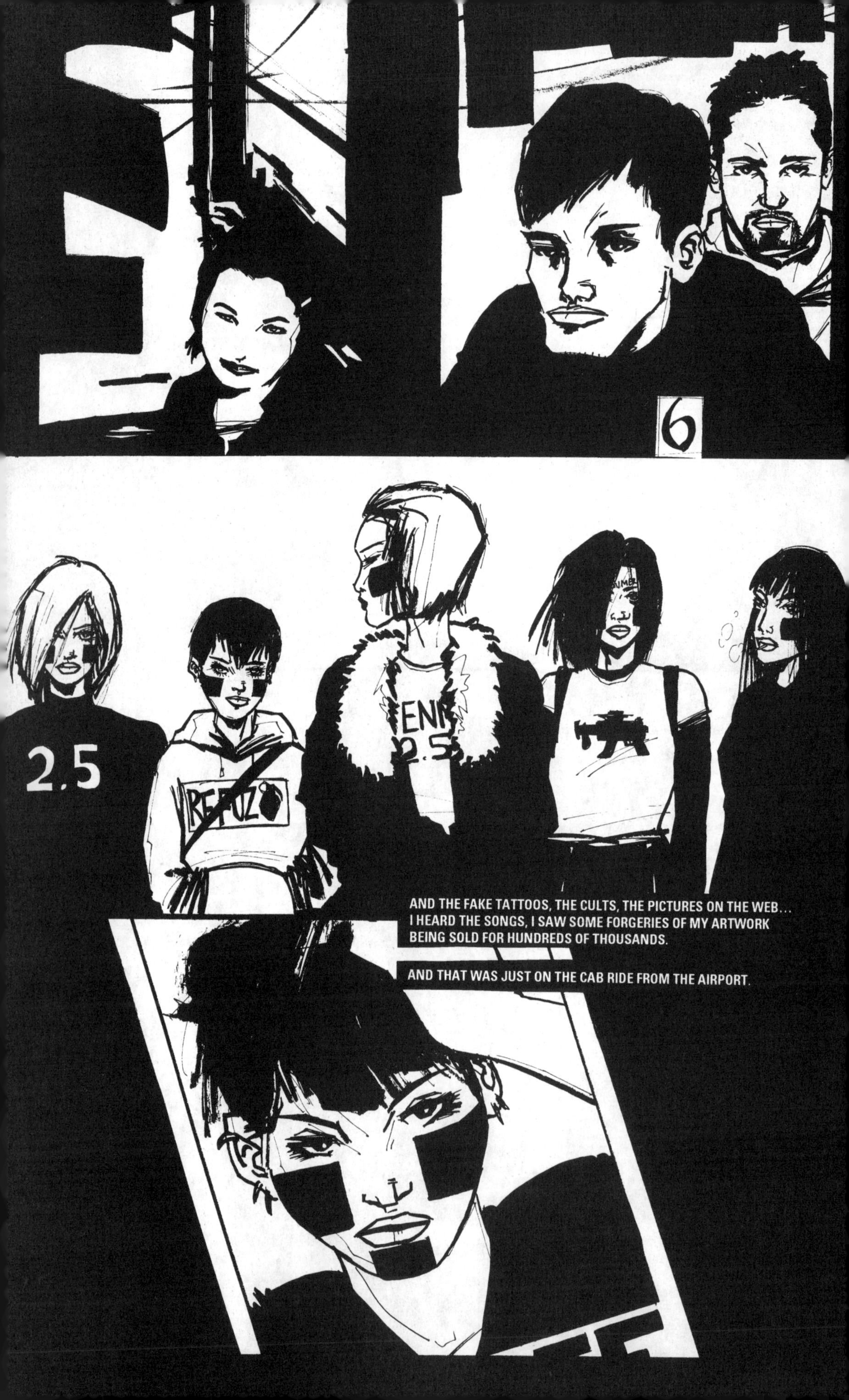
6
2.5
AND THE FAKE TATTOOS, THE CULTS, THE PICTURES ON THE WEB...
I HEARD THE SONGS, I SAW SOME FORGERIES OF MY ARTWORK
BEING SOLD FOR HUNDREDS OF THOUSANDS.
AND THAT WAS JUST ON THE CAB RIDE FROM THE AIRPORT.

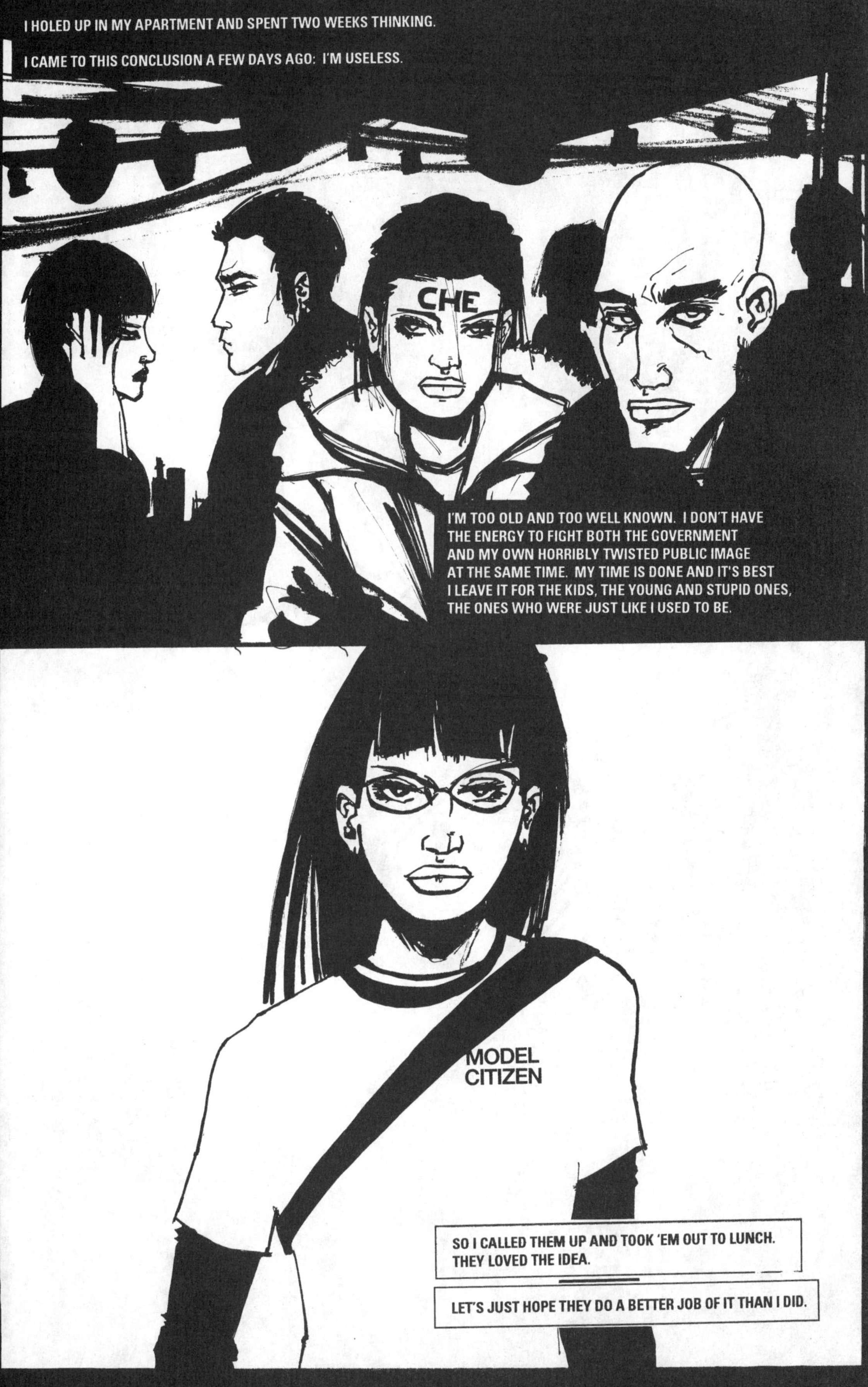
I HOLED UP IN MY APARTMENT AND SPENT TWO WEEKS THINKING.
I CAME TO THIS CONCLUSION A FEW DAYS AGO: I'M USELESS.
CHE
I'M TOO OLD AND TOO WELL KNOWN. I DON'T HAVE THE ENERGY TO FIGHT BOTH THE GOVERNMENT AND MY OWN HORRIBLY TWISTED PUBLIC IMAGE AT THE SAME TIME. MY TIME IS DONE AND IT'S BEST I LEAVE IT FOR THE KIDS, THE YOUNG AND STUPID ONES, THE ONES WHO WERE JUST LIKE I USED TO BE.
MODEL CITIZEN
SO I CALLED THEM UP AND TOOK 'EM OUT TO LUNCH. THEY LOVED THE IDEA.
LET'S JUST HOPE THEY DO A BETTER JOB OF IT THAN I DID.

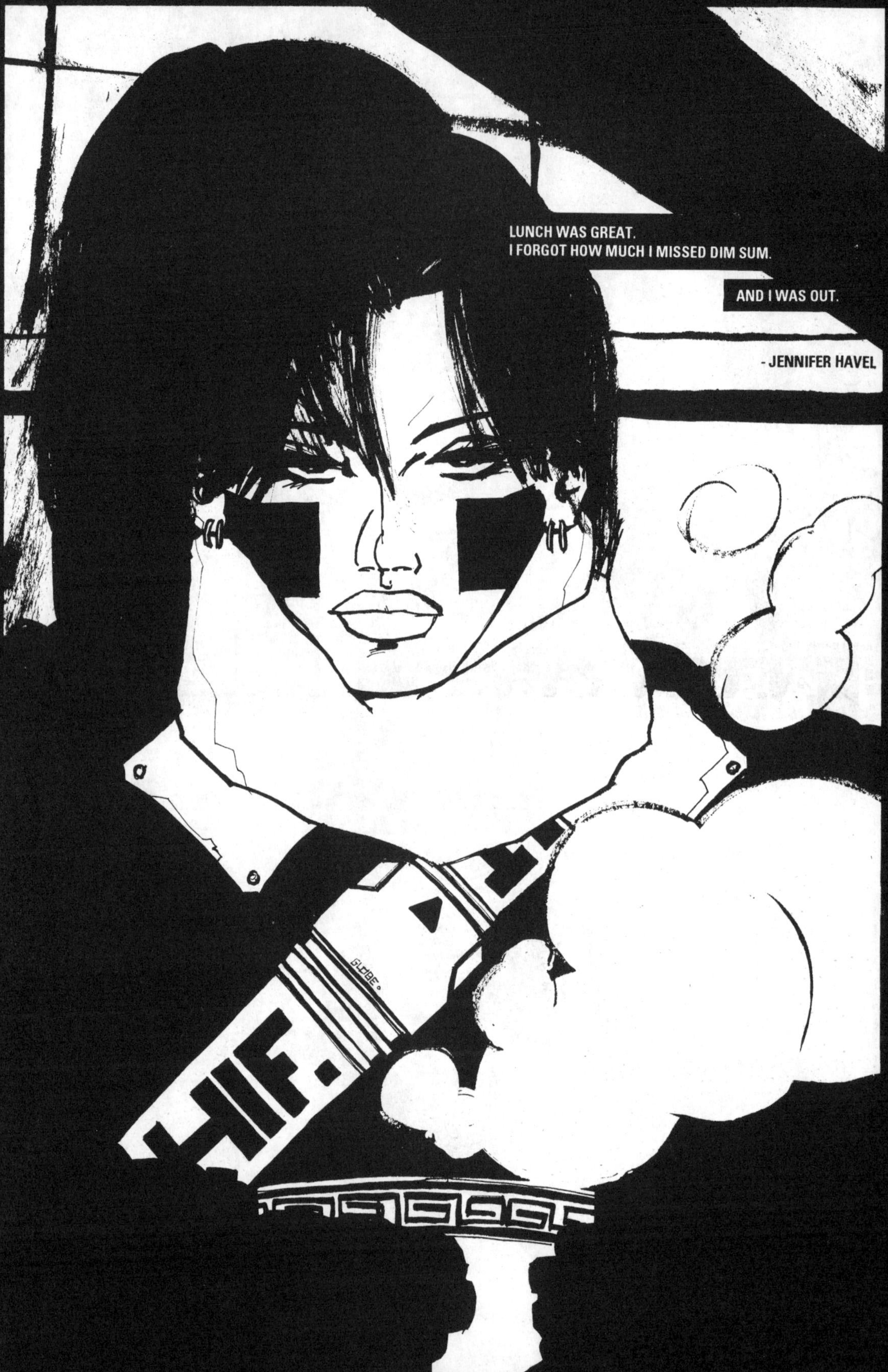
LUNCH WAS GREAT.
I FORGOT HOW MUCH I MISSED DIM SUM.
AND I WAS OUT.
- JENNIFER HAVEL

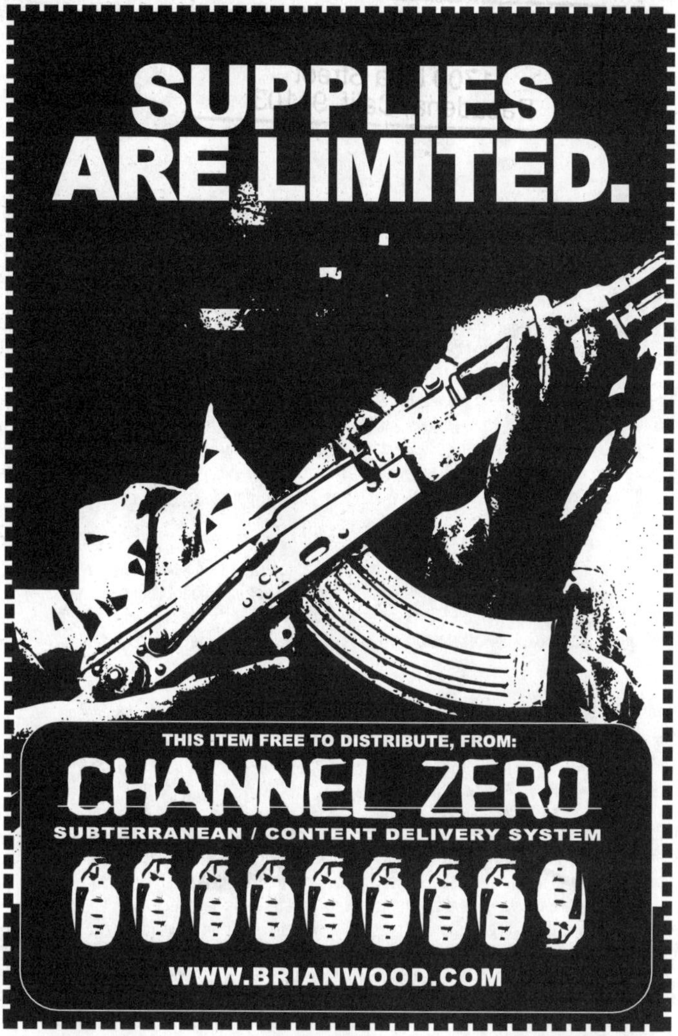
SUPPLIES ARE LIMITED.
THIS ITEM FREE TO DISTRIBUTE, FROM:
CHANNEL ZERO
SUBTERRANEAN / CONTENT DELIVERY SYSTEM
WWW.BRIANWOOD.COM

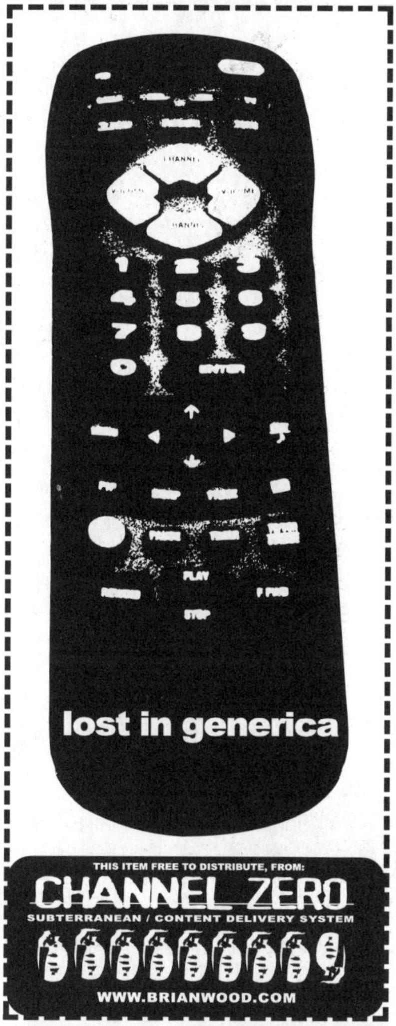
lost in generica
THIS ITEM FREE TO DISTRIBUTE, FROM:
CHANNEL ZERO
SUBTERRANEAN / CONTENT DELIVERY SYSTEM
WWW.BRIANWOOD.COM

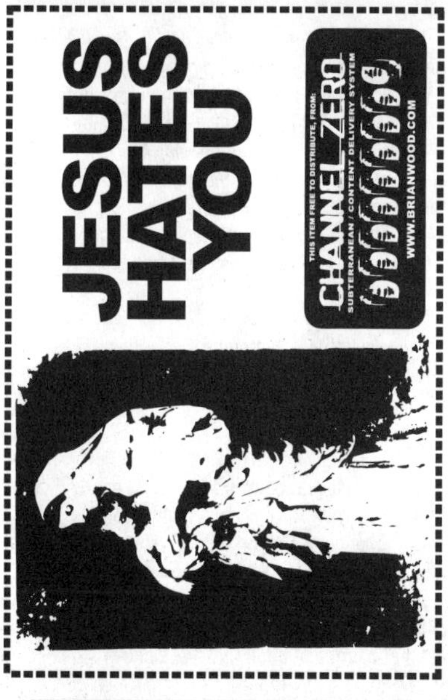
JESUS HATES YOU
THIS ITEM FREE TO DISTRIBUTE, FROM:
CHANNEL ZERO
SUBTERRANEAN / CONTENT DELIVERY SYSTEM
WWW.BRIANWOOD.COM

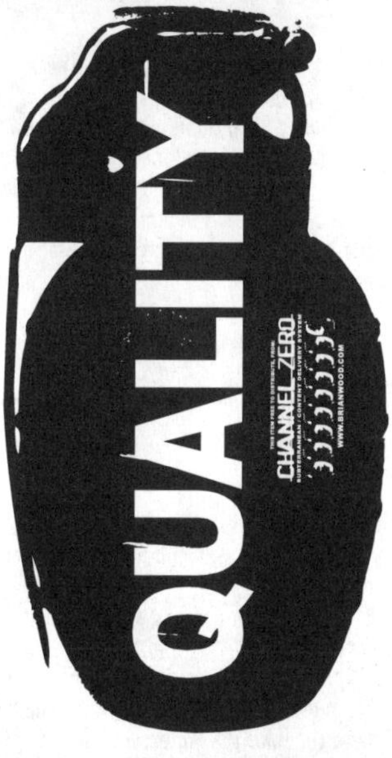
QUALITY
CHANNEL ZERO
SUBTERRANEAN / CONTENT DELIVERY SYSTEM
WWW.BRIANWOOD.COM

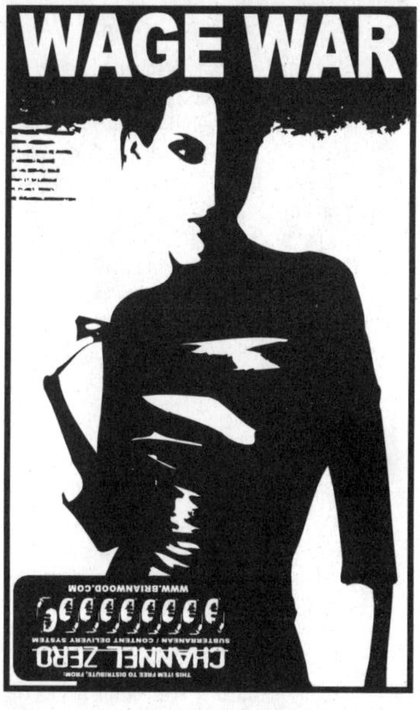
WAGE WAR
CHANNEL ZERO
SUBTERRANEAN / CONTENT DELIVERY SYSTEM
WWW.BRIANWOOD.COM

PHOTOCOPY THIS PAGE!

These are copyright-free images you can use for stickers, flyers, t-shirts, and petty vandalism. They may not be used for profit, or altered in any way. Scratchbomb the system! Help spread the message.

CHANNEL ZERO
CREATOR'S NOTES

First projects are usually things creators prefer to let fade away. Except in rare cases of genius, they're flawed, amateurish works usually followed up by something better. "This is what I meant to do the first time," says the creator. "My work is much more professional now. Please stop looking at that first one." I've heard it a million times. I've said it once or twice myself.

James Sime, a retailer in San Francisco, likes to sell *Channel Zero* to his customers by describing it as (and I paraphrase), "Brian Wood not really knowing what he was doing, just trying all sorts of things, getting a feel for the medium. It's not the best book he's done, but it has a hell of a lot of soul." I agree.

Channel Zero is my first professionally published graphic novel, and to me, it's my baby, flaws and all. I really didn't know what I was doing. I didn't know how to do a comic book by the rules, if there really are any rules. At the time, I barely read comics. But I knew I wanted to try it, and I felt I had some things I needed to say. It took me a year to get it done. And I love it dearly. It's a relic from my creative past, an artifact I can dig out and remember exactly where I drew every page, how I felt, what reference I was using, how the medium felt wide fucking open. I can do anything with comics, I remember thinking. Who cares what anyone else says? I knew as I drew it that some pages stunk, but fuck it, move on to the next page.

I feel a strong sense of pride that *Channel Zero* still exists in print today. I'll never be able to recapture that same creative moment I had working on this book. I've moved past it; I know how the comics industry works now. I have to worry about sales numbers and editors and publishers. My personal standards have changed - no way could I work with such a "fuck it" attitude. I'm a different person now. I'm eight years older and have other things I want to do, other stories I want to tell, other genres and storytelling techniques I want to explore. *Channel Zero* is-- was-- a one-time deal.

And it sells. It sells to readers who look back at this early work and see it for what it is now, as I do, a relic, a first work of someone who's progressed on to other projects. It also sells to people who are affected by the energy and attitude the book possesses, its call to arms. To them it's a brand new book. *Channel Zero* is different things to different people. I think its success over the years is due in large part to that.

Which brings us to this edition of the book, and this essay I'm writing. Any writer I know, any type of artist I can think of, would kill for the chance to go back in time and improve on an earlier work. And why not? If they know they can execute something better now, the urge to "fix" an inferior work can be overwhelming. That's why things like director's cuts and new editions of films exist, to name just one example. But in the case of published works, like novels, like music, and like graphic novels, most people never get that chance. I've been lucky that with each edition of *Channel Zero* (because this book goes back to press every year or so), I can make minor tweaks to things, update my essays, swap out a panel or do a new cover. These little things enable me to keep it current and fresh looking, and satisfy that creative urge. I've been lucky that people keep buying the book, and lucky that my publishers, AiT/Planet Lar, see the value in these creative updates, and give me the opportunity to make them.

Channel Zero was born out of a very specific time, culturally and politically. These days, one can draw very direct and scary parallels between what happens in this book and what's happening in the world right now, totally valid comparisons that, unfortunately, are pretty accurate. But *Channel Zero* is a direct reaction to Rudy Guiliani's rule over New York City in the mid-90's, specifically his "Quality Of Life" crackdowns. While there is no doubt that he left NYC a safer city in the end, it was at the expense of a lot of people who didn't deserve the trouble it caused them. For a few years the city looked and felt like a police state, with City Hall barricaded from the public and under armed guard, artists under constant attack, street vendors driven out of business, rampant police brutality, any valid and legal protest or criticism of Rudy's policies suppressed, journalists fired and blacklisted... the list goes on. This was the environment that *Channel Zero* was created in. I was young, poor, and pissed off. I didn't so much create *Channel Zero* as I just let it happen. It was my reaction, my reflex to the times.

While there can never be more *Channel Zero* such as it was, *Jennie One*, the *Channel Zero* prequel story I wrote and Becky Cloonan illustrated, has us revisiting a lot of the same political themes, but written from a post 9-11 viewpoint, subtle as it was.

On a technical level, *Channel Zero* is very much a product of its times, and of the tools I had at my disposal back in 1997. Very nearly everything was done by hand, with a quill pen, a brush, ink, and a photocopier. I used a computer only for the cover photo illustrations and to type out the text for the dialogue and narration captions. Those were then cut out and rubber cemented onto the Bristol paper. I didn't own a computer at the time, so I stole time on the machines at my school and work. I remember the section of *Channel Zero* dealing with The Cleaner was drawn during an exceptionally hot and humid summer. Anyone who's spent time in NYC during one of those summers knows how horrible it can be. I had no A/C and suffered some setbacks due to the fact the weather prevented my ink from drying on the pages in anything resembling a reasonable amount of time. And even when appearing to finally have set, one brush of my damp skin against the pages would smear the ink. The "interview" section of the story was drawn during a three month span of time when I lived in four different apartments in New York and Jersey. In an effort to apologize to readers for the lateness of that issue, I extended the page count from 24 to 40 pages.

Today, when I draw, I make an effort to stay as analog as possible, still using a brush and ink, never spotting my blacks in Photoshop, but my scanner's replaced the photocopier for the most part, and I tend to layout my projects in InDesign now, rather than delivering the actual art boards to the printer or client.

In addition to the politics of the times, *Channel Zero* was heavily influenced by sf and cyberpunk fiction writers like Neal Stephenson and William Gibson, television shows like *Max Headroom*, east coast hip hop, Korean comics, *Judge Dredd*, and that first glorious year of *Wired* magazine.

Channel Zero runs about 130 or so final story pages, pulled from the 400 or so pieces of paper I actually produced. I sketched a lot, drew several versions of many pages, clipped and edited, and drew alternate scenes I would later reject for one reason or another. I'm fond of comparing this process to mixing music, where one starts with an excess of material and edits and mixes it all down to a coherent, tight final product. Some of this extra material made it into the *Channel Zero* designbook, *Public Domain*. Most of it remains hidden away in the bottom of my closet.

Since completing *Channel Zero*, I've spent more time as a writer in the comics industry, working for a year on Marvel Comics' *Generation X* with writer Warren Ellis, as well as *Couscous Express*, the *Couriers* family of graphic novels, and *Demo* for publisher AiT/Planet Lar. I've written *Pounded* and *Local* for Oni Press, *Supermarket* for IDW, and *Fight For Tomorrow* and *DMZ* for DC Comics/Vertigo, all of these with extremely talented artists lending their skills.

On the visual side of things, Warren had me do the covers for his 12-issue Wildstorm series *Global Frequency*, and I've contributed the odd short story for small press anthologies such as *Project: Superior* and *Ragtag*. I've worked for a string of internet startups before putting in a solid 3+ years at Rockstar Games as a senior graphic designer, working on the *Grand Theft Auto* and *Midnight Club* video-game franchises, as well as *Manhunt*, *Smuggler's Run*, *State Of Emergency*, and *Max Payne*.

Currently I'm living in Brooklyn, hard at work writing and drawing my upcoming projects for the 2006-07 year.

Keep track of me at: *www.brianwood.com*

-bri
1/15/06
Brooklyn

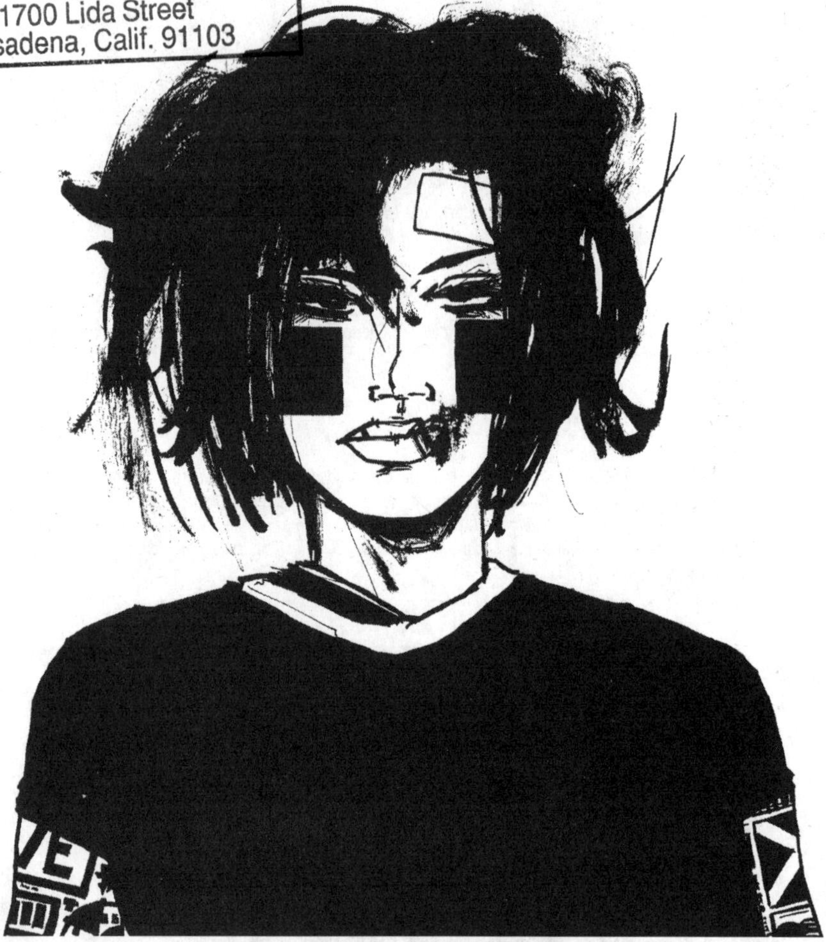

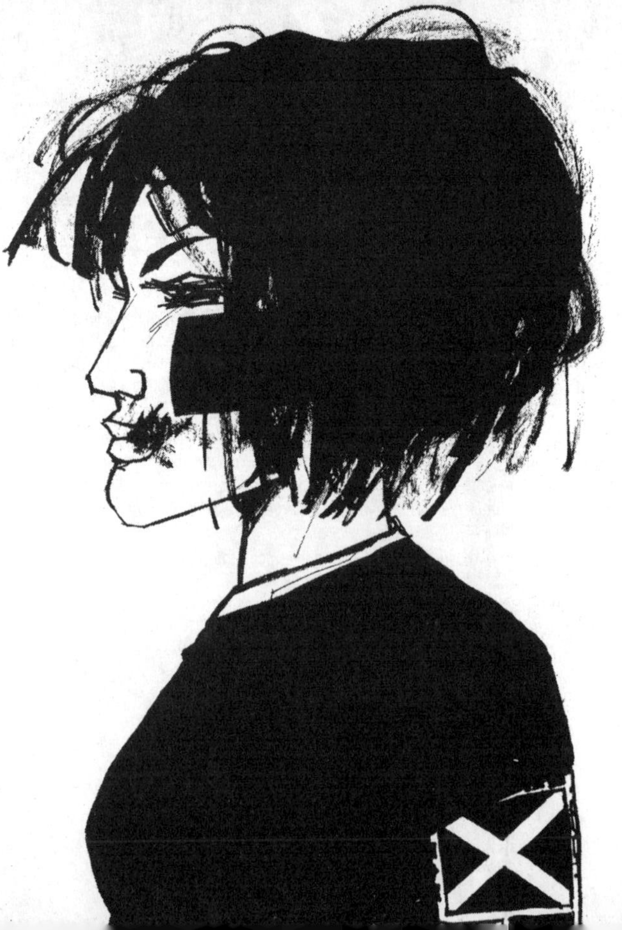